The best example of th
is the personal testimony of o
done so in a candid, authenti
the present as a called, anoint
of the questions we struggle to answer regarding God's response to our
prayers, His providence for our lives and encouragement for the often
inevitable divine silence. This is a book I would hastily recommend for
those who are on the move from low self-esteem to the championing of a
new life in Christ. In fact, it should be read by anyone who wants to have
better ammunition for the diabolical volley and disappointing encounters
along the way to victory in Jesus.

Hyveth B. Williams, D.Min.
Professor of Homiletics
Seventh-day Adventist Theological Seminary
Andrews University, Berrien Springs, Michigan

Within four days, amazingly, I read this book while on a short
vacation in New York. I was captivated by the author. I remained at the
edge of my seat as if listening intently to every word, wanting desperately
to know the end but grasping every moment that led there. The writer
weaves superbly within and between chapters recounting an inspiring life
story. It is an encouraging autobiography that people can identify with –
real, honest. It encourages you to look deeper into your own life and
recognize that though your situation may be different, the underlying
conditions are not that far apart from that of the writer. It helps you to see
the pain in others, and inspires you to do better by them. As the father of
three children I could see how this book could be helpful to young people
as well as to parents. The book beckons you to trust God, and the writer
testifies of God's faithfulness based on her experiences along her life's
journey. The writer's questions about God brought the realization that
God was with her all along the way even in her pain, hurts and
frustrations. The testimonies are compelling, and you are taken through
her life of despair, fears and insecurities, to one of total surrender to GOD
where she finds real peace and Joy. What an inspiring life story!

Kent Vital
Economist at Caribbean Development Bank
University of London and University of the West Indies

Josian's writing conveys a message for every one of us to cherish and apply in our daily lives. She expresses her sentiments and experiences with a genuine sincerity that is so admirable that I found it difficult to interrupt my reading. Actually, her writing mesmerized me. She is truly "Chosen by God" to write for us as we all desperately need guidance, leadership and inspiration. She causes the reader to understand that the problems we face are human and can be solved if we parallel our strategies to hers. She depicted "The Devil at Work" just as it truly occurs for all of us at one time or another in our daily lives. Her final commitment to God is the answer which the reader desperately seeks and searches for just as she did. She shows God's power at work when we request His help and show our whole hearted loyalty to Him. Surely, this book is the answer to the human needs of mankind. This book is not just an inspiration but a spiritual example of God's divine purpose. I sincerely believe this is God's personal spiritual message to each of us through Josian.

Marie Notaris Professor of English
Mercy College, Bronx, New York
Retired Board of Education, New York City School Teacher

He Leadeth Me

One Woman's Amazing Journey of
Faith and Miracles with the Invisible God

J osian

F rampton

COVER DESIGN BY ALCOLN THOMAS

CONTENTS

i

ACKNOWLEDGEMENT

With Sincere Thanks

My sincere thanks to all the people in my life who have helped make the writing of this book a possibility. Your care, compassion and support have helped birth this God story.

To My Loving Mother

You have been a good mother to your children. Your hard work and self-denial showed you wanted us to succeed. Your commitment to praying continually for our safety and care is a great attribute that I appreciate very much. Thank you for the love you have shown and the many sacrifices you have made for me. I do love you.

To Avis and Bruce Berry

Through you, God gave me the parents I didn't have in America. Your self-sacrificing love is one that I can never forget or repay. Your care and compassion, your consistency and commitment have touched and blessed me in more ways than I can ever express in words. Thank you so, so much for all you have done and the many, many ways you have allowed yourselves to be used by God to bless me.

To my immediate and extended family in the United States and Dominica especially, Vanessa, my Aunt Yvonne-Maria, Juliette, Debbie B., Debbie J. and Carmella, as well my extended family

Thank you for the support you have given throughout my life. I thank God for your countless contributions to my growth, maturity and now my life in ministry. You are amongst my greatest fans. Your rooting for me and the ways in which you have stood firm by me from the beginning of my journey keep me going strong in my life and ministry. You are loved and appreciated deeply.

To my Pastor Dr. Abraham J. Jules and my entire church family at the Mount Vernon Seventh-day Adventist Church

I have found in my Pastor a true friend, colleague and mentor. You have helped my ministry in many positive ways. Your respect for my life and work in ministry has inspired and motivated me. I appreciate you very much. I also thank my church family for the wonderful care you have shown and the many ways you helped me survive my ministry journey at Andrews University. Your financial support, spiritual encouragement and prayers kept me enduring.

To Darlene Thomas

God gave you to me as a gift at seminary and I am more than blessed to have you in my life. You are amongst the most sincere people I have ever met. You are a true Christian, a devoted and trusted friend and confidant. I thank you for always being there when I need you. You occupy a special place in my heart.

To Marie Notaris, Dr. Hyveth Williams and Debbie Willock (Editors). **To Alcoln Thomas** *(Graphic Designer of the entire book including covers).* **To Stein + Partners Brand Activation** *(For photograph layout on covers).* **To Timothy Lampson** *(For photography of covers).*

Thank you to each of you for sacrificing your time editing, formatting, graphic designing, photography and further editorial review of the book. May God richly bless you.

To God My Father

I never would have made it this far without Your watchful eye on me. Thank You for Your unconditional love. My life will never be the same because of You.

PREFACE

The making of this book has been an adventure and miracle. I felt inspired to write it during my last year of seminary while enrolled in the Masters of Divinity Program at Andrews University Theological. On May 26, 2009, while serving as the newly elected President of the Seminary Student Forum (SSF), I had the opportunity to share my ministry journey at a seminary chapel service. That night, when I went home, I felt deeply inspired that I should put on paper the testimony I had shared. In June of 2009, I began writing. When the intensive sessions ended in July 2009, I only had thirty pages written. I wrote nothing over the course of the rest of the summer, as I was actively engaged in Field Evangelism in New York. This city has more life than any other I have visited. This cosmopolitan center never sleeps. Its active twenty-four hours a day, seven days a week. I love New York. Writing just wasn't happening.

Upon my return to school in September for the fall semester, to my satisfaction, I resumed writing. By February 2010, I had completed all twelve chapters, then spent the following months making changes, additions and adjustments as my experiences evolved. Working on this book has been an inspiration. There were times I couldn't wait to get back to it. Many times in the beginning stages of writing, I would awake at nights. Thoughts of events in my life which I had almost forgotten were racing back to memory. There were times I would write for hours and not realize how much I had written until the next day. I thank God for His help and direction and the courage that He gave me during the process of compiling these pages.

INTRODUCTION

One of my greatest amazements is how much I have often missed blatant realities of God's providential workings throughout my life. The reality of God's existence wasn't something I readily embraced. I could not reconcile my human reasoning to the faith walk I had been called to tread. Living in a very visual environment, I went simply by what I could see. I would come to learn that to experience God is to grasp the true nature of His invisibility. When Hebrews 11:6 elaborated on the concept, "Faith is the substance of things we are hoping for, the evidence of things not seen," I still missed it. As I am reminded in scripture, in the same way that the wind blows and I do not see it, neither can I trace where it comes from or where it is going; I cannot deny God is present just because I cannot see Him. Just as there are undeniable evidences of the wind's effects around me, so, too, I have come to see the glaring realities of God's presence in my life.

Although I must submit and surrender daily in order to maintain spiritual focus and to not lose my way, God's hands continue to lead me along my path in life. Like the children of Israel, I could have entered my "Promised Land" of peace much earlier and foregone years of wilderness experiences. These experiences have literally taken over three decades, and I am still learning and growing. The beauty in my journey is that teaching me is not nearly as difficult as it used to be. I am a lot more teachable. Allowing Him to do this for me has led me to love and trust Him so much more. Living in surrender and submission to God cannot be explained; it has to be experienced.

It is true I cannot see Him and I am often unable to trace Him, but His undeniable workings in my life are very real. It has been said that every human being has been created with a void. Revelation 22:17 calls it a "thirst." I believe only God can quench this thirst. This book is a revelation of my faith journey with God and His unseen hands which have miraculously led me from birth to this point. This is a story about God and His true existence in my life. The stories are real and continue to forever change my own belief in and view of God. Although the beauty of this reality seemed to have taken a lifetime for me to realize, I am content in that I have found the "Peace of God which surpasses all human understanding" (Philippians 4:7). It is evident from the experiences shared along my journey in life that finding such peace was not an overnight process. It took time, years and many object lessons. Today I share in a life with God that only He could have made possible.

My fight for survival began in my mother's womb.

GOD HAS BEEN LEADING ME

Chapter 1

God Has Been Leading Me

My journey of struggle, hardship, fight for life, and survival began in my mother's womb. A deep, long phone interview with my mother in the fall of 2007 while in Berrien Springs, Michigan gave me an in-depth look at my journey into this world. The world received me at Princess Margaret Hospital in Roseau, Dominica. The strain of financial hardship and feelings of abandonment by my own father forced my mother to reconsider my birth. Persuaded by many that my coming into the world would be a huge mistake, a close friend at the time brought her a local unofficial, medicinal drug for her to abort my unborn fetus. My mother recalls holding the substance in her hand while cleaning fish outside her home. As she contemplated the possibilities of a better life without an extra mouth to feed, she heard a voice clearly communicate to her, "You may be killing a teacher, a doctor, lawyer, etc." Compelled by the unseen presence, she dropped the substance into the bloody fish water. Then in tears she prayed and begged God, "Since I cannot take its life, please take this child's life when it is born." Thankfully, God did not answer her prayer, but my journey through life would be a long painful one.

Josian Frampton

Growing up in Dominica was an interesting but meaningful aspect of my formative years. Dominica is sandwiched between the French sister islands of Guadeloupe and Martinique. It is called the "Nature Island of the Caribbean," mainly due to its rich natural resources explicitly manifested in fertile soil, lush forests, three hundred sixty-five rivers, waterfalls, fresh water lakes, including the second largest boiling lake in the world, hot springs, and rugged terrain. Sitting at home on a given afternoon could bring the pleasure of watching a pod of whales come up to breathe. Spending time alongside the fresh water riverbed of the Layou River, while sipping on an island Fanta (soda), and eating a hot loaf of bread with butter were glory days. Pretending to be a fish as I practiced holding my breath under these crystal clear waters holds wonderful memories.

As the summers rolled in, Dominica exuded a beauty of greenery ushered in by rain showers poured out in the earlier months. The fruits welcome these showers of blessings by bursting their buds and bringing a beauty of colors which can only be seen to fully appreciate. Many of my young days were spent climbing guava, mango, and other fruit trees to comfortable heights for feeding. There were days I would have eaten so many guavas that my bowels suffered as a result. Too many mangos also left me many discomforts but I still indulged in these island pleasures. At the time, with almost no crime rate, the peace and safety of the island greatly promoted the enjoyment of life. The black sandy beaches welcomed our bare feet although we were unable at times to endure its heat. Bathing in the deep water at the Castaways Beach while gazing into the vast horizon of the unknown world beyond, brought a welcome feeling of Dominica's beautiful and peaceful life. Amidst these external pleasures,, however, were deep emotional wounds accompanied by countless unfortunate circumstances and life experiences.

Although I was never sexually molested or physically abused, my life in many ways was emotionally rough as a girl. I had seven aunts and uncles while growing up. They all were very respectful and kind to us. I do not have a single aunt or uncle who abused us physically or otherwise although, without a doubt, we had our conflicts. I believe my other siblings and cousins can attest to this. The curse of sexual abuse which has plagued many households did not, to my knowledge, exist in our family. Everyone played an active role in helping raise us in the best way possible. They bathed us, combed our hair and fed us. They instilled values and assisted in our sound upbringing. Those who migrated later on in life also contributed to our basic needs as we grew up. When someone was ill, everyone bore the concerns. Our family almost competed with medical professionals to care for any family member in their care; this has not changed to this day. We have had our family dramas but, when one is hurt, we do pull together. Still, the emotional nurturing a child should receive in its formative years from its biological parents was lacking. As children we had to sometimes play an active role in assisting with and participating in the care and provisions for our home. My grandparents, who raised me, were obviously not wealthy. So, I definitely was not born to privilege. We had to walk from door to door to sell avocados, cocoa, spice packs, and other things my grandmother made to sustain our income. I really dreaded those days. I did not enjoy selling. I took each turn down from a poor sale very personally. I could not handle the rejection. I still don't particularly enjoy selling, although I've done much marketing in my adult years.

During the Christmas holidays, we sometimes sold coals to make ends meet. Since we made the coals ourselves, we had to search for wood to burn. I can recall being with my cousins and aunts in the forests close to home and dragging huge logs several miles back to our house. It took several trips to accomplish this mission. My little hands were blistered and sore by the time the ordeal was over. Once we fetched the wood and set the fire for the coals, we were often awakened in the wee hours of the morning on certain days when the coals seemed to not be burning the way my grandparents knew they should in order to get the best price for them. I also dreaded those days. I did not like chores. Since bananas were the main export on our island, almost every family farmed. When harvesting time came, my siblings and I often had to forego school days to help with the harvest. These were very embarrassing times for me. Our grandparents thought more from an economic standpoint than an educational one. It's not that they did not value education, but they went with what made more sense at the time. Their decisions, however, severely affected my esteem and sometimes gave me the impression that I was not loved.

Home life, however, truly was not unpleasant. We had many fun moments with our grandparents. They enjoyed telling us stories and cooking us delicious meals. We were blessed to have fruits of many kinds in our own backyard. There were two huge mango trees, Star and Sugar apple trees, sour sop trees, sugar cane, passion fruit, papayas and guava trees. We also grew our own vegetables, such as lettuce, watercress and tomatoes.

We also raised many animals, which became our food once they were grown enough to be eaten. We raised goats, sheep, pigs, cows, dogs, cats and fowls as pets and food. We also helped to take care of the animals by grazing them in nearby fields. This gave me a better understanding of the sheep and goat parables in the Bible. Our goats had absolutely no manners. They pulled us and butted at us and gave much resistance when being cared for. The sheep, on the other hand, were much more cooperative. We were happy to have freshly laid eggs from our hens. We had done our own studies on these hens to learn when they hatched. They often came back clucking away to indicate that they had laid an egg somewhere. My grandmother was often frustrated that the hens laid in places where we could not find the eggs. She often performed her own physical examinations on the hens to see if they were ready to hatch. If they seemed ready, she would toss them in a cage where they wait until they laid their eggs. These were quite humorous moments for us kids.

I also learned much about sex by watching roosters exercise no restraint as they chased hens around the yard for mating. I often wondered why the roosters did not just accept the fact that these hens were not in the mood. I got some insight into male dominance at that point. The animals often bred and we had to help nurture their young. We usually had pups because one of our dogs, named Whitee since she was white with black spots, was very promiscuous. So she was always giving birth. This dog suffered a lot of verbal abuse due to her behavior. She must have had very low self-esteem because of the things she was told. I think we were just upset that we had to care for her puppies on such a frequent basis. Our house was filled with excitement.

My grandfather loved the bottle. Whenever he came home drunk, he sang very interesting songs with strong messages directed toward my grandmother. Those songs were humorous to us, but she did not find them funny at all. His drunken days made our house a live comedy stage. One time one of my aunts bought him a t-shirt which read, "A bull like me is always charged." He took pride in wearing that t-shirt. Although my grandfather was a devoted alcoholic who could drink alcohol like it was water, he was a very loving, caring and gentle man. He was never, ever abusive to his spouse, my grandmother, or to any of his children or grandchildren. He never compromised caring for his family to drink alcohol. He was an excellent provider and a very hard worker. He worked hard during the week and drank hard on the weekends. He also was a heavy smoker which he continued until his conversion in 1987. Interestingly, not one of his children or grandchildren, to my knowledge, smokes today, although they may have experimented at times in their earlier years. He made sure that we did not develop this habit, but a number of his offspring inherited his love for alcohol.

Although my grandfather was not a weak man, my grandmother wore the pants in their household and ruled with an "iron fist." She was the disciplinarian. She'd give one look and you knew that you were in serious trouble. She had never known another man besides her husband, my grandfather. She lost both her parents early in her life. My grandfather became her support in every way until they were parted by death. Their personalities were very different, but they had a strong marriage. It was understood between them that separation or divorce was never, ever an option. They taught me, through their example, what "for better or for worse, in sickness and in health," truly meant. They suffered a lot and struggled through many hardships together in order to raise a good family.

My grandmother told us funny stories of how she fought women who attempted to come between them. She often called herself "Joan of Arc" and "bowik lachet wed" (the donkey with the hard tail), to emphasize her strength. Her strength manifested itself in the way she comported and carried herself. She walked and talked in a way that commanded attention. She was of reasonable height and seemed to fear no one and nothing under the heavens except snakes. She never backed down from a conflict. I must also confess, I dreaded being anywhere with her, not knowing what could occur. Her outings were never uneventful. She did not necessarily bother others, but if she was ever bothered, then "woe be unto" the person who trespassed against her. She had great strength. I never thought I would say this, but it was humorous growing up with such a character. She, along with my grandfather, wanted us to have life values. I remember them telling us how we should be treated by men. "Being abused or disrespected is never to be an option," we were reminded.

My grandparents also believed greatly in self-preservation. So, being a virgin when we married was top on their list of moral values. We dressed to command self-respect, which was a huge rule in our home. Sitting properly like a lady, speaking articulately, and comporting ourselves as ladies and gentlemen were important rules which we learned in their house. Sometimes I wasn't sure if they were more concerned about their reputation or ours. I remember my grandmother telling us girls that if a man, especially a raster (a man who locks his hair and smokes weed), would be so bold as to even look at us the wrong way, we should let her know and she would take them to the police where she would ensure that their names were written in "red," indicating that their record would be tarnished.

I recall the day when a raster said hello to me and then proceeded to follow me in an attempt to make conversation. With the fear already instilled in me by my grandmother and the reminder that we were to report such incidences, I could not wait to get home to tell my story. Without delay, my grandmother flew up, left whatever she was doing and, barefooted, headed for the nearest police precinct where she proceeded to give this man a record against his name. I felt so terrible and embarrassed. It was the last time I recall reporting anything of such a nature to her. Fortunately the young man was not harmed or in trouble. Maybe he just received a warning. My grandmother knew all the corporals and sergeants very well or maybe they were also aware that she was too much to handle and let it go. I really don't know, but I can only say I never wanted her to fight those kinds of battles for me. Since she thought that I was too fragile, she took a particular interest in my issues. Whenever my grandparents had to go to work to fend for our family, they left us in the care of our aunts, uncles and cousins, who all did a great job caring for us.

Often, when we would not behave and we were disobedient, she expressed her frustrations through angry words. She often threatened to ship us to our mother. She also frequently reminded us: "If Mahomet cannot go the mountain, the mountain will have to go to Mahomet." To this day I do not know what "Mahomet" means, but I do know that my grandmother wanted us to know that if our mother would not come to get us we would go to meet her. During these moments I felt unwanted, but I knew she cared greatly for us. I probably appreciated my grandparents a lot more after their deaths. They were wonderful care givers for us.

Sibling Rivalry

I grew up in the same house with my brother and sister, yet we were very different. My sister had a lean yet beautiful frame. She stood erect with beautiful curves and a gorgeous butt. She had a head full of hair and looked great in a pair of jeans. She, like my grandmother, was fearless. She moved at the speed of light. She was bold, defiant, brave, daring and would do or try anything. She got into trouble often but never concerned herself with what others thought. Although she got into trouble a million times, which led to constant discipline, it taught her nothing in that moment. Since she was very attractive, she explored dating before our recommended dating age. So, she concealed her dating adventures a great deal. She did not seem to concern herself at all about her reputation or how she was viewed by those at home or in our community. She was such a free spirit. My brother was just as daring and shared a lot of the same personality traits as my sister. As a result they got along better with each other than I ever did with either of them.

My brother is tall and handsome with a quieter disposition. Yet deep within he possessed a silent strength. He seemed to be in his own world at times and he always appeared to be on a mission. I cannot to this day say what it is. I only know that for years he and my sister were tight partners: Interestingly, they often could not get along because they shared so much in common. I loved my siblings but I always seemed on the outside looking in. Looking back, I realize that they were loving people who just enjoyed their youthfulness. They enjoyed having a lot of friends and sharing what they had with others. They were real social butterflies and the life of the party. They knew how to have fun and felt no inhibitions, reservations or shame about it. My very introverted nature, combined with my need to keep everyone happy, along with an intense desire to maintain my perfect image and reputation even at such a young age, did not always sit well with my siblings, especially my sister. I feel at times she disliked me probably for good reasons. My understanding of what being good meant posed some serious challenges to our bonding as siblings. Looking back, I seem to have related better with my brother than with my sister, although we had our close moments. I felt my brother was protective of me and he often related to me in a much gentler way than my sister did. I often felt she was probably frustrated, because we were always being compared. I did not like the comparisons and felt badly about it. Especially since it seemed her free nature kept getting her in trouble.

One night, in the summer of 1987 we had a church event. My sister disappeared for most of the day and word came back that she was with her boyfriend. My grandparents and uncle were very upset. She was forbidden from attending the church function that evening, while all the other children in the home were allowed to attend. That night as we all got dressed and left, she yelled at the top of her lungs in a very angry tone. Even after we left the house for the church, which was across a little river which separated the church from where we lived on Church Lane, I could hear her screaming. I felt hurt for her. I tried to negotiate giving her a chance before I left, but I was asked to stay out of it. I don't recall a girl who got into as much teenage trouble as my sister. She has grown up and is now a married adult with four wonderful children, but that free spirit has not changed much.

I continue to pray that the Lord will move and work on mellowing her. She has made great strides in that respect. Our relationship still sometimes feels strained for the same reasons that existed in our childhood, our personality differences. I love my sister and I have sought many ways to express this to her over the years. She has also shown her love in many ways. We are simply different and we've both accepted that.

Childhood Memories

In addition to these growing up joys and discomforts, some unfortunate circumstances seemed to follow my childhood course. I recall being still a young girl sometime in the early eighties; I remember it as if it were today. I came to visit my Aunt Helen. I was wearing a pair of shorts with a matching top. They were a pretty baby blue color and the material was quite thin since we lived on an island. That particular Sunday afternoon my aunt cooked a delicious soup to serve her family. Fresh from the fire and still boiling from the heat, we collided as I made my way into the kitchen she was exiting.

I was scorched with third degree burns over the right side of my chest, inches more and I could have been disfigured. I was taken to our local health center where my burns were treated. The nurse placed fish-like mesh gauze over the severely burned area. Then she placed some thick cloth bandages over it and wrapped the area around my chest to keep the dressing on. I had to return to the health center every week to have the dressing changed. This process was painful and gruesome to my young mind. The mesh would stick firmly to the burnt area and had to be pulled to release it. My flesh seem to have parted with each release. I screamed in pain. Healing seemed to take forever. My aunt's daughter would take me to soak the burn in the sea, before going to the clinic for my bandage changes. The sea water truly helped with speedy healing. I still bear a huge scar from this incident.

Just a few short years after this incident, I fell into a flooded river and was drowning. I was still a young girl and could not swim. I had been on my usual routine of getting water from a public tap since we did not have running water in our homes at that time. It had rained heavily and the concrete platform which held the standing tap became slippery. Without thinking, I stood on the slippery concrete which slightly overlooked the now flooded river we called "pooporie" due to its murky and disgusting nature. I fell into the river. I began to sink. As I sunk, I recall the struggle as the filthy water hit my face. I took several drinks of the green, dirty and contaminated water as I made my way to the bottom. Everything was happening really fast. I felt sure I was going to die. I could feel the fear, but there was nothing I could do to save my life.

There was a local soccer game going on in the community. The neighbors, across from where the tap stood, began to scream but they seemed immobilized and unable to jump in and save me. This could be for many reasons. Maybe it was the murkiness of the river which had obviously overflowed its banks. Or maybe people debated who should jump in first. Suddenly, a young man jumped into the river and fished me out. I stood in shock and fear, fortunate to still be alive. I looked terrible with all the green filth and debris from the river still trapped on my face and hair. I felt very humiliated making my way through the thick crowd which gathered to witness my rescue. My life was spared and I lived through this experience.

In 1988, three girls in our neighborhood had surgery to remove their appendix. I suddenly became fearful about mine rupturing. I had been experiencing similar symptoms. I went to my doctor and examinations confirmed that my appendix was in fact ripening. This news totally unsettled me. I spent weeks fearing that my appendix would rupture and kill me. Since death was my greatest fear, my anxieties increased. One Saturday morning our family was planning to attend some tent meetings on the Northern part of the island. Fear enveloped me as I felt a slight pain on my right side. I unsuccessfully tried to conceal my fears. Suddenly, I felt sharp pains on my right side where the appendix is located. I began sobbing. My family quickly grabbed me, and took me to the hospital. My doctor, fearing a rupture, performed emergency surgery. My recovery was painful. My wound became slightly infected and reopened after the metal stitches were removed. This kept me out of school longer. It was a traumatic experience, and I was very afraid, but I survived the physical and emotional trauma.

I have seen how Satan has set traps over the years, and orchestrated pits of danger for my demise. He has worked through human agents to make my life difficult and to frustrate my walk with God. Part of these difficulties includes my character and reputation often being attacked and viciously assaulted. I have felt rejected by people even in my own family, whom I don't recall ever harming. There are those who have plotted my demise and have rallied others to hurt me without any just cause. Through every event I now see avenues where God has rescued and delivered me. Although in my spiritual ignorance I failed to see God working during all of these moments, I can see now that He has been there with me throughout all of these life occurrences, consistently leading and protecting me.

In an interview with my mother just months after moving to Berrien Springs, Michigan to fulfill my call to Pastoral Ministry, I was amazed at what I was discovering about my life journey. I was left by my mother to be raised by my grandparents. I had not always understood all the details of my life but one thing was clear, there was a lot I did not have and amongst those things was the presence of my biological parents in my formative years. My father was always a distant part of my life. I was born to a black mother and a half white father who was very handsome. He never committed to any woman by marriage during his life, although he had many relationships. I have a number of siblings on my father's side, and interact quite well with a few of them. My mother's involvement with my father seemed doomed to failure from the beginning. As a single parent, she was my sole provider. Part of supplying that provision was leaving me and my two older siblings to be raised by our grandparents when I was only three years old. She went in search of a better life overseas. The next time I would live in a home with my mother was when I turned fourteen. It felt strange at first, although she was always a part of my life growing up. To my recollection, I missed certain parts of my upbringing, things I guess were meant for one's parents to do. There were things I desired to know concerning my conception and birth which only my mother could relate. Yet, it was years before I ever mustered up enough courage to ask her about these things.

Relocating to Michigan in preparation for my pastoral journey was when I would understand more deeply the circumstances surrounding my coming into the world. For the first time in my life I engaged my mother in an in-depth and detailed dialogue concerning the circumstances surrounding my conception and birth. This discussion came about one night after being drawn into a state of great sadness, perplexity and bewilderment about my calling. As I poured my heart to God asking that He would help me cope, and after sobbing uncontrollably, the Spirit of God led me to the Jeremiah 1:5 which read: "Before you were ever formed in the womb I knew you...." It was then I felt a strong desire to call my mother and have a heart-to-heart talk with her about my life in the womb. For years I had resented any discussions which involved my father and her involvement with him. For most of my formative years I found my life on this earth to be more of an embarrassment than a joy. I saw myself as an unfortunate soul not having both my parents in my life.

I envied the ideal of the wholesome family life, although I never mentioned it. Although there were many nuclear families in our community, single parenting prevailed. Students were often teased in school for having a stepfather instead of their biological father in their lives. There is a song I learned while I was growing up that spoke loudly to me as a child. The lyrics went: "Nobody's child, I am nobody's child. Just like a flower I am growing wild. No mommy's kisses and no daddy's smile, just like a flower I am nobody's child…." Tears ran down my face each time I heard the song. I appreciated being raised by my grandparents, but I really wanted a life with both my parents. I vowed that so long as I lived, I would never bring a child into this world if it would not be raised in a stable family. It is not in my own strength, but through the mercy and keeping of God, that I have upheld this principle. I am grateful for the care and sound upbringing given to me by my grandparents, whose example gave me a strong foundation for family life. They were married for more than forty years by the time my grandmother died, in 1995. Yet, it simply wasn't the same without my biological parents in my life. I even resisted hearing stories about the little cute things I did as a child. I simply was not interested in this aspect of my early childhood years.

Looking back, I see there were times my mother tried sharing events concerning my conception. I simply was not interested in hearing it at the time. Had it not been for the gift of going into pastoral ministry, I am not sure if I ever would have been prepared to have this discussion. I am therefore convinced that the night our conversation took place was unquestionably led by God through the guidance of His Holy Spirit. I believe the time had also come for me to face the reality of my feelings concerning my childhood. I realized through this encounter that sometimes to move forward one has to look back. The conversation with my mother turned out to be a very emotional one.

For the first time, I got to hear her version of the story. I saw through the pain of her past errors and choices. I believe it was only then that I truly got an understanding of my mother's feelings as a mother. Having had failed relationships myself, I felt empathy for the way things turned out in her own life. In that moment I wholeheartedly forgave her and felt a more sincere connection to her. Over the years, although we've had a fairly good and cordial relationship, considering that most of my life has been spent without her physical presence, I still feel some disconnection, although I have never told her this. I was only three years old when my mother migrated and left us with my grandparents. The disconnection I felt was not because she had not cared for us over the years, since she is a very caring and considerate mother. I later realized I had in many ways held her accountable for the discomforts about family life I felt during my growing years, particularly the shame I internalized being raised without the continued presence of my biological father. The economic circumstances which allowed her to migrate to the French island of Guadeloupe to provide better financial opportunities did not ease my discontent. That night, however, she agreed to take me down memory lane. It turned out to be a tearful and emotional journey.

A Harsh Reality

My mother recounted how unwelcome many found the news of my arrival into the world. Since she was already a single parent of two children, everyone found her irresponsible for bringing another child into the world. She recounted her mental anguish and turmoil over the pressure to abort. The strain of financial hardships and feelings of abandonment did not help the situation. She said a friend, convinced that I should not be born, brought her a local and unofficial medicinal drug which would abort my unborn fetus, especially since she was still in the early stages of pregnancy. She said as she held the substance in her hand and contemplated what she was about to do next, an internal voice clearly communicated with her saying: "You may be killing a teacher, a doctor, a lawyer, etc." She said to me, "I never thought I would have been killing a pastor," and she began to sob.

The most heart-pounding detail of our conversation was when she said, "I did not want to take your life myself. So, I asked God to take your life when you were born. I said, 'Do not let it live.'" She then wept again uncontrollably. My heart sank, realizing the fresh pain she still felt. She expressed her remorse for having asked such a thing of God and the guilt she carried over the years. It was indeed the most heart-felt conversation I ever had with my mother. It was encouraging to be reminded that from conception God had been a present influence, guiding, leading, and protecting my life. Psalms 139 states; "You knit me together in my mother's womb… you know my rising up and my sitting down." Due to the overwhelming conviction my mother felt that day as she contemplated aborting me, she decided to carry me to full term. It was not an easy decision. She was often depressed during her pregnancy.

Having to work menial jobs to make ends meet, she was subjected to the physical strain of bending and lifting throughout her entire nine months of pregnancy. As a result, I was born into the world on May 13 in the 1970s with a crippled limb. The emotional effects of these occurrences surrounding my birth were later manifested. I was born with my left leg stuck to my underarm. My mother recounts the doctors being very perplexed about my deformity. They quickly got together to plan a strategy to try to correct this bizarre medical condition. Although different family members tell variations of this story, one thing is certain. I was born with this problem. Finding a medical solution was not an easy task since it was the 1970s, and we lived on a very small island that lacked the best in medical expertise and proper health care. The odds of healing were slim. There were no known specialists in these areas, at least not anyone known to my mother. Most doctors were General Care Physicians. They undoubtedly were not in any position to attempt any work on my condition without the risk of killing me.

They seemed quite eager, however, to operate, and concluded it would take many attempts of breaking my leg with the hopes of ever correcting it. As the doctors debated their next course of action, my mother said she prayed to God in her own humble way for help. Although it is evident by her life choices that she lacked spiritual maturity, she knew enough to call on God in a moment of crisis. She remembered growing up as a Roman Catholic. So, she knew God existed and she knew how to pray. She also attended many Protestant services as a young woman. She said she silently called on God asking Him to help. During this time, God was working on the heart of a woman, who was a local from one of the neighboring villages where my mother lived. In the days following my birth, as this woman continued to observe and hear the interactions between my mother and the doctors, one day she made the most unusual proposal as a means of healing.

The hospitals only had open wards separated by drawn curtains. This made it possible for the woman to hear conversations between my mother and the doctors. When the doctors left the hospital ward, the woman spoke confidently to my mother and said: "Do not let them operate on the child. Rather, here is a prayer...." My mother is sure this prayer was the reason for my healing, since not one doctor has ever performed any medical procedures on me to this day. The woman who gave this prescriptive prayer simply instructed: "Pray this prayer for three days in a row every morning before speaking or communicating with anyone; then try moving the baby's leg." It would be great to read the prayer that moved God to perform the miracle which corrected my limb. No record or memory of such a prayer is available. She only recalls that with the prayer came very specific instructions as if prescriptive. According to my mother, upon finishing the prayer, she tried moving my leg from its paralyzed position into a stretched out position. Realistically, this made no sense.

It is true Faith can seem unrealistic. I do not know if my mother was exercising faith or rather was desperate and would have tried anything to see my deformity corrected. I recall stories in the Bible such as Luke 6:10 where a man with a crippled hand was healed. Also in John 5:8-12 a man paralyzed for 38 years was also healed. The power with which Jesus healed these infirm people is the same power I believe He extended in healing my leg. I learned that the decision to operate on my leg was still being debated as this prayer regimen, mingled with some works, was quietly being implemented.

My mother said the first day nothing happened. My leg did not budge when she attempted to move it as she was instructed. The leg remained fixed in place. She recalls being discouraged. Remembering she had to continue this process for three days, she proceeded. Still no change came in day two of this prayer regimen. This brings me to a story found in II Kings 5. Naaman was plagued with leprosy. The instructions from God for his healing were to dip in the murky rivers of the Jordan seven times. It appears God is precise in His care for His people, although He does not always ask that we do things which are reasonable, sensible, or even traditionally or socially acceptable. When I think about what my mother had been asked to do, it seems foolish. Yet, I am so glad she obeyed. I am also especially glad she did not give up when her first two attempts failed. On the third day, when she performed the identical routine, this time my leg slightly moved from its fixed paralyzed location into its proper position.

Realizing something did take place, my mother recounts, she quickly repeated the step to which my leg responded, and it has remained in an outstretched position until today. Though over the years and while growing up I did have certain challenges with this leg, it never again returned to its crippled and paralytic state. There have been different versions by family of where my healing ultimately took place after this hospital prayer encounter. One thing is clear. I was born with this condition and it was corrected without medical intervention. Without this divine intervention I do not know what my life would be today. To confirm that He had performed complete healing, my mother assured me, I walked the day I turned exactly six or seven months. Even I had a difficult time wrapping my mind around this revelation. My mother says she recalls it as if it happened today. It was very early and way before I ever learned to creep. One thing is certain; the day I walked she said family members went flying out of our home in fear. It was one beautiful Saturday morning, and just about six or seven months after my miracle took place. The only two Seventh-day Adventist Christians in our family at that time were getting ready for their morning worship at the local church in the community.

Uncle Peter, whom we called Malachi, and Uncle Mozart were in the middle of their preparations when I went from laying flat to getting up and walking. So frightening was the experience that these two adults left me alone in the house and ran out screaming, "It's a miracle, it's a miracle." This open knowledge of God's manifestations in my infancy and adolescent years, unfortunately, did not register enough on my growing mind to have made a positive impact as I grew older. I grew to forget those things as I matured and never again revisited their impact until my call to pastoral ministry. This neglect of the supernatural robbed me of an opportunity to always remember that God had at least at some point in my life considered me. This would have been extremely helpful to me, since at different intervals in my life I often felt neglected by God. I felt unloved by Him due to certain unpleasant life experiences. I particularly blamed God for my emotional state. Although no one would know it if not told, low self-esteem and a sometimes depressed, fearful, paranoid, timid, and overall psychologically unbalanced state enveloped my young life. My quiet demeanor concealed these conditions quite well. I do not fully remember how or when they began. It seems I had always felt that way. With age, healing and maturity I later learned that many of these

21

mental challenges were due to my innate melancholy temperament and the possibly unhealthy emotional state of my own mother during her difficult pregnancy with me.

As a child and teenager I did not fully understand why my emotional state was so troubled. When I discovered I was not wanted, a shock wave went through my heart. I found comfort and gratitude in knowing that God has been with me since conception. He spared me from an inevitable death. The understanding that God knew me "Before I was ever formed in the womb" became quite clear (Jeremiah 1:5). My mother pleaded for my forgiveness. I assured her she already had it and that I did not hold any resentment or anger toward her. Instead, I felt relief knowing that God has been with me before I was even a thought. These details of my life helped me put into perspective the turmoil and searching that took place throughout my life. By the time my calling to ministry came, I had already been at a good place spiritually and otherwise. I can see now that knowing these things about my earlier years helped me understand who I am. God adopted me into His family at a time when it seemed that no one wanted me.

My mother later confessed that the way I have cared for her over the years has simply increased her guilt. She lamented that the way in which I contributed to her well-being has sometimes brought her more suffering than joy. She said I was the child she rejected, yet I seemed to have given her many reasons in her life to be happy. I had the pleasure of having my mother present at both my Undergraduate and Graduate Degree ceremonies. Both events were incredibly emotional for her. I do love my mother. I do not hold any of the things she has shared with me against her. I reminded her that God has forgiven the mistakes of her youth a long time ago. I told her that I have also forgiven her and that it is time for her to forgive herself.

Fear consumed my life. Dying was my greatest fear.

TROUBLED YEARS

Chapter 2

Troubled Years

Throughout my life, fear undeniably consumed me. Of all my fears death was, without any question, my greatest. This fear of death I believe came as a result of the way death was viewed on our island. In any land death is a horrible thing, but some cultures do grieve differently than others. When someone died as I was growing up, darkness seemed to cover the entire village. Then the church bell would sound a most dismal ring to alert the community that someone had passed. Longevity is most definitely prevalent in Dominica's culture. We have had a number of centurions. So, it was mostly very old people who died. Seldom did a young person die. When they did it was often from freak accidents and not illness.

At funerals people would wail and bawl and even try to throw themselves in graves, asking to go with their loved ones. The songs sung at those cemetery services were sad, dark and dreadfully painful to listen to. As I saw more of such things while growing up I realized that death was a dreadful thing. So terrifying were its effects on my life that I spent most of my young days trying to avoid it. I would mentally plan my days to avoid the possibility of encountering death. Then the nights brought with them their own careful watch. It was draining keeping track of my life this way, but I had no clue how to fix it. I also tracked any physical symptoms which appeared to be life threatening. I mimicked many illnesses when I learned that someone died from them. My little life was consumed with loads of care. Sadly, this demon followed me for many years. Looking back, I see that these fears existed as early as I can remember. I now know that God did not give me this "spirit of fear" (2 Timothy 1:7). It is also my belief that God wanted to free me from this life of fear from the time it began, but I needed to trust Him through faith to heal me. I just sincerely did not know how to do that. For years I battled occasional depression, but I did not know then that it was depression. Existence in such a fearful, depressive, and psychologically unbalanced mind set made it decidedly difficult for me to enjoy a full and happy life even as a child.

Although I had a dry wit and sense of humor at times, which has stayed with me, I was unquestionably an unhappy child. I cried often, mainly because I was afraid of being alone. I feared something terrible would happen to me. I did not care for crowds either, but I hated being anywhere without someone else present. I was also terrified of people I did not know, including my own father. Although my father did not welcome my coming into the world, just like my mother, he received me after my birth and accepted me when I was born. My father, who was mixed, looked more Caucasian than black. He was born to a white father from Britain and a petite, dark woman from Dominica.

I was frequently told by my mother's parents, with whom I was raised, that I looked like my grandmother on my paternal side. This was mainly because I had her dark complexion. The fact that my father looked white made me very fearful of him. I feared just about everything. So, he was simply an added fear. He tried hard as I grew up to establish a relationship with me, but I didn't know how to let him. Whenever he visited me as a child, I would run and hide under beds. I was covered in dust by the time I was found. My father was a nice man, and he had a gentle, quiet spirit. I missed never bonding with him.

As I became older his visits tapered off, and he became less and less of a presence in my life. My heart grieved in April of 2001 when he died before we ever came to establish a father-daughter bond. In the months before he died I craved a relationship with him. I had been in the process of contacting my sisters on my father's side to find out how we could bring him to America. The last time I saw him alive was in the summer of 1995.

It was not just my father I feared. There are different times throughout my growing up that visitors would come to our home, and my reaction to them was no different from that which I exhibited with my father. There was one particular guest whom we called Mark. He was from a neighboring village where my grandparents claimed to have had many relatives. Mark was probably the darkest human I had met to this point as a child. In the same way I was fearful of my father's white complexion, I was equally fearful of this man's extremely dark complexion. I would run, scream, cry and hide so that I did not have to see this man on his visits. None of these people ever hurt me. None were unkind to me. I was just afraid of them. Being fearful was my norm. So, I found things and people of which to be afraid.

I believe my emotional instability overwhelmed and distressed those who cared for me, particularly my grandparents. My sensitivity to my fears made it almost impossible at times to bring me joy. Whenever I had happy days my care givers were happy. In retrospect, my family tried to help me get better. They wanted to find out what was happening with me. I often heard my grandmother in conversation with a close neighbor about her concern for me. I don't think they ever really knew what was wrong. I never verbalized that my issues were fears. I simply acted out my fears and anxieties by being withdrawn, crying often, sleeping much during the day and refusing to talk sometimes, except when I really had to. I often refused to eat, and shadowed adults. Since those who cared for me were not particularly knowledgeable in regard to psychological disorders, they never suspected that my concerns were of such a nature. Besides, I always attributed my ailing to something physical rather than emotional.

Childhood Dramas

As a child, I was a very picky eater and barely ate. This is because I feared dying from food poisoning. This particular fear of food came when one of my cousins had a bad case of food poisoning. Her condition was so severe she spent an extended period of time in the hospital. When she was released, she was frail and looked quite sickly. I remember her saying that she almost died. Well, I most certainly did not want to die. So, I made sure I stayed away from the beans she had eaten and would not eat any peas or beans for many years. I personalized her illness so much that I eliminated a number of other foods from my diet. As a result, I looked like a twig. I had a sickly, unhealthy frame for most of my life until my early twenties.

I recall a most humiliating visit I had with a doctor in Brooklyn, New York around my twenty first birthday. As the nurse got me ready for my visit, she proceeded to take my weight. The doctor stood over her looking at the scale as they tried to determine how much I weighed. The scale said ninety-nine pounds. They looked at each other and chuckled. Then the doctor said, "Give her one pound to make it a hundred. She could use it." I looked unhealthy, and I did not like the way I looked. The doctor had no idea how much this one statement affected me for quite a long time and the damage it did to an already unhealthy self-esteem. Life was not normal for me emotionally and I knew it. I did not enjoy being this way but I sincerely did not know how to be otherwise. I do not even fully have an explanation of how these fears originated except for my knowledge of my melancholy temperament, combined with the difficulties of my mother's pregnancy. My fears were with me from childhood and seemed to follow me into adulthood. I got better with age and maturity by simply adjusting to life as I grew older. I sought the best ways I could to find peace amidst my fears, but I did not know how to bring such peace into my life. I tried to engage in activities, but my fears always hindered me from being fully involved in anything. I loved the idea of swimming, but I did not learn to swim properly until my late twenties. As a teenager, I hiked, I climbed trees, I ran races by getting involved in athletics, but I did all these things with a heart filled with fear.

Often, I had to be coerced, challenged and begged to undertake many of the things I ended up trying. Fear paralyzes and I was in many ways paralyzed. Knowing now that this life has been given to me as a gift from God to enjoy to the fullest, I see how much of it passed me by. I focused so much on dying that I forgot about living. It was not possible for me to sincerely enjoy living while fearing just about everything. My frequent moments of sadness and my need for security and protection consumed me. It also consumed my family and care-givers.

Things were not always dismal for me, though. I played dress up and house. My siblings and cousins would come together on holidays and weekends to play house. We built shacks on the vacant lots near our home and played Mommy and Daddy, Shop and Police and Rasta's sometimes all day. We stole the milk and sugar and other groceries from the house to support our pretend grocery stores. We were at times rebellious and would do sneaky things such as steal the frozen pops my grandmother made to sell to earn extra money. One time I hid under our bed and ate quite a few of those pops. They were so sweet and well prepared. What I did not know was that my grandmother had already calculated how much they were going to generate financially. When she did her inventory and came up short, my two siblings, two cousins and I who lived with them were called into a meeting. We were each asked, "Who did it." Everyone including me declared innocence. Now my grandmother did not take lying very lightly. Neither did she tolerate dishonest behavior on any level. She believed firmly in walking the "Straight and Narrow."

When things began to heat up and it was evident that we were all going to be in very big trouble, I said that my sister had stolen the pops. She wailed and cried but I maintained she did it. Everyone believed me because she had a history of getting into trouble and disobeying. I was less likely to do things like that. It broke my heart as I saw the way she cried proclaiming her innocence, but I never told the truth. I believe she despised me for a while because of this incident. I do not know if she remembers it, but I never forgot it. I cannot recall if I ever did something like that again to someone. It truly had brought me too much guilt and pain. I wanted to tell the truth of what really happened and clear her, but fear of my grandmother's harsh discipline kept me quiet.

This incident sent me back into my shell for a little while. What I did was wrong and unkind. I caused my sister pain and I never liked seeing her hurt. I think she thought I enjoyed her pain because I was often so quiet during her moments of discipline. As we all grew, we adapted to each other's home life and learned better how to interact with each other without hurting one another. I can truly say we did well in that. Though our personalities clashed, we shared a mutual closeness. I love my sister and have missed seeing her due to the distance which miles of ocean put between us. She told me she loved me and I believe she does.

Unforgettable Moments

I was a little girl when Dominica was hit by a Category Four Hurricane. The one hundred fifty miles-per-hour winds hit the island on August 29, 1979. I remember the event as if it happened yesterday. We knew the hurricane was coming and we made all preparations. We packed our valuables into boxes, secured whatever items of significance we had, and watched as the skies became dull and gray. As I recall, it was in the morning when what seemed like a whistle blew, and the winds began to pick up. Before we knew it, things were flying all over, the heavens opened and rain poured as if we had a repeat of Noah's flood. People were screaming, trees gave up their posture in strength to the one hundred fifty miles-per-hour or more winds. Debris gathered as if by someone's hand. The oceans raised, the waves beat angrily on the shores and the winds echoed their fierce sounds to those who became victims of this storm. Suddenly our roof collapsed and water poured in without mercy as we helplessly watched. All we had worked hard to protect absorbed the waters from the sky. We watched years of valuables and collectable items destroyed right before our eyes. The waters mounted and soon we were taking refuge in our basement apartment. It was not that much more secure except for the fact that we had a roof over our head.

Dominica had never suffered such a disaster of this kind before Hurricane David struck the island. It was a terrifying experience. I remember one of my uncles saying as our roof departed, "Oh Lord our roof is gone." Witnessing the obvious fears of the adults in my life added to my insecurities. Before long the storm had passed. Its effects on the island, however, were devastating. The physical damage left to the inhabitants paled in comparison to the emotional impact. In the days following the hurricane we found ourselves lined up for food distribution. With bananas being our main export, the country literally lost its economic foundation. It was a great disappointment, but more so a bleak future. With our clothes, food and income gone, bouncing back would be no easy task. Actually, it is over thirty years later and we still feel the effects of this disaster on the island. This was truly an unforgettable moment in our nation's history and in the personal lives of many. It was after Hurricane David that many American foods such as sardines, corned beef, ham and spam and the like found their lodging on our shelves and in our local kitchens. Up to this point many of us ate from the earth.

Since farming was known to most households, organically grown foods and animals were where we found our nourishment. Canned foods were luxury items. Life after the hurricane brought new meaning to the words wind and rain. I never saw another cloud the same again. Clouds were no longer to be trusted and overcast weather conditions meant harm. I had now found a few more things to be afraid of. Years had now passed since Hurricane David had devastated Dominica, but the passing of time brought no healing for the fear I developed of strong winds and rain. So when we made a trip to our farm lands, which was a regular custom in 1986 or 1987, I was not surprised by the weather drama which unfolded. In the country, Atly, we had a little house where we would lodge while away from our regular village home. This was a bit more primitive and most certainly did not reflect any touch of luxury.

One day, as we made our way back to St. Joseph, our home town, from our country home, a terrible thunder storm arose. My grandparents waited for a while to see if the storm was going to let up so we could depart. No change happened in the weather, however. Determined to make it back, my grandparents prepared us children for the journey. We had our rain gear on and our little parcels of food from the farming done over the days we were there. We children tried to negotiate staying longer but that was not going to work. We were instead saddled with our little parcels and encouraged to be brave because all would be well. My grandparents were both very brave individuals. They wanted us to also be strong and courageous. Besides, island life like the one I grew up in did not include an 'aristocratic' way of living. We simply learned and knew just what was needed to function in the world. My grandparents did not want to raise weaklings. Rather, their objective was to raise men and women who had backbone, ambition, motivation and drive. My fragile and troubled mind was not grasping those things very well. I instead found them harsh and unbearable. The way to transportation from where we lived in the country was quite a walk. There was a very long, steep hill with a deep precipice on one side. My grandparents were resolute in their decision to go ahead with their plans no matter what. The weather had cleared a bit but only for a short while. So we were quickly rushed out of the house to where transportation awaited us. No sooner were we out the door walking up this long hill, when there was the loudest burst of thunder and lightning clashing from the heavens. I dropped my little parcel.

In frustration my grandfather who was right behind me pleaded with me to move along briskly. I would not listen to him but to the loud sounds of the thunder. I seemed to have frozen with fear. I began to yell and scream as if I was being kidnapped. He then got really angry because I was slowing down their movements and could have caused us to miss our only ride home. I kept dropping my little parcel of produce placed on my head. It was not until I was threatened with punishment that I sped up the hill wailing at the top of my lungs. We eventually made it to the top of the hill where we caught the truck home. Once in safety I was highly embarrassed by my fearful outburst. My siblings looked at me in such pity and sympathy. Maybe they were embarrassed for me and them, too. They just never told me. I never forgot that day. Although I can laugh at it now, I know these experiences were not presenting me in a favorable light with my siblings and cousins.

It may have been a year or two after the hurricane that my grandmother encountered a Swedish couple who were lodging at the Castaways Hotel in Mero, a small village outside of St. Joseph where I grew up. The couple appeared to have fallen in love with me and wanted to take me as their own. I do not recall exactly how and when we first met them. I can only remember the many trips made to their hotel room as plans were under way to give me to them. During those times many European couples came to Dominica and brought children back to Europe with them. Adoption procedures were not necessarily needed on the island back then as is mandatory these days. Many children who left with couples over the years returned to Dominica as adults to reconnect with their biological families, but some were never heard from again. I do not recall the conversations my grandmother had with the couple when we met with them. I do recall being told that I would be going to another country to live there. I felt afraid and somewhat happy at the same time. Times were rough in Dominica and, although I was only a young girl I already had dreams of a better life. The couple gave me candy and money when we visited. I remember the last visit I had with them. I was wearing a black dress with many colorful circles all over it. I felt as bright as the many colors on my dress, but it was the last time I recall ever seeing or meeting with this couple. It appeared my grandmother kept such details from my mother. When my mother heard of it, she did not approve. She was not happy to say the least. She said she would rather come to get me than give me away. My grandmother was not happy with her response either, but she had to agree since my mother did not give her approval.

My mother took very good care of us as we grew up. Though she was not present physically, she made great efforts to ensure that our needs were met. There are times that she also fell on hard times and could not sufficiently provide for us. This often frustrated and angered my grandmother since it made her own challenges greater. Maybe this could have been one of her reasons she wanted to give me away. Or, maybe these people promised her better financial opportunities once I left with them. I do not know why I was the one chosen of the five grandchildren who lived with her to be handed over to these foreigners. I am happy my mother stepped in. There is no telling what would have become of my life had I been given to these complete strangers. There are stories of girls who left who had terrible lives, including those who had been given over to prostitution. Although I do not know if these stories were true, I thank God for His intervention.

My Teenage Years

My teenage years came with their own challenges. The fact that I was sheltered and naive did not help very much. We grew up in a strict, sheltered environment. My grandparents adamantly discouraged us from becoming teenaged or unwed mothers. This was not acceptable in our home. The idea of preparing for boys by discussing contraception or subjects along those lines would never have been a discussion in our home. Abstinence at all cost would be our only option. My grandparents created such a fear of pregnancy in our minds I concluded that, if I even sat where a boy sat, I could become pregnant. So for years I did not realize sex was the problem; I thought boys were the problem. So, I stayed away from boys altogether. In addition, I did not feel that I was attractive anyway. I did spend a lot of my time day dreaming of what it would be like to have sex. I wondered why it was such a scary thing. Since I was denied this pleasure, I simply allowed my imagination to run wild. I spent hours hiding in secluded places to read romance novels. We were not allowed to read such books either for good reasons. The likelihood of trying what I read was very possible. These stories, though they were not pornographic in nature, were quite sexually motivating. All the details of the romantic rendezvous outlined in the pages left a lot of room for one's imagination to run wild.

I also went to the home of friends after school on the pretense of doing homework. What I was really doing, in addition to doing homework, was watching soap operas where I experienced on screen romance highs. When I was about fourteen, while visiting a friend who lived just a few houses down from our home, there was a hard, strong knock on the door. I knew right away that it was my grandmother. I dived for cover. She angrily told my friend that she should not let us into her home to watch television. I was so displeased with her conduct. How embarrassing to have your grandparent angrily come to retrieve you from the home of a friend! No boys and no T.V. was not a lot of fun. I did try to find other ways to have fun as a teenager. We played skip rope, high jump, hide and go seek; I still played with dolls and appreciated sports. I spent a lot of time reading educational books that I obtained at the local library. We had to read in our home as children. As teenagers, we were also encouraged to read a lot. Reading helped in positively shaping our minds as young adults. One particular book I read was "On Becoming a Woman." I learned many things about maturity which my grandparents could not find the courage to tell us or weren't educated enough to share. Bess, my lifelong friend, and I would always try to do things together. We met in preschool and have been in each other's lives ever since. We had sleep overs in my later teenage years and we spent much time day dreaming about life away from Dominica.

I tried to be more involved in church life, but this posed challenges for me because of my fear of being up front. Despite these means of developing a social life, I struggled in my emotional health. By the time I was twelve or thirteen years old my grandmother took me to one of our well known island doctors, Dr. Winston. He was a general physician and not by any means a psychologist. On this particular visit I had come in for my regular complaint of stomach pains. Over the years I had learned to mask my emotional fears with physical complaints, although my emotional troubles did bring me some physical challenges as well. Headaches, chest pains, nausea, abdominal pain and insomnia, amongst others, were always constant. Some of these symptoms were undoubtedly mind over matter. Due to these physical symptoms I always needed medical attention. My insomnia, interestingly, mainly existed because I feared I would die in my sleep. To ensure I did not die in my sleep, as if I could have kept it from happening, I stayed awake often for many years of my life. I remember at times I was hit by my siblings and others because I would wake them in the middle of the night to tell them I could not sleep. I got jabbed in the side and pushed aside so they could enjoy their rest.

I recall one night as they lay sound asleep, I sat up in the middle of the bed between them, poking them and asking if one of them would accompany me to the rest room. I was totally ignored by both of them and brushed off with a few pokes, elbow jerks and nudges. I then came to a very simple solution to take care of business right where I was. So, I did. I chose to wet my bed rather than walk to the rest room just inches from my door. My siblings were not amused. Yet, we have learned to laugh at those things.

On this particular visit to Dr. Winston's office, he asked me some pointed questions. By the end of the visit, he assured my grandmother that my troubles were not physical but emotional and psychological. I believe it was the first time that she had a sense of what was really happening to me. He prescribed valium for my sleepless nights. I only took them a few days, but did not continue as they made me feel very strange. I knew then that I hated medication. I could see signs, though, that I was getting somewhat better after that visit. It's as if I also was able to face my troubles. It gave me consolation to know that I was not the only one who knew something abnormal was taking place with me. Help was on the way, I thought. I did not enjoy living life this way, but I did not know how to change it myself. In 1984 or 1985 my grandmother converted from Catholicism to Adventism. She attended the graduation of my Uncle Mozart who completed a degree in Theology at a Seventh-day Adventist University in Trinidad. Her return to Dominica, after her three-week stay in Trinidad, was an interesting one. With the exception of our grandfather who remained a humble, yet committed alcoholic, the entire household had now become Seventh-day Adventist Christians without notice or warning. I was in the middle of preparing for my first communion. I had, for months, looked forward to wearing the pretty white dress which girls wore on First Communion Day. Now this expectation was gone.

Life at our new Adventist Church turned out to be much fun. I

37

made a new friend; her name was Esther. We remained quite close until she migrated to the United States in 1987. I was very sad when she left Dominica. I was eventually baptized into our new denomination at the age of fourteen. Bess, whom I had known since preschool, had a great sense of humor. Our friendship continued to develop and we are dear friends to this day. My friends had no clue I was experiencing emotional struggles, especially since we laughed much when we were together. My religious upbringing in many ways was improving my life. I loved going to church as a young girl. My sister and I looked forward to the many fun activities in which we participated at church. I attended as often as the doors were open. For me it became a great outlet. My cousins poked fun at me by calling me "Sister Frampton." It was not common to address a teenage girl as "Sister" at church. This was saved for much older members. Although I was extremely reserved and did not enjoy public life, I did what was needed to fill my void.

My sister enjoyed singing and had a powerful voice. She could be a mighty tool in the advancement of God's work. Once the church members realized she could sing, they began encouraging me to sing as well. I avoided such possibilities as often as I could. Sometimes I could not escape it. One day, at an afternoon worship service, I had to sing. My heart raced as I made my way up front. As I looked and saw all eyes on me, I began to sing and weep all at the same time. By the time I was finished, I had to be consoled, and escorted to my seat. I decided in my little heart to stay away from such public displays. Aside from my desire to avoid any up front roles, I loved my new life at church. I joined the Pathfinder Club. This is a club much like the Girl Guide and Boy Scouts. There I learned much about the Bible and the history of our church. We took many trips to camps and visited other churches across the island. This exposure helped me greatly in my social development. For years I experienced social anxiety. I broke out in cold sweats when in large crowds and my heart palpitated as if I were completely out of breath. I grabbed onto the hand of almost anyone near me to make it through a large crowd of people.

One such situation occurred while at a political convention when I was about seventeen. Thousands of people milled around, and gigantic speakers were blaring loud music. There was much going on and I tried hard to act normal as we made our way through the crowd. It wasn't long before my anxiety kicked in and I began grabbing tightly to a friend who could see that something was wrong. She commented on how I was doing as we made our way to a less packed location. I had the same reaction in church, too. I would often make my way down the aisle of church shaking and with teary eyes, doing all I could to shield those symptoms with false bravery. No sooner had the service ended than I would literally rush out of church to avoid contact. No one outside our family ever knew these things, because I did an excellent job of concealing my fears and insecurities. Many people in my family were aware of my mental instability. I saw signs where I was improving, although I was a long way from healing. Interestingly, my religious beliefs were not enough to give me the confidence I needed to reach out to God for help. I did not know Him that way. I had not yet understood the difference between attending church and having a personal encounter with God through faith. I knew how to pray. So, I would talk to God vaguely about my troubles, anticipating immediate results. When I saw no change, I concluded He did not hear me or did not care. This attitude was what defined much of my religious experience. I read the Bible but never with the intention of becoming transformed. Many of the passages I learned and verses I memorized came as a result of teachings through our church. I myself did not earnestly search the scriptures. I did not find the Bible to be an intriguing book as a teenager. I read 'Mills and Boons' and any other romance novel on which I could place my hands.

Somehow, I did not see God as a real presence in my life or in the world. In spite of this disconnect, I believed enough in His existence to do all I could to serve Him. Much of my servitude was misguided. Since I had often felt that I was rejected due to my emotional instabilities and insecurities, I worked hard to ensure that I did all the right things, so that God would love me. Part of pleasing Him meant living to perfection. I remember distinctly a verse that read: "Be ye perfect, as your heavenly father is perfect" (Matthew 5:48). I took this verse literally. For years, as I continued in my religious walk, I chased this perfection with the intent to please God in such a way that He would not reject or be angry with me. Of course, the human that I am, I could not always keep up and I would do things not always conducting myself well. So, I feared being punished by God. I would sometimes not perform my chores. So, I wasn't always obedient, since such acts of "sin" took place. For weeks I would be depressed thinking I had lost favor with God. It was not long before I started realizing that I could not keep up with this standard I had set for myself. It would be helpful if I fully understood what it meant to "Cast all your anxieties on God" (1 Peter 5:7).

By the time I was about fifteen my grandmother had a huge falling out with my mother over her children's care. My mother rented a home for my two siblings and me. This decision mostly resulted from the pressures of my sister and brother who could not live amicably with my grandmother anymore. Needless to say, this was a poor parenting move. Of course, my poor mother just wanted to know her children were happy. We were three teenagers on their own in a three bedroom house. My brother, who is three years older than I am, began drinking heavily. My sister was often out all day with friends. Sometimes we only saw each other at night when they came home after long periods outdoors. They had a lot of friends and always had many things to do. I was too busy pleasing our community and my family and maintaining my reputation. I was a people pleaser. With maturity I have realized this is no way to live life. It's a killer. I totally separated myself from the drama. This did not sit well with my sister. We had a fight one night where we expressed exactly how we felt about each other. Since I had been brewing over her conduct, we spoke some extremely choice words to each other. It was not pleasant.

She told me I thought I was better than she was, and she was probably right at that time. It's not because I wanted to feel that way, but because many people compared our conduct. Our personalities clashed big time.

I felt my sister did not trust me. She thought I reported their behavior to the rest of the family. I did not. I was at times too ashamed about the craziness of our living situation. My brother could not handle alcohol since he was so young. He often vomited when he drank. It was disgusting. My sister and I would slap him and yell at him for having us clean up his mess. My siblings were social people so they brought all kinds of friends to the house. They played loud music and stayed up late at night, as teenagers do, which often disturbed our neighbors. I was embarrassed by their social lives. My sister and I fought much over this and she seemed to only grow more resentful toward my "prim and proper" attitude. I failed to understand them at the time, and it was a deep struggle for me. I felt torn between being the supposed "good girl" and the pressures that came with that reputation. In some ways I envied them and wanted to be free like them.

One summer during the local elections on the island, my siblings and other family members sought to show our loyalty for the party we supported, the Dominica Freedom Party. We attended all the events held by the party and participated in the conventions. When election night got closer, many block parties were held. I was certain I would never join any of those block parties, although I saw many of our local church members letting their hair down. As I saw my brother and sister let loose, which was not unusual, my tapping feet on the sidewalk suddenly accompanied me to the thick band of party supporters waving their rags and flags in solidarity. Before I knew it, I was in the center of a jump up. By the time the morning broke and Sabbath rolled in for worship, we were the talk of the town. I was quite embarrassed. I decided in my heart that it would not happen again. Needless to say, it would not be the last time I violated the church's principles on parties during my Christian journey. Every so often

I ventured out and did something out of the ordinary.

One of my greatest religious struggles during my preteen and teen years was the issue of faith. It did not make any sense to me. Each Sabbath we attended church I heard countless stories about angel encounters in relation to answered prayers. Then there were all those Biblical examples such as Abraham, Enoch and Job who had great faith in God. Despite all these evidences, I was having a difficult time attributing these possibilities to my walk with God. I could not recall having any personal experiences of answered prayers except for one time when I had lost a key I should never have touched. I feared getting into trouble. Silently, I begged God to help me find the lost key. Not long after the prayer, it turned up in the most remote of locations. I remember that I was very surprised, knowing I would have not looked for the keys where I discovered them. As far as I can recall, this was up to that point my entire answer to prayer repertoire. I felt God did not hear me because I did not have the faith spoken of in Hebrews 11:1-11. I quickly concluded I would never have this kind of faith. So, I gave up trying to be like those men in scripture.

Identity Crisis

I wanted so much to find my place in this big world; although I never verbalized it. For a long time, I doubt I knew for sure who I was. Besides my name on my birth paper, who was Josian Frampton? I felt so lost at times. I already knew my mother was not present in my life due to distance. My father and I lived in the same community, but for years we had not communicated. While my grandparents cared for us to the very best of their ability, I cannot recall either of them hugging, kissing, caressing, wrestling or playing with us. They had already raised a large family of their own. They now had to raise five grandchildren, my mother's three children and two of my aunt's children. Such affections therefore were not displayed in our home. I also do not recall affirmations such as you are beautiful, you are smart, or I am proud of you.

It is not that they did not think it, or that they did not love us. They were simply not expressive in that way. Whenever we did not perform well, however, we were often compared to other smart kids in the neighborhood who were doing well. They thought by speaking critically we would be motivated to do better, but it only damaged further the way I saw myself. Somewhere deep inside I felt I did not belong to anyone. My petite, skinny frame and chiseled facial features caused me a great deal of suffering while growing up. I was often the subject of much ridicule at home and at school. My family did not intentionally wish to break me down or be deliberately mean or unkind. It's just that island life was about finding humor in everything. We did not have the use of televisions the way we do now. People found creative ways to entertain themselves. So we poked fun at each other.

Everyone, when I was growing up, had some kind of nickname. This appears to be prevalent in black culture. There are people I grew up with whose birth names I never knew because they had always been called by some nickname. I remember one of my aunts and her partner for years never called me by my name. They always addressed me as "Sheep and goat face." I smiled, but inside I ached. They were never harsh and did not laugh at me when they said it. I guess they genuinely felt that, since my face was so small, it looked like either of those two creatures. So that's all they called me for years. What it did, though, was convince me that something was significantly wrong with my face.

I recall longing to be in an accident so that my face would be crushed, allowing my cheek bones to disappear. I did not know then that high cheek bones were a sign of beauty. I felt them quite a curse for many years until my relocation to America. At school I had other names such as skinny legs, broom stick, Zozyo (means bird in Creole). I was called "Zozyo" because my birth name was Zozian. I hated that name with a passion. It simply added to my life struggles and contributed to my insecurities since I was teased so much about it. What mother would give this name to a child? I wondered. My sister and brother had lovely, normal names. I often thought to myself, whatever happened to Mary, Jane, Martha, Beverly and all the other lovely names you'd give to a girl? The kids at school had a field day with this name for years.

I Will Give You a New Name

By the time I turned eleven and was preparing to take my "Common Entrance Examinations" to enter high school, I needed a birth certificate. When we went to the registry's office, we asked for Zozian Frampton, but that name could not be found. There was only a "Josian" on record. There was no concrete evidence to explain the reason for the change. It was then we learned for the first time that no one existed by that name and that my birth certificate named me Josian Frampton. The news sounded like music to my ears. My mother and I have often wondered what really happened to the name I was given at birth. The only possible explanation could be found when a huge fire in the city of Roseau burned down the registry's office on a Saturday afternoon, June 16, 1979. Many records were destroyed. I believe that while recovering the records some changes were made to files. I do not know for sure. I can only say I loved my new name. With the submission of the new information to the school my teacher announced that as of that day my new name is "Josian" and that I should acquaint myself with my new name.

Although some trouble makers sought to continue in their folly of calling me "Zozyo," it did not last very long. Many years later, in my mid-teens, out of my new name came "Josie" which I also greatly love. As I see the twists and turns my life has taken over time, it is my sincere conviction that God changed my name because with the name change came a new appreciation for myself. All these treatments and teasing severely affected my self-esteem. It is difficult to think highly of oneself when others work

44

so hard to belittle, discourage and break one down. This is one of the reasons why in my adult life today ,and even while serving as a minister of the gospel, I try with the grace of God to make a deliberate attempt to maintain a healthy self-esteem by keeping ever present in my mind the fact that I am created in the image of God.

Created in God's Image

I was about twenty-four years old, living in Mount Vernon, New York. One weekend when my cousin and best friend Juliette braided my hair, we engaged in a deep dialogue about our lives. To this point opening up seemed almost impossible for me, because for years I had bottle up my emotions. I did not enjoy talking much, and found it to be a lot of work. I particularly did not like having conversations about myself. Plus, I truly did not particularly trust others enough to confide in them.

Throughout my young life, I had few close friends I felt I could trust. One such friend is my lifelong friend, Bess. Today my circles of friends have expanded and I share in a lot more close friendships. With maturity and growth I learned to be somewhat more open. However, I still have a great regard for my privacy and enjoy when it is not invaded. As I shared with Juliette some of the struggles I had with self-esteem, confidence and beauty, she seemed surprised. It was then she affirmed me by saying: "You are not just pretty, you are a gorgeous woman." Those words pierced through my heart like arrows. Growing up, if ever I heard I was pretty it wasn't with such conviction. Besides, I would be told I had a pretty face, as if the rest of me did not exist. My frail, skinny frame commanded no attention. Every black woman knows that to attract a date you must be curvy and have a healthy looking butt. Not possessing any of these requirements, I simply did not qualify for the dating life.

Even my sports teacher would chuckle when I showed up for practice, as he looked at my little legs struggling against those of the giants

I stood next to. I always felt unattractive, inadequate and second best. No one ever said those words to me. I believe those feelings developed because I was teased so much. One would not know I felt this way about myself because I never verbalized it. It was not in my nature to be expressive or talkative. I could also have fooled people into believing that I was confident and beautiful, not intentionally, but because I was always nicely dressed. My mother sent my sister and me lovely things from Guadeloupe. I also loved being dressed up. It somehow became my escape. In many ways, however, it was a cry for attention at that time. I kept screaming in my heart for attention. I wanted to be viewed for more than my frame. No one seemed to hear me. My concerns were invisible. People often ask each other, "How are you doing?" But they never stick around long enough to get a sincere response. My self-esteem issues were a pivotal aspect of my emotional crisis. Its effects showed up in a number of ways: shyness, isolation, dress, tears, intimidation and lack of confidence amongst many other negative emotional responses. It would be years of grooming to correct this demon.

At church some of the girls disliked me because of the fact that I always looked good. They talked about me badly. At school we wore uniforms. So, the issue of dress was not a bother. I found creative ways to blend clothes and to alter them to meet my taste. For me it became a hobby which has remained with me to this today. It was an outlet. I had somewhere to center my focus and attention. It gave me a sense of fulfillment to put something together which made me feel good afterwards. I had a creative way of altering clothes to accentuate styles. My work wasn't always tidy because I did not have a sewing machine. So, some girls would laugh if they saw a fault, and others would criticize. I felt hurt but it did not stop me. I still enjoy wearing beautiful clothes. Except today, I dress for very different reasons. I sincerely feel very good about myself and I now know and understand my place in the world.

Amazingly, and in spite of my physical setbacks, I succeeded in just about all my sporting competitions at school, but not because I possessed a competitive drive. I guess I just put my heart into the things I did. People treated me based on my shell (my outward appearance), but I had a heart and I operated from the heart. Somewhere deep inside, and I do not know where the thought came from, I knew that someday I would overcome my obstacles and be someone who would command respect and attention.

School Days

The high school I attended was not a regular high school. It was one for students like me, who did not pass the proficiency exam to obtain admission into the regular high school. If we failed the test, the J.S.P (Junior Secondary Program) would allow us to continue to the tenth grade, which is the third form in British culture, and no further. The students who failed this entrance exam were ones of whom the teachers did not think favorably. They were treated like rejects, ones who were not smart or those who did not make it. We were treated differently from those who transitioned to the real high school. At the end of the tenth grade the students were allowed to take a School Leaving exam. It's somewhat like the G.E.D program here in America. If a student scored high, they would possibly go on to college level classes and if not, they'd learn a trade. The ladies learned sewing and cooking; the boys learned agriculture and woodwork. The possibility of advancing academically was bleak for someone in this program, but I had a dream. I had friends who entered the regular high school, but Bess and I stayed back. My future did not look so promising. I had other cousins who later obtained scholarships to high school. They were exalted, talked about and praised as I looked on, hurt and silent. They did deserve to be acknowledged. They had found success and this was a reason to celebrate. On the other hand, losers fade in the celebration of those who succeed. It's how it is in life. I was happy for them but sad for myself. They did not gloat over my failure;

47

they were just happy for their own success. In my heart I longed for the time when I would celebrate something.

Many of the students in this program seemed to have had a chip on their shoulder, possibly for a number of reasons. I believe it is because they knew the stigma attached to being in this program. So, they simply acted out. Needless to say, the fact that I was also in this special program did not help my already damaged self-esteem. I felt such humiliation being there, but I had made my way into this group by my own fears. For a long time my anxieties about taking exams made it difficult for me to do well. Never having verbalized my concerns, they went unattended and unnoticed. I do not believe anything would have been done even if I had informed anyone that I suffered with test anxieties. Our system then did not make contingencies for those kinds of issues. Things may have changed since. In any event, when the teachers came to teach our classes, they seem unenthused and many of them made certain negative remarks to the class concerning our intelligence.

Some students including me remained quiet. Other students laughed. I guess this occurred out of embarrassment, but I know it was painful to many of us. It is my belief that the teachers felt convinced that we were not interested in our education. So, they treated us accordingly. I wondered what my life was going to be like without receiving further formal education, when this had been my dream. I knew I was not dumb, I was simply fearful. My fears in turn affected my performance on almost all levels in my life. I compensated by doing well in sports. I had become in our own little school circle some sort of a "Star athlete." I even won "Most Outstanding Student" one year during our seasonal sports competitions. I still do not recall how I did it. I had been nervous throughout all my training and the actual races. I would not even look behind, or beside me to see who my competitors were. I just ran. Still, each time I ran I won. It remains a mystery to me. I won many medals by the time my school running days were over.

It felt good accomplishing something. Feeling good about myself was a constant struggle when so many people teased me and poked fun at my petite frame and fragile demeanor especially at school. There was a boy in grade school with a real mean streak. He looked pathetic, himself, with blood-red eyes, and was always sucking his thumb. Almost every day after school he waited for me as I walked home. He would flick my ears with his fingers, poke me in the back and call me silly names. I was a coward so I was afraid of him and he knew it. This just spurred him on to abuse me more. He did this for a long time until it finally stopped. His treatment toward me did not help my fears or esteem. I did not date while in high school although there was one boy who really liked me. He had a deep, gruff and unattractive voice, which I very much disliked hearing. He tried really hard and even sent friends to speak on his behalf but I did not respond to his interest. I was not interested in boys or dating at the time either, so I left dating alone.

There was a boy, though, that I liked a lot. He wasn't interested in me or any other girls, as a matter of fact. He seemed shy, and so was I. So I ended up never dating in my school in Dominica. Things changed when I spent time with my mother for a summer vacation in Guadeloupe. I was sixteen at the time. There I met a handsome Indian seventeen year old who was horny and very excited about dating me. I never had a boyfriend before so I was nervous but truly flattered. George sent my heart racing. He was tall and lean with bushy eyebrows which lay flat and gorgeous. His skin oozed a softness highlighting his natural bronze complexion. His lips were beautiful and cried out repeatedly to be kissed. It's not surprising that he was the first guy I kissed.

George made it clear from the beginning that he loved me very much and wanted to make love to me. He didn't try to polish it. He said it was what people did when they loved each other. I told him that I didn't believe in sex before marriage. He wasn't happy about that. So he negotiated only kissing. This is how I got my first kiss. I saw stars the first time we kissed, though it was broad daylight. We had been told we should not date until we were eighteen. I was very nervous about dating earlier or being caught. We found creative ways to meet each other and we used codes to meet. Since we were neighbors, this wasn't hard to arrange. I won't forget what love felt like for the first time. All kinds of movement went on in my stomach. I was so overcome by emotions that I could barely concentrate or look him in the eyes.

I fell so deeply in love, or lust, at that moment. I certainly experienced my first emotional and or sexual high that day. There is something about sneaking around as a teenager and kissing that does not have the same thrill as when everyone knows you have a boyfriend and you're entitled to kiss. I was never more pressured to be intimate in my entire life as when I knew George. If I hadn't been so afraid of becoming pregnant and not being a virgin anymore, I would have unquestionably lost my virginity at sixteen. I'm glad I was afraid of something. By the next summer when I visited George, he said he had a girlfriend who was willing to make love to him. I was very hurt and tried to work on some negotiations to make our little romance work but he wasn't having any of it. I had my first heart break that second summer. It took me a long time to heal. George is not the only relationship I lost during my dating experiences for not having sex. One valuable thing did come out of my relationship with George. He taught me French, the language of love and romance. We wanted so badly to be able to communicate with each other I was forced to learn his language. I still speak French to this very day.

My Search for God

It was during that time I began having some serious questions about God. These inquiries were present before I turned sixteen, but they intensified then. Subconsciously, I decided that I was never to question God. I am sure this line of reasoning came from somewhere in our church's teachings. To this point in my life I knew all this information about God: what He expected of me, His rules, commandments, His teachings and how they were to be applied to my life. To the very best of my ability while growing up, I tried hard to please God. God had never been presented to me as a loving, caring, considerate or even a real being. The teachings I received introduced me to a demanding, distant, abstract, impersonal and harsh God.

For years I felt God would punish or disown me if I disobeyed Him. I saw Him as a disciplinarian who waited until I did wrong to punish. Serving Him therefore did not come from any deep love I had for Him as a being but from fear and obligation. This is no way to love someone. It would be the only way I knew until God Himself taught me how to love Him. While on the French island of Guadeloupe visiting my mother one year, I sat and gazed deeply into the sky. I took in the majestic look of the heavens filled with beautiful white clouds which created great designs across the sky. I became filled with expectation that God would reveal Himself in the sky. For hours I sat imagining what it would be like to finally see God. To this point in my life He had been so absent. All my injustices I felt were unattended by Him. My pains were overlooked. I wondered where He was when I suffered these things. I grew disappointed, sad and frustrated. I think I started losing hope then.

It would be years before I fully comprehended the meaning of "The Great Mystery of God" (1 Timothy 3:16). As I approached my seventeenth birthday, a deep yearning in my heart came for an exodus to some cosmopolitan country. Guadeloupe, though a very beautiful and well-to-do French island, had not done well for my esteem. Still traditionally committed to the whole French-English revolution, with those from my island in particular not liking the English, my life there felt unsettled. It was time to leave. Granted the issues I had been having in my life, I truly did not want to be in a place where my presence was not welcome. Since a few of my relatives lived in the United States, I was able to convince my mother to let me go to America. On March 26, 1993, I left for my first visit to the United States of America. I would soon learn the history of race relations in America where new challenges of identity awaited.

Upon arriving in America,
I realized it was not what I saw on T.V.

JOURNEY TO AMERICA

Chapter 3

Journey to America

Upon arriving in New Jersey, I first took up residence with one of my cousins, Debbie. She was very kind to me. She often took me shopping and gave me pocket change each week. She also gave me clothes and made sure my needs were met. I think being with her was the most comfortable I had been in staying with relatives while initially being in America. I felt closer to her because she is such a wonderful, caring person. We are still very close to this day. Once here, my primary goal and dream was to go to college and get an education. I was also eager to do something about my sickly frame. I still weighed below a hundred pounds at this time. Being as petite as I am bothered me immensely. I felt that I looked like a child and not a young adult. Being in a diverse environment such as the Tri–States, and New York in particular, I found myself studying young women whom I felt were in my age group, just admiring from a distance what it would be like to look that healthy. I began a campaign to gain weight. I became acquainted with fast food restaurants and found myself eating foods which I would not have eaten previously. This is because I came from an island where I ate organically grown foods.

In desperation to improve my looks, however, I was willing to try almost anything. I drank so many Ensure, Nutriments and other weight-gaining drinks but my weight didn't budge. It wasn't long before I could not keep up with this regimen, particularly financially. I had been worshiping at the Bethel Seventh-day Adventist church in Jersey City, New Jersey. Maintaining my religious life in spite of my frustrations meant a lot to me. After spending six months in America, I returned to Dominica. The West Indian community knows that if you travel abroad, particularly to countries like Canada, the United States and England, you must reflect physical change upon your return. Well, since I had not gained a pound while on my visit to the United States, you can only imagine the embarrassment I felt when I returned.

Once I was back home my cousins, aunts, grandparents and friends bombarded me with questions and comments about my return home and the fact that I looked the same as I did when I left. Since I knew how hard I tried not to face criticism, the experience was humiliating. Although I had not improved much physically, I did have a more polished look since the months I spent in America had encompassed spring and part of the fall. The cold temperatures brought a beautiful glow to my complexion. Over time I blended in again and the nagging stopped. In the summer of 1994, I returned to the United States. This time I was determined to do something positive with my life. My first step in doing this would be to get an education. There were two obstacles in my way: finance and my immigration status. To study here I needed an adjustment of status and money.

Reality Check

My fantasies of life in America through the world of television, movies, and soap operas were far from any reality I was experiencing. I did not want to simply live life in this country without any direction. I knew that I was on my own, though I had relatives here. I also knew that asking them for help to fulfill any of the dreams I had, wasn't an option. They had their own struggles with which to contend. In the late fall, I worked as a nanny in New Jersey. I worked for two Caucasian families at the same time. They were two sisters who lived down the street from each other and hired me together to save money. I took the children to school, did their laundry, and fed them their meals. I lived in their home Monday to Friday and earned $150.00 a week. The sister with whom I stayed had a little boy about three years of age and a girl about six. The boy had some demonic tendencies. He had a midget-like build with a mean countenance. He had a rage in him which scared me. One day while I prepared their dinner, he took a baseball bat and pounded on the kitchen window till it cracked. When his parents came home, they blamed me. It seemed interesting that when they were home neither of them could control him. Yet, whenever they came home to a report that he had done something wrong, they would say I had not done a good job supervising him. I grew extremely frustrated with their unreasonable attitude.

One morning while I got the boy ready for school, a mean look took over his countenance. He grew red, angry and violent. He began kicking me very hard. I tried containing him without success. Then I began to grow angry. I held his feet strongly enough to let him know that I was in control. Nothing worked, however. Like a possessed individual this three year old kicked and screamed and fought me. Finally, his father came into the room almost afraid of him. He was contained enough to make it out of the house. It was that morning I knew for sure that my time left with them would be very short. When the mother realized that I would not stay long, she began accusing me of things. One day when she came in from work she confronted me and said she noticed that every time I did laundry the children's clothes were missing.

This was a backhanded way of telling me I was a thief. Well, I grew up in a home where if twenty five cents was missing, there would be a meeting to inquire where it had disappeared to. We were to report every coin we found in our home. The understanding was that we did not work so no monies belonged to us. Also, while growing up in our home, we were specifically told that when we were old enough we would have to work. Regardless of where we worked we should never touch any loose change or monies we found lying around, as it was a test to see how loyal we were. If I would not take a coin which could be so easily overlooked, why would I take something as obvious as clothes?

While working for the family in New Jersey, I had enrolled in some G.E.D courses. Since it was only a three-month course, I completed it by the time my tenure with the family ended. So something good came out of my working with that family. Enrollment in an American university was now a clear possibility. I still needed funds and my immigration status adjusted. Since I didn't want to be a burden to my family here, I knew I could not approach them for help. My stay in New Jersey was very short lived when my two cousins argued over a guy. While still at the home of the family where I lived and worked in New Jersey, one of my cousins called to tell me that I had been involuntarily relocated to New York, where she was now going to stay. It wasn't a shock to me as their relationship had become very estranged. Things had been brewing for a few months since a sleek African-American man had supposedly swept my other cousin off her feet. Her sister really felt she had been swept of her senses, because this Casanova was up to no good.

West Indians and black Americans for decades have had their stereotypes of each other: but it wasn't just because this man was African-American that my family rejected him so much. There were major character issues which everyone on the outside looking in could see but my cousin in love could not. The tension escalated and I was caught in the middle. So when I found out one day, while I was still at work, that my belongings were in Brooklyn, a new journey began. As the New Year approached, my search for a sponsor to assist me with my studies here continued. I now had been attending a church in Brooklyn. The pastor and his wife were wonderful people but I felt quite lost in that congregation. In my estimation the people were self-absorbed. In my understanding there appeared to have been a great emphasis on social status and education. Not that anything is necessarily wrong with social status or education. But when those things keep us from paying attention to people amongst us who are less advantaged or seeking a place to belong, we must revisit why we attend church. I was never once invited to a member's home for lunch in the two and a half years that I stayed there. I also cannot recall once that an interest was taken in who I was. A young single lady, attending a church week after week for all this time, I had hoped for a better interaction.

Shackled

Feeling alone and in many ways helpless to improve my challenges, I tried my best to stay afloat. I had to provide everything I needed. There was no one I felt I could ask or depend on. Everyone seemed to be experiencing similar financial struggles. I didn't really have a close friend at the time. I rented an apartment with one of my cousins. We had a roommate whom I had met at the church I was attending in Brooklyn. She was extremely secretive. Since I was a deeply private person, this made any real bonding a great challenge. This new friend and my cousin were present only on the weekends, since they worked jobs where they stayed during the week. Their contributions helped to financially sustain the $700-a-month apartment.

Prior to branching out on my own I lived with different relatives who each helped in their own way, particularly with providing a place to stay. I continued to center my objective on remaining focused. I found myself often alone, so I grew extremely lonely. Many people were around me living in a busy, crowded city like Brooklyn, New York. Yet, I felt alone and isolated. The struggles with my earlier childhood fears had not vanished. I had learned better how to control, as well as disguise them, but I wasn't free from them. While alone in my Brooklyn apartment, most nights I was sure I heard things. I would often get up, look around, check all rooms and corners to find nothing and no one. My fears were simply driving me. Before long, my insomnia had intensified and I walked around like a zombie sometimes from lack of sleep.

Spending so much time alone did not help my emotional health. My unhappiness intensified. I began entertaining thoughts of self-hate. Although I struggled with my self-esteem, I cared about myself. When my continued attempts to improve my appearance had not started working, these negative feelings grew. My teeth were crooked and needed to be straightened by braces. But since I was without any form of medical or dental insurance at the time, I remained unable to do anything about it. My confidence only decreased from these setbacks. My desire to eat diminished also, so in my mind I looked worse rather than better. My understanding of who I was also became severely challenged by issues of race here in America. The social stigma and negative ideology associated with blacks here in this country posed additional stresses to my self-esteem. Growing up in Dominica I was simply a girl. I never had to worry about race. People generally had a healthy understanding of themselves racially. It was here in America I was informed that I wasn't just a girl. I was a "Black girl." This knowledge deepened my identity issues. I did try my best not to allow it to add to my emotional challenges. As I wrestled with my appearance, I often stood in my bedroom mirror staring at my frame and overall appearance. One day as I looked at myself I grew very angry at God. "How could I be made in Your image," I cried. "Look at me."

After speaking some very unkind words to the girl in the mirror, I reached for a sharp object. While holding the object in my hand, I wept uncontrollably. With tears rolling down my cheeks I stretched my arms out with a desire to cut them and other parts of my body. Though determined, I couldn't hurt myself. The flashbacks of my mental and emotional hardships while in Dominica filled my mind. "Where is God?" I pondered. "How could He possibly be real in the midst of such confusion and struggle?" I really wanted freedom from my fears, discontent, self-dissatisfaction, unhappiness and loneliness; but how? I had prayed for years for God to help me, but He appeared to remain absent and silent. Suddenly, a deep prompting on my heart overwhelmed my thoughts, urging me to drop the sharp object. Almost in submission to the thought which encouraged me not to hurt myself, I dropped the object then fell across my bed and wept bitterly.

I made it to work the next day with my head hung low, trying to shield my puffy tear-soaked eyes. The thought that I am fearfully and wonderfully made by God, based on Psalms 139:14, angered rather than encouraged me. By the summer of the following year I began working a nanny job in Manhattan. It was then I met a man who worked as a security officer for the private housing complex which was home to many working families. Up until this point, since my return to America, I had not dated anyone. Still a virgin, I fought hard to preserve my purity. In addition, the influence of American television seriously challenged my values and beliefs. During the months I had not been working, I spent many hours watching daytime talk shows. The moral decay of the value system here both troubled and intrigued me. The assertiveness of young men and women met my envy. Until this point in my life, I was still an introverted and reserved person. I spoke if I knew someone well, but generally I did not associate very much with people; although I was quite personable when I did interact. I also did not always particularly care to be bothered by others. I wasn't open and I wasn't really friendly. It's not because I wasn't nice. I sincerely did not know how to initiate friendships. I would be a good friend to the friends I made, but it always felt safer if I did not have to go make friends. I believe I operated in safe mode most of my life. Much of my time was spent trying to avoid pain. The more I tried, though, the more pain seemed to find me. Writing became my way of expression. This explains why I have almost thirty journals. This is also why my current life as a minister continues to challenge the core of my innate personality traits of quietness and solitude. I always found talking to be a lot of work. I no longer desire solitude as often as I did during my unstable emotional days but, after hours of teaching, preaching, and interacting, I must go into seclusion in order to recharge. Though I am a lot more sociable than I have ever been, I will always value quietness and tranquility.

It was a blisteringly hot July weekday as I sat on a park bench in a Manhattan neighborhood cradling a beautiful baby girl in my arms. I had just a few months earlier begun caring for her and another child, a lovely boy from another family. As I reminisced on the thought of one day having my own family, a good looking, and calm spirited African-American security officer came behind me fully dressed in uniform and asked my name. The security officers in this complex operated almost like police officers. This man possessed a respectable demeanor, was soft spoken and had a lovely smile. He proceeded to engage me in conversation, appealing to my attention with his flattery. Hungry for love and affection at the time, I gravitated to the bit of attention I was receiving. No desperation showed in my demeanor but in my heart I longed to be loved, nurtured and cared for by someone during that period in my life. Since being in America, I had been on my own. I had no one that I was really accountable to. All I needed came from myself. I felt lost and alone although I never said it or showed it. He soon asked me my age. I told him exactly how old I was. He quickly blurted out, "Wow you're young! I am twenty nine." I later learned that he was literally twice my age. Since I was extremely naïve, I had no reason not to believe his words. I felt a sense of security in that he worked in a job which promoted safety.

I also discovered his professional life did not equal his moral life. We exchanged numbers and soon we were talking on the phone. There were so many tell-tale signs that this relationship was a recipe for disaster, but my naïve mind could not process those warnings at the time. As I later looked back at the blatant things I overlooked, I became more aware of where I was mentally and emotionally. My need for attention and affection blinded my ability to think clearly or rationally. Within weeks of conversation, this fox knew that I was a virgin. He seemed shocked that I still was one. I shouldn't have been surprised when he became conveniently unavailable after I had given myself to him.

As a result of losing a relationship in the islands because of my decision to abstain from premarital sex, my fears mounted that I would have another failed relationship. An inner battle arose to uphold these standards. This struggle came to a halt when I feared not having the strength to fight in that moment. At the slightest pressure, I had succumbed to my new lover. Moments after the encounter, I knew I had made a horrible mistake. The days and weeks following being intimate with this man, he would not return my calls and completely avoided me in the area where we worked together. Realizing that I was a mere experiment, I sank into a deep depression. One time in conversation, he told me that he had never been with a virgin. An emotionally stable girl would have sensed danger. Ashamed that I had to continue to work in the same environment, I seriously contemplated suicide. It's not that I wanted to die, but I most certainly did not feel like living with the shame.

One day, as I felt I had reached a breaking point, and again considered suicide, a very strong thought of my mother enveloped me. My mother has a very worrisome nature. I knew if I killed myself, my family would possibly bury more than one person that day. My mother would not survive my death. I could not be this insensitive. If my mother had not been alive, I would have taken my life. There was no one else in my life at that time, for whom I felt I needed to remain alive. I thanked God for keeping my mother alive. The loss of my virginity severely wounded me. I developed an acute fear of men. I never thought I would have been able to open up enough again to let another relationship develop.

By the fall of 1996 I returned to Dominica to work on obtaining my student visa. I had traveled back and forth between the United States and Dominica during the time I had been here to keep my status open. In December of 1996, after praying much for a sponsor, I received sponsorship. That year I had my status changed to allow me to further my studies in America.

A Dream Comes True

I returned to America in preparation for my studies. My attempts to save money to help with my college expenses had not paid off well. I only saved money for two semesters. In earlier times as I had looked for ways to raise funds, a woman told me of a live–in housekeeping job on Long Island. I recall showing up for the interview and a tryout for the job. It was a Tuesday afternoon around three when I arrived. Eager to raise some funds I quickly accepted the job although in my heart it was not what I desired to do with my life. No sooner did I walk away from the chair, but I was shown to a bottle of bleach and Lysol along with other cleaning supplies and a list of the many areas I should clean that very moment. Soon I had been escorted to an ironing table filled with shirts and other items to be ironed when I finished my cleaning assignment. Distressed, I proceeded to work that Tuesday until almost seven in the evening. When I retired later, exhausted, I cried all night.

The next two mornings, I walked their dog, Leo. Leo was a huge and very active dog. As I walked him around the block, he pulled and tossed my skinny frame around. It was quite evident in that moment, that I was not walking Leo, but rather Leo was the one taking me on daily walks. The possibilities of a future with such a life disturbed me. It was then I asked the family to take me home that very Friday morning. I did not know how I was going to survive, but I knew it was not this way. As we drove to the train station, the woman seemed visibly upset because I would not continue in her home. She criticized me for being very thin and said I needed to get on a chicken diet to gain some weight. She quickly concluded that looking the way I did, I would not have been able to handle her job anyway. Incidences like these motivated my ambition to get an education and make something of my life. Just a few months after this incident, I received a call from an old friend in New Jersey where I once lived. She informed me of a nanny job available in Manhattan. I was interviewed for a position working for two couples, a black and a white family. We shared a fairly nice working relationship until they no longer needed me. I felt a great connection to the children who were each only a few months old at the time. I still maintain a lovely relationship with these families to this day. From this work I was able to save sufficient funds to cover my first year of college. I worked as hard as I could to make my dream of obtaining an education come true, but I think I was pushing myself way too hard.

One day, I left work from Manhattan headed to Brooklyn where I lived. I was extremely tired and stressed, and poorly nourished because I did not eat well. I looked very thin and sickly. I got on the crowded New York City subway train that evening feeling somewhat strange physically. The train was filled to capacity, standing room only. I wished for a seat but you don't ask a New Yorker to get up so you can sit. I dared not be so bold or brave, but held onto the metal pole above me as securely as I could. I felt weak and sick. The train passed through its usual stops on my route as I felt more and more light-headed.

Soon, I could feel that I was losing focus and I grew exceedingly dizzy. The next thing I remember is a faint voice in the distance asking, "Ma'am, are you okay?" I never had a chance to respond. As if in slow motion I could feel myself losing my grip on the pole and slumping down.

Before long I was lying on the train seats with a bottle of smelling salts below my nostrils. People were pushed aside to give me air. I do not know for how long I was out, but the train went out of service and the paramedics were attending to me. They soon escorted me off the train to the platform, where two of New York's finest checked my vitals and tried getting me to go to the hospital. I assured them I would be okay; I convinced them to let me go home. They asked that I remained hydrated and go to the hospital if I felt worse. I made it home, still wondering how I so quickly collapsed. By the next morning I was back at work as if nothing had happened, but I made a conscientious effort to take better care of myself. I had been saving nearly all I made for my tuition. It wasn't much, but on the little funds I had, I began preparing for college in Manhattan.

I attended the Borough of Manhattan Community College before later transferring to Monroe College in New Rochelle, New York for undergraduate studies. Certain of my family members in America did not receive very well the news of my education. This was not because they did not care, but I believe they did not wish my ambitions to become their responsibility. I had a dream, however, and I knew the only person who could make this dream a reality was me. One day, prior to beginning classes, as I finalized my application process, a relative approached me, with a frustrated look, and said: "Don't think the burden of your college will rest on me. I suggest you find a domestic job to support yourself in this country and forget about this college affair." I was hurt but I knew nothing or no one would stop me. My dream to have an education did not originate in America. Rather, the dream was the reason I was in America. Somewhere deep inside there was a dream buried beneath the rubble of despair, depression, belittlement, low self-esteem, unhappiness, sadness and insurmountable fears. Maybe I wanted to show those who looked down on me that I had it in me to succeed, or maybe I wasn't trying to prove anything to anyone. I just wanted to improve my quality of life. In my heart I felt convinced that only education could open the door to fulfilling that dream of improving my quality of life. With money saved up to cover only two semesters, I needed a plan to pay for college. My tuition was only $1,500 a semester. After my first year I got on a tuition program that allowed me to make payments over a four-month period. This plan made it much easier to manage things financially and stay in school. But the same year I began college, I fell on hard times. I could not find work on or off campus.

By February of 1997 I relocated to Mount Vernon, New York with my cousin and best friend, Juliette. We are distant cousins but I didn't know it at the time. So, I related to her as a friend, not a cousin. I received a call from her some time in 1996, when I was at an all-time low, and when I still lived in Brooklyn. She had just relocated to America for studies and decided to try to find me. We were not particularly friends back in Dominica, so I was most surprised by the call and her need to search for me. We were complete opposites. I was a seasoned introvert greatly inhibited by my fears. She feared nothing and no one. Older by a few years, she had already accomplished much in life. She was well traveled, and already had a degree; I had not even been to college yet. She also possessed a great sense of self. I was still learning who I was. Strengthening our friendship was not easy. I clearly had issues. But it remains my strong belief that her being in my life was extremely providential.

One of my primary issues had to do with trust. I had been emotionally hurt so often, it became difficult for me to venture out. With each episode I reentered my shell and as a result, I was often misunderstood. These misunderstandings led to speculation and gossip, even viciousness at times by others. I recall one incident with a woman from my island whom I met in New York City while working as a nanny. She had become quite cordial after she pursued a friendship with me. Sadly, this individual's tongue seemed quite loose. She said very unpleasant things to me about the nannies where we worked and she also told them very unpleasant and damaging lies about me. When I met her, I was still a virgin. She knew this because she was presumptuous enough to ask. Yet, she worked hard at soiling my reputation with men in the community where we worked as nannies. Before long, barely any of the other nannies were speaking to me, thinking, no doubt, that I was promiscuous and a threat to their relationships. It wasn't until several of them became victims of her gossip that they sought to repair relations with me. Eventually I had to make a difficult decision to move on from having any connections with this individual. We have never interacted since then. It is my understanding that, years later, she has not changed a bit. Some people are not good for our health.

Juliette's presence in my life, on the contrary, had been having some incredibly positive impact on me. Being a very sensitive and insecure person, I found it hard at times to bond with her due to her strong personality. Yet, her sincerity, honesty, and openness served as a safety net for me. For the first time since leaving Dominica, I began feeling a sense of hopefulness. My weak personality I know irritated her at times. She would often get frustrated with my frequent tearful moments. I felt it in the way she would sometimes address me when she asked me to "Pull myself together." I cried at the simplest things. If I had been looked at too long or too hard I would also weep. My insecurities were insurmountable and I was helpless in doing anything about them. Juliette's presence in my life in time truly became impactful. Since our religious beliefs and denominational affiliations were the same, we became real girlfriends hanging out at many events and occasions. Her inner strength challenged me to believe in myself. I benefited greatly from our friendship. Since being in America, I had not established any such bond with anyone else. I truly craved having a female friend with whom I could do things and go places.

New Beginnings

As time went on, Juliette became a mentor in addition to a friend. She poured words of encouragement and positive thoughts into my mind. She taught me to walk erect and to stand confidently in my skin. She reminded me often not to be intimidated by anyone. Her strength greatly helped my esteem and confidence. I also think she wanted me to be better as soon as possible, because my weakness was not helping her to maintain her own strength very well. My family back in Dominica had in their own way tried to reach me. They cared greatly about my physical needs but I never allowed them into that dismal side of me enough to let them help me emotionally. How can a person truly help someone who has not asked for help? I reached out to Juliette for help by opening up. I allowed her into my life and told her things I never felt comfortable telling anyone else. I shared with her the pain of losing my virginity

For the first time she helped me restore my dignity. She reminded me that I reached out for love in a sincere way. Someone saw an opportunity and took advantage of my trust and inexperience. Although I had not been raped and had willingly placed myself in that situation, she explained that someone of character would have handled things differently. Once she counseled me, I was finally able to stop blaming myself or even this individual and find peace to move on, but the effects of this incident would remain with me for years. Living with Juliette and her sisters, Carmella and Debbie, created an atmosphere of happiness although it was not always perfect. There were moments of tension as is expected when four women share a space.

Granted my then fragile nature, I had many happy yet uncomfortable moments with them. The passing of time kept making things better. Eventually they introduced me to live theatre, which I greatly loved. We started spending much time on Broadway in Manhattan. One of my favorite shows, besides Miss Saigon, was the

Phantom of the Opera. We dined out often, shopped, had facials, manicures and pedicures, baked, cooked, danced and laughed a lot. Almost every Saturday night we'd have friends over. We cooked Dominican style meals and danced to island music as if there was no tomorrow. We would reminisce on times back home when St Joseph, our village, held its village feasts. We laughed at the island jargon of the locals as well as the want-to-be Calypsonians (Song Artists). The isolation I once felt was gradually wearing off. Juliette had a freedom of spirit which had not been altered by the supposed restrictions of denominational teachings. She had a mind of her own. After years of being imprisoned in my mind, dancing brought me a freedom of spirit I cannot express in words. Though I still appreciated moments of solitude, no longer did I deliberately seek isolation. Having spent so much time alone in my earlier years in America, being with my cousins in their home eliminated this desire for isolation. Occasionally, I still experienced depressed feelings, but this did not occur as frequently as in past years.

Earthly Angels

For about eight months while in college I could not find work. These were tough times for me financially. Without financial help, I struggled to get by. The two $500 credit cards I had received from the school were now maxed out, as I had used them to pay certain bills. I paid rent where I lived with the girls. I had tuition, plus my basic needs needed to be met. When I was not able to meet my portion of the rent for a few months, I felt terrible. Tensions occurred as my lack of contribution forced others to make adjustments in their budgeting. This was understandable. We all studied and had major expenses. I sensed my unhappiness beginning to show.

Things for a while seemed to have been working, but now I was back to square one. I continued to attend school which undoubtedly became my number one priority. One day while still at school I grew very hungry. I went to a Jamaican restaurant a couple of blocks from the school to purchase a West Indian meal. I knew I was not able to afford anything large so I ordered the smallest size meal on the menu. The meal was only $5.00. I handed the cashier my credit card but my $5.00 purchase was declined. As the cashier stretched her hand to take the food, with tears in my eyes I stretched out my hand to give it back. Then a tall dark man with an accent said, "It's on me." He paid for my meal and wished me a good day. Teary, grateful and humiliated all at the same time, I wondered about the kindness of this complete stranger. I had never seen him before and I never saw him again in that community during my three years I attended that school.

I met another person who touched my life while at school. We were both international students, so we understood each other's plight very well. We would often gripe to each other about our hardships. He shared his girl troubles and I shared whatever troubles I had. We encouraged each other. When things really got rough, he often brought me cookies from the cafeteria. I was aware he did not always purchase them, but I ate them though I felt bad afterwards. After a few times of sharing with me, I began refusing them. This encouraged him to stop. It was best that we die of hunger than fatten ourselves on that for which we did not labor.

For me, dignity in death, even then, was much better than an insincere pleasurable life. My grandparents would not have been pleased knowing I encouraged anyone in wrongdoing. I usually took a bus and a train to school. The bus fare was only $1.15 then, and the subway fare was only $1.25. There were days, however, when I could not even pay these fares into the city. Sometimes I left home in faith hoping to run into a driver who I knew. There were a few instances when I got to the subway entrance to make it home and realized that I had no money. I would crawl under the subway turnstile in order to make it back home from school because I could not afford the fare. Doing this could have posed problems for me, but obtaining an education was the reason I had begun this journey. Besides compromising my self-respect, morals or integrity, I was willing to persevere through almost anything to help me reach my educational goal.

My days were very long as I had an interesting class schedule to accommodate the times when I did have to work a job. One night, as I traveled home after 11:00 p.m., I crossed a vacant parking lot to get home. A store has since built on this spot in Mount Vernon. As I approached this point, I saw a car sitting there and immediately sensed danger. I began to pray in my heart, while the car filled with young men began yelling things out at me. They then put the car in motion and began circling around me as if to scare me. I thought I was going to be hurt or worse, kidnapped or raped. I know that God protected me that night. It was late, dark and not a soul was in sight. They could have done anything to me and walked away. Suddenly they stopped and I ran all the way home in tears. That night I felt terribly exhausted mentally, physically and emotionally.

The weight of my life burdened me. Frightened, I cried hard. In time my friend at school spent much time convincing me to try marijuana. He assured me it would help with my studies and help me cope with my problems. Remembering the repeated warnings of my grandparents and the stigma I knew was associated with the use of illegal drugs, I did not feel any desire to follow his advice. My academic life at the college wasn't going well either, because I still had trouble taking tests. I had failed my college entrance exam, placing me in remedial math and English classes. Most of the students in the English remedial classes were ESL (English as a Second Language) students. English is my first language. This did not help my already damaged self-esteem. As time went on, I made my way out of these classes into regular classes, but my grades continued to suffer. I performed poorly my entire first year. Finally one night when I had grown very tired of watching other students celebrate their successes on exams while I cried in the school bathrooms, I poured my heart out to God in a prayer. It had been a while since I had talked to Him so earnestly. I knew I had not been doing many things right, so I had a difficult time going to God and asking for anything, especially when I had been so withdrawn from Him.

My first few years in America had truly affected the spiritual strength I felt back in Dominica, though I had my religious struggles there as well. Something about the support of friends and family back home kept me from venturing into dangerous territory. That night I called on God in desperation, but sincerely. I prayed something like this: "Dear God, You said your children are to be the head and not the tail. I know I have not been your best child. I shouldn't be asking anything of you, but how come I am not doing well and you won't help me? Please help me to do well in my classes and please help me not to be humiliated anymore. Help me to do well on my exams. In Your Name, I pray, amen." I cried in embarrassment and shame, feeling so dumb even though I knew I wasn't. God heard me. I know he did because my academic life forever changed after this.

It was during that same semester of praying this prayer that I made the Dean's list. My grades continually improved until I transitioned from that college to my undergraduate studies where I had even greater academic success. After that day, I saw God a bit differently. I felt grateful He had heard me in spite of my failings and shortcomings. I felt encouraged to pray more earnestly about things in my life and to return to God more fully. In the fall of 1998, after pleading with God to help me find a job that would pay me well enough to meet my financial needs, I responded to an advertisement for another baby-sitting position, this time in Pelham, New York. Thus began a long baby-sitting career there with many families with whom I still share great relationships today. One such family is the Lampson family. I had the blessed privilege of caring for their two precious daughters whom I feel so connected to. I have had the blessing of attending recitals, plays and even their graduations and many other family events as they grew older. After twelve years in each other's lives we have grown so close in our friendship.

The job I initially responded to also allowed me to meet another lovely family. I enjoyed working for them. They had two very bright children and they did an excellent job raising them. It was a pleasure to see how they worked together to ensure that their children were well rounded. Their son was particularly smart. They were fun to work with. Their home was only walking distance from where I lived in Mount Vernon and the new college where I studied, which was only a seven minute drive away. I could not have been more satisfied. This was a lot less stressful than my New York City work and study experience. Plus, even better, it paid me more than I had made on any other job since working here in America.

Once again I saw evidences that God was listening to me. It felt refreshing that He was not angry at me as I thought. I had always felt He became angry if I didn't behave or I disobeyed Him. Yet, for the past few years it seemed that I had not lived in the most committed relationship with Him, and He still helped me greatly. Though I never left the church, my heart had not always entirely been on the things of God. So engrossed in my life and its hardships, I lost sight of the anchor in which I had once felt safety. The financial blessing of my latest job remained until my services were no longer needed.

My enrollment in undergraduate studies resulted in higher tuition payments. My troubles were far from over. When I discovered I could earn scholarships by making the honor roll, I pushed myself even harder. I made the President's and Dean's lists each semester for the two years I was enrolled in the University. Midway into my second year, I almost had a mental breakdown. I remember the night I stayed up all night into the morning preparing for exams. As I saw day break, I could not remember anything. I had studied all night, but I could barely remember who I was.

I felt highly disoriented and unsettled. A fearful thought came over me that I may have confused my mind. I stopped and rested my brain before coming to the conclusion that I did not want to die for a degree, though I most certainly wanted to live to have one. In August of 2002, I finally graduated from Monroe College with an undergraduate degree in Business Management. To my surprise, I even graduated with honors (*Cum Laude*). I had never even heard the word until graduation day. Amazingly, I went from remedial classes to the Honor Roll. God knows how to meet the needs of His children. I recall the moment my name was called to receive my Diploma. I choked back tears, and an overwhelming sense of emotion flooded my heart as I crossed the stage. I reflected on all that I had been through and God's role throughout the process. My heart was glad. The dream had become a reality. I had amazingly beaten my financial, emotional and relational odds. I also could not deny "God was with me."

Where is Jesus in the Church?

Having been raised in a Christian home my whole life, many if not all of my values, principles, standards, core beliefs and world views have undoubtedly been shaped by religion. Although most of the things I learned religiously to this point came mainly through hearing and observation rather than personal study of the word of God, I still continued to have expectations regarding God's people based on the teachings I had received. Even an unbeliever knows there is a certain lifestyle and conduct expected from one who is supposed to be a Christian. I am fully aware that at many intervals during my Christian journey, I did not live above reproach. I have not always been obedient to all of God's commandments and teachings, and I have made many decisions out of harmony with the will of God. So, if anyone is empathetic to Christians who struggle in their life's walk, it is I. Still, when I knew that my practices contradicted what I professed to believe, I kept a low profile. I refused to hold any church offices and I would not speak to people about the way they lived their lives. Not that I ever really did that. I also did not publicize I was a Christian. Many people, interestingly, always identified me as one. Like the apostle Peter, even when we go to great lengths to not be identified with Christ and deny Him, others will still see that we have "been with Jesus" (Matthew 26:59).

Having this Christian background, I found myself experiencing great disappointment in my church life. By the time I went to my new congregation, my cup of church discontentment was practically full. I had by now dealt with church in Dominica where all the church members there seemed to do was nitpick people's wrong. It appeared there were more religious police in the church than the government. Nevertheless, I had many enjoyable times at church and there were many moments of great fellowship and Christian love exhibited amongst members. Despite the fun times, it still seemed apparent to me that people lived for discovering who fell into sin.

Once a person joined the church, there were people who spent their time following this person's course to find something on which to condemn them, or to see how long the person would last. This was a judgmental and prideful way to practice religion, in my estimation. It was all about who lived better in Christ. Religious pride appeared to be a dominant part of our religious practices. People were often ostracized depending on what sin they committed. If you became pregnant out of marriage, committed adultery, or someone knew you were committing fornication, you were finished. We seemed to show no compassion to those who struggled in their walk with God. This often confused and frustrated me. Such practices gave me a highly negative view of God and religion. How could this be, I pondered, when God is supposed to be compassionate and merciful? So after attending congregations for two and a half years in Brooklyn without ever establishing any solid bonds with anyone, I felt lost in church. While it is true that I had my own issues, I would have certainly adjusted if someone had taken an interest in me.

In February of 1997, when I moved to Westchester County, I began attending services at my new church in Mount Vernon. This church was the largest Seventh-day Adventist congregation that I had yet attended in the United States. It was a lovely edifice then, but is absolutely gorgeous now since its new renovations. I experienced a culture in my new church at the time that's similar to that which I had at my Brooklyn congregation. I didn't feel that sense of warmth I expected from a group of Christians. I also cannot neglect that my own internal issues may have made it difficult to connect or bond with others. It has been my observation that if you grew up in the church, your treatment is often different to that of one who is newly coming into the church. I don't believe this is true of all our churches. Also, since becoming a pastor, I have traveled to preach at many churches around the country and have both seen and experienced great warmth and care. We are a globally recognized denomination, and in each culture the care temperature varies. Yet, the feelings of isolation, rejection and unimportance that are at times manifested in certain churches, are not a good reflection of the love God is hoping to exhibit.

I had been attending church for almost seven years at my new church and people were still greeting me: "Welcome, pleasant Sabbath and please come again," indicating I was a visitor. It is true ours is a very large congregation and I did not make myself visible. I can see how I could have been overlooked and become lost in the crowd. Still, we are to be intentional about reaching out to each other. If each person reaches one person, no one will be left behind. In the same way that God kept placing people in my path to help me up, Satan kept placing his own agents to keep me down. I saw this exhibited when some overly zealous Christians who took their roles way too seriously were causing me some grief at my new place of worship.

In the summer of 2005, Robert, who had been trying hard for years to get me involved in church activities, asked if I would do the

Intercessory Prayer for the Worship Service that morning. It was in celebration of our Annual Youth Day. I was very nervous since the moment I was asked. I showed up the day of our worship shaking as I sought the rest of the platform personnel. I entered the lobby, where one of the organizers of the day's events greeted me. With a very intentional study of my attire and overall appearance, I heard the disapproving words which landed on my ears like clashing thunder, not because she was loud but her dissatisfaction was.

The words fell on my heart like tons of needles fighting for space in my flesh. "Your skirt does not meet pulpit approval," she said. "It has to be on your ankle and right now it is knee length. Our committee has met and we have found someone else. Thank you." "The committee met?" I questioned. I had only been in the door for less than ten minutes, how could a committee have met to decide on my attire? She left me standing there and walked away. I continue to be amazed at what sins we decide are acceptable. We disown people for adultery and fornication, but tolerate those who harbor prejudicial behaviors of all kinds, under the pretense of preference and "Gate keepers" for God. I choked back tears as I felt so insignificant, so unwanted, so out of place.

The committee member who requested my service later came to apologize to me. I had given so much care to choosing my attire, especially since I knew I had an upfront role. I knew all eyes were going to be on me, so I purposed to look my best. My suit was a mustard-like shade. Its conservative look was reflected in the blazer which buttoned from the neck down, with long sleeves, fully lined and a pencil shaped skirt which met at the knees. I felt respectably attired. It was okay to be dishonest about the committee meeting to decide on my attire, but I could not wear a knee length skirt in the pulpit. May God have mercy on His earthly children!

At the end of the year I was asked again to pray for our year end youth day. This time I still did not wear an ankle length skirt, as I knew very well by then no such rule was applied. Modesty is the key to

Christian attire. I poured my heart out to God that day. I asked that he would take authority from those who abused it. Many had never heard me speak so openly before. They seemed shocked that I actually had a voice. One time, I was at a gathering with a few ladies from our church. One of them reminded me of the shock and amazement they had when they first heard my speaking voice. She said, "We went wow, to indicate our surprise." Just one year later I saw evidence that God heard my prayers since that committee member was relieved of all church responsibilities and duties. We've had wonderful pastors during my time at my church. Our new pastor whom we inherited in 2006 implemented many changes which, I believe, forced members to be more careful and considerate of others in their work for God.

There was another time that I had been asked to lead in some songs during our morning worship. There is usually a break between the lesson studies we conduct and the commencement of the eleven o'clock service. During this short break, there tends to be much activity as people try to transition to the next phase of the service. Still having reservations about leading in upfront roles, I reluctantly agreed. For about two weeks I led out in a few songs. One morning, one of our sisters stood in the back waving at me to stop. I kept on singing since I was in the middle of conducting a song. It was then a pair of hands was sent to gently usher me out from before a packed congregation. If there was a hole in the floor I would have entered it and disappeared. As I made my way to my seat, I sat with tears rolling down my cheeks. Humiliated and embarrassed, I purposed in my heart that so long as I lived, I would never again take part in any thing that had to do with church functions. Today I have respect for these individuals and share in a much better Christian relationship with them. I now have a deeper understanding of who they are as my family in Christ. I do not in any way hold these incidences against them. We all have at some point in our Christian walk hurt others in some way. It is my belief, however, that we focus our time so much on serving the church, that we forget to lovingly serve God by the way we interact with others. We must move forward together to grow and uphold unity in the body of Christ.

The Day I Met Jesus at Church

I feel chills at the thought that, though we are forgotten by humans, we are never forgotten by God. It is why I am fully convinced that it is He who placed me on the hearts of a wonderful couple at my church. My knowing the Berry family marked a turning point in my life. I later found out this couple particularly sought those with whom no one else bothered. Themselves the parents of two young adults, they were intentional in caring for young people. Since my life spoke of one who unquestionably had concerns, it is not surprising that they picked me out of the crowd. My insecurities were apparent if one cared to notice. Within a short period of time Avis and Bruce invited me to their Bronx home.

Soon I was treated as their very own. This gave me my first sense of belonging to a real family since leaving Dominica. Their genuine care for my life brought an additional security which I had begun experiencing since meeting Juliette. They did not just give of their time but also of their finances. I never asked anything of them. Yet they always seemed to know when I had a pressing need. It had been the first time since being here that anyone had been so intentional about contributing to my life in every way. Through their love, I saw God's care for me. In time there were others who expressed their kindness and found ways to involve me in church life. Mrs. Berry worked hard to have me integrated into church life. She often asked me to sing special music which I felt afraid to do. Wounded and broken hearted, I felt unenthusiastic about participating in any church functions, so I often gave her a very hard time. There are times she would ask me to sing at our worship in the morning. I would mostly say "No!" After saying "No," I would not go to church on those mornings for fear she would call me out anyway after I had refused. Still feeling separated from God, I also felt unworthy to participate in any church activities.

Gradually I lent myself to service but my struggles had not in any way diminished. For years different individuals worked hard to keep me integrated at our church, but I remained uninvolved. In time, God showed me that a few experiences by a handful of individuals who themselves are still struggling to practice Christianity right, is never sufficient to overrule the countless other loving and caring individuals who are yet to cross our paths and show us God's love.

Since my ministry journey began a few years ago, my church has been an undeniable support, not just with words but with strong financial support, prayers, encouragement and a love which could only come from God. With my own spiritual maturity and growth, I am able to receive the love of others. My life is now very wrapped up in this congregation. My heart has grown to deeply love my Mount Vernon Church family. I stand in amazement at what the Lord has done in blessing me with such a loving and beautiful church family. They have loved me with an exceptional love. The spiritual temperature of our church has improved remarkably. There is vibrancy and life in the people. I see a greater integration of fellowship and brotherhood in Christ Jesus. I am happy, encouraged, and blessed at what God has done through his people.

My Search for Love

As I fought hard to integrate my Christianity and social needs, I kept struggling in my desire to keep my affections on the things of God. I continued to seek to quench my thirst and feed my hunger with things and people who could not satisfy.

In the fall of 1997, two years after the painful intimate encounter, I attempted to give love another try. I came to the point of reopening my heart to a relationship. This turning point came after a conversation with a friend, Jim. He had for months pursued me, but I had no interest in a relationship with him or anyone else at the time. So he settled for a friendship. While on a visit with him one day, he must have felt the tension in the air when he attempted to sit near me. As I drew myself away from him with a tense look on my face, he looked at me with pity and concern. He cautioned, "Someone has hurt you very badly, but do not let them ruin your opportunity to love someone else or be loved by someone." I had never once spoken to him about the pain I had experienced in my previous relationship, but he sensed I had been severely wounded. He offered some advice which I believe helped me find confidence to open up to the possibilities of loving again. He said, "Don't commit to a serious relationship for a while. Instead, just go on dates, and learn how to interact with the opposite sex again without fear." This was a cultural challenge. When we were growing up we were always taught never to go out with a man or accept anything from him if we do not share in a committed relationship with that person. Almost two years after Jim's advice, I opened my heart to trying the new dating approach. It went well, but I still exercised all safety measures.

When the summer of 1997 ended, I felt ready to open my heart to a real committed and long-term relationship. It was also that year I centered my attention on school and finding strength to succeed in my studies. Though I continued to attend church to keep up with my Christianity, my relationship with God became decidedly strained. Having blamed Him for many of my life's difficulties and disappointments, I felt separated from Him. Feelings of guilt from losing my virginity still burdened me. My indoctrinated understanding that I should have preserved myself until marriage made my worshipping experience a major challenge. I felt highly unworthy and hypocritical. I stopped singing certain songs, particularly "I Surrender All" and "Have Thine Own Way," amongst others.

I had not fully surrendered many areas of my life to God. For many years I had, in numerous areas of my life, piloted my airplane, captained my ship and paddled my own canoe. Even when I thought I had surrendered at earlier points in my life, it is evident that I controlled my destiny for a while. Besides, having held God accountable for most if not all of the problems in my life, made it impossible to surrender to Him. I most certainly did not know how to do this. This explains why I would never have asked Him to "Have His own way." So I failed to sing any of those songs. I did not want to lie or say something I did not mean. Speaking the truth means a lot to me even in situations such as the one just described. This disconnect from my spirituality opened the door for more errors and poor life choices. So it was not surprising when, after two years of not being in a relationship, my loneliness began to again set in. Like the "Woman at the Well" I kept seeking. As my hunger for love, appreciation and affection kicked in, I recall almost suffering from not having found a special someone with whom to share in a loving and caring relationship.

As I reflect on my dating journey,
I never trusted God to find me a life partner.

DATING WITHOUT GOD

Chapter 4

Dating Without God

One thing became apparent to me as I reflected on my life journey: I never trusted God to find me someone to love me sincerely. I controlled this aspect of my life for a long time. I quite truthfully did not think He would find me a handsome hunk that had charisma, energy and zeal. The men I knew in the church always seemed so boring and geek-like. I no longer feel that way. The most attractive man, in my view, is a man who truly, deeply believes in and loves God. I learned this through some exceedingly painful dating lessons. I always wanted to share in a wholesome and healthy relationship with someone. To do this, I had much healing to do in myself as well as from my previous relationship.

The pain of my previous experience affected the new dating course in my life. I had long been taught as a young girl while growing up in the church that I should not develop romantic relationships with men who did not share my faith and beliefs. I held this teaching dear to my heart for many years until I began to lose my grip on my spirituality. I began wrestling with this Biblical and denominational teaching. I felt frustrated about this need to control my dating life. It was during this time that I began reasoning, if a guy is nice and he does not engage in harmful habits, I don't see why I can't date him. I later learned that if you compromise one area of your standards, it only leads to an open door to many relationship pitfalls. It is not surprising that after two years of not dating, and finally finding the courage to date again, I met a handsome Canadian, former professional hockey player with a career in sales and marketing. This guy was gorgeous and he knew it. He was quite a sexy man. He had strong features, dazzling green eyes, and he wore a bang which he often tossed to the side. He exemplified the men I read about in my romance novels. He was sharp, daring, strong and a real man's man. He just exuded shear confidence. I rather liked that. Maybe it was because I lacked confidence myself, that I always admired it in others. In time I discovered he was very cocky. When we first met he was so gentle with me, and treated me nicely.

My sheltered life, innocence and naivety could not be concealed. He told me often I was every guy's dream because of this innocent aspect of my personality. I eventually learned it truly was his dream. As time passed I saw telltale signs that he was very controlling. I noticed his gifts were carefully picked. He soon began telling me what to wear as well as how I should comb my hair. I still attended services, as I fought hard to maintain my connection with God. This man often suggested that I did not have to attend services all the time, but I would not listen to him. Somewhere deep inside I felt I could win him to my faith. I was sadly mistaken. Only God can change a person's heart, although we can try to inspire, motivate and influence others to change. He seemed intrigued by my physical appearance and it appeared he felt intimidated that I might leave him. Soon he began telling me I did not need to look pretty all the time and particularly when we were out together. He began asking me not to wear anything that would enhance my beauty, except when he had special requests. He did not like it when I let my hair flow. He wanted my hair in a ponytail almost all the time. He was always telling me how I should look and he worked hard to tear me away from my cousins and friends. He also tried hard to have me relocate with him to another state, but I refused. It angered him that I told him "No." When we were in the city together and I was complimented on my beauty, he lashed out at me afterwards and blamed me for the compliments. When we dated, I was at the height of my internal renewal. I truly looked like I modeled. I had gained some weight. My complexion was fair and beautiful. My broad shoulders with naturally muscular toned arms drew much attention. I had a glow which radiated, but I wasn't sure of myself or my beauty.

My new love was not handling my beauty well even though he seemed so intrigued by it. In time I was forbidden from wearing certain clothing and other things he felt added to my beauty. I was only dating this man for a few months and all these changes had already been implemented into my life. I was still a novice at dating relationships. So, this behavior was new to me and I was ashamed to tell my cousins about it. They did suspect that I could not be my true self with him and that my personality was too fragile for his domineering style. My cousins did not care for this man but they tolerated him because of me. Juliette, who had deeper insight into our relationship, told me, "Your presence in his life is like tossing pearls before swine." She kept encouraging me to walk away from him, and I purposed to do that. He quickly became verbally abusive at times particularly when things did not go his way. I knew for sure he was not someone that I wanted in my life.

I was raised in a good Christian home. My grandparents had long taught us how we should be treated by men. It should be nothing shy of great respect, they often reminded us. This man had failed miserably in meeting these requirements. I wanted out, but I knew it required caution. One day we came back from a drive in New Jersey. For the entire two hours of the ride I barely spoke a word as he dominated the entire two hours of conversation. I have no trouble being silent, so I just listened without interruption, since there's no telling what his reaction would be. As he dropped me off at home, and I got ready to leave the car, he verbally assaulted me expressing some very hurtful words. He told me that "Your laid back attitude is useless to this country, and it will not bring you any success, here in America." He further told me, "You will never make it here, it is best you return to the dirt roads back in Dominica, where nothing is happening." This was characteristic of his approach by this time. Mentally I had long ago left the relationship. I only remained for the present, trying to find the best time and way to move on.

As I made my way to the door of my apartment, his unkind words painfully pierced my heart. I dropped right there outside the main entrance door of my apartment and wept terribly. How could someone who professes to love me hurt me so much, I pondered. It wasn't settling well within me. So, I further determined in that moment that he and I would never have a future together. it was after this incident that I pleaded with God to make me a stronger person. Some weeks later I told the man that I was moving on because I no longer desired to be in a relationship with him. I already knew he was not going to be nice about the break up, but I was not prepared for what I heard next. He got very angry and began saying some unpleasant things. I did not interrupt him. Suddenly he said, "I will have you killed for trying to make a mockery of me." My heart sank at the magnitude of his rage. I remained on the phone as he detailed to me how he was going to take my life; it was unpleasant listening to his details. He told me, "I am not so foolish to have your blood stains on my hands and let the police trace me. I will pay a thug to ensure that you disappear." He reminded me that even though I went to the police it would not keep him from proceeding with what he had determined to do. I did not take his words lightly, but I also knew he intended to scare me into staying in the relationship. Ridding my life of him took awhile after this conversation. Although our relationship lasted less than a year, its impact was severe. For several months I lived in fear of my life being taken, until one day strength visited me. Deep in my spirit I settled that it was better to die than to live enslaved by this man's threats. I stopped looking over my shoulders and determined to free myself of his control even if it cost me my life.

Almost a year after I had seen or heard from him, he contacted me one day to tell me how much he missed having me in his life. He said I had a goodness that he had not found in any of the many women he had dated, and he dated a lot of women. I think I fit perfectly into his need to control someone. He asked me to marry him and start a family. I was not willing to raise a pet with this man. So, I most certainly would not raise a child with him. He promised me all kinds of life comforts for starting this new life with him. I would have rather died in poverty than have anything this man was offering. I listened attentively as he detailed all the contacts where he could be reached. By this time I had a made up mind. He would never again be a part of my life. Despite the errors in my choices, I had a strong foundation growing up. Character was the foundation on which we were groomed in my home. Even through my mistakes my grandparents' words were ever ringing in my ears every step of the way. I understood clearly what the Bible means when it says that "A child should be trained up in the way he should go and when he is old he will not depart from it" Proverbs 22:6. I centered my focus on staying connected with God and repairing my spiritual walk with Him. Sadly, my search for love continued to take me into painful places.

I don't believe I ever deliberately sought to live in defiance against God, even when I often rebelled against Him by rejecting the church's restrictive teachings. I simply went on throughout my life searching for peace, joy, contentment and happiness outside of God. I knew it came from somewhere. The church told me joy and peace came from God, but at times they did such a poor job showing how this could ever be obtainable, that I wasn't ever convinced it could occur. So my search continued for peace, joy (real joy) and happiness. Yet, peace can only be found in submitting to God (Job 22:21).

The invitation in 1 Peter 1:5 which asks me to "cast all my cares upon Him" had been extended, yet I consistently held on to my cares. The more I held on to them, the more my search to fill the void in my life continued. Unable to fully receive the love of God, I hoped to find it in the perfect relationship with a loving man of character. Though I appreciated very handsome men, I tried not to compromise character for beauty. In our growing years, my grandparents enforced character over beauty. The human's desire is to be loved. We all want to be loved. So in the spring of 1999, when I opened my heart to a gorgeous stately hunk, I believed love had finally arrived. Yet, something about the timing was scary. It occurred at the highlight of trying to recapture my early years with God. I had been praying more and spending more time learning about the things of God.

All had not been perfect, because I still struggled in my emotional and psychological health. But there still existed in my heart a void and yearning for God. I tried hard to stay on track, but I still felt weak in my spiritual walk. I had grown much over the years, but much work needed to be done. My journey with this handsome man began in July of 1998 as I made my way home from a job interview on the Upper East Side of Manhattan for a part-time nanny position. I had been slowly followed for several blocks by this man. Being followed in the city had not been an unusual thing for me since I was living and working in New York. Because I have chiseled facial features many people thought I modeled. For years I was approached by photographers when in New York City. I also collected stacks of business cards from modeling agents and photographers over the years urging me to model.

In 1995, I met with my pastor at the time to ask him what his thoughts were on being a Christian and working as a model simultaneously. He agreed that it would be a great opportunity for someone. Then he laid out the dangers for a girl who may not be strong enough to handle life associated with the industry. Since I knew my emotional history, this possibility died for me that day. I did not wish to further lose myself or my Christianity for the sake of fame. I welcomed all the compliments from those who thought I was beautiful enough to be a model, especially since prior to coming to the United States, I never received this kind of attention, but at times felt cursed for the way I looked. These were extremely flattering times, but I decided to center my attention and focus on education rather than becoming a famous model. Since I had become accustomed to this kind of attention whenever I was in the city, I thought I was being stopped that day by this sharp business man concerning modeling possibilities.

He complimented me on my beauty and then confidently told me he was certain that I wasn't American. With an almost embarrassed smile I waited to hear his reasoning. I soon discovered his solid connection to the Islands and mine in particular. I was immediately intrigued by this hunk who had discovered this hidden Caribbean treasure which only Dominicans seem to know about, my island. His bright blue eyes stared at me as if communicating to me without any words. His voice was beautiful. There was something about the way he spoke; it was sweet. He laughed from deep inside his belly. There was life in him. That was attractive to me. I wanted life; my timid and reserved nature often robbed me of real belly laughs.

My lack of confidence and introverted nature had also robbed me of my ability to freely appreciate life. I always admired people who were not inhibited by their fears the way that I was. His knowledge of Dominica told me he had genuine connections to the island. Here is this man in a city with millions of people, but our paths cross only to find out that he is totally connected to where I grew up. For at least eight years prior to our encounter he had traveled and stayed on Dominica. I was fascinated by that.

Dominica has not been a much publicized tourist-based island.

So, Dominicans are very pleased when we meet anyone from any nation or even island who attests to knowing and loving our island. As the sun went down on this meeting of the minds that day, we purposed to stay in touch with each other. For almost a year we interacted but never dated each other. I had attempted dating two years after that painful encounter to no happy ending. I then centered my attention on strengthening my relationship with God. As the spring of 1999 rolled in, I felt a sense of newness. I felt strong in seeking God more earnestly again. With relationships behind me I wanted to learn to fall in love with Jesus. Satan is cunning, however. He was not going to let me strengthen my walk with God so easily.

So, in May of 1999 when I received a call from my friend with whom I had been interacting for almost a year, to go out for my birthday, I knew things were about to change. Our conversations prior to our getting together for my birthday were strictly platonic. I found him attractive and he felt the same about me but something kept us from pursuing a romantic relationship. This something was my desire to rebuild my relationship with God. I had been open in our dialogues about my faith and spirituality, though I had never told him of my emotional hardships, struggles and my own frustrations with religion including my own denomination. I also did not tell him I wrestled with my own spirituality and the things of God. Not having seen him now for months since we first met, seeing him again was refreshing. He looked amazingly handsome. His hair, brushed slightly to the side, accentuated his big blue eyes. He stood tall, had a flat stomach, a beautiful body and a lovely smile. He dressed immaculately, as if he was intentional about being irresistible to me that day. My calm composure and tamed demeanor did not give away my pounding heart and sweaty palms.

One voice said "Run." The other said, "You deserve to find true love." I wanted true love. Maybe this was it. I would not know if I ran, would I? Having spoken to him for several months now while building a friendship, I had grown to appreciate his mind. He was a brilliant man. A deep thinker, he engaged me in many subjects. We had a wonderful time at dinner the eve of my birthday. We became inseparable from that day. Ours was not an immediate sexual bond. I had made it clear from the beginning that I wanted to live a godly life, but only time would tell if I could stand by my word since I was so attracted to this man. I asked if this is something he could live with and he agreed. I was way too naive or afraid to ask how he satisfied his sexual desires. We did find ways to be passionate in our relationship. He respected me greatly and he was quite a gentleman. He never pressured me in any area where I said I would not do something because of my belief, not even one time. Though I had struggled for months in my decision not to engage in a romantic relationship with him, it seemed so natural once it began. This relationship, however, would climax any that I ever had on all levels to this point.

A Life-Altering Decision

Since the evening of our meeting for my birthday, we had regular meetings. We spent almost every weekend together. We could not be apart from each other. I missed him the times we were not able to meet and he missed me deeply. He called me every morning at ten. His deep masculine voice would pierce my heart as I heard "hello-o-o-o there." What joy it brought my heart when he reminded me, "I can't stay. I just want to hear your voice." He called me several times a day throughout the entire time of our relationship. He expressed his love for me in many wonderful ways. He gave me flowers even when there wasn't an occasion. He sent me cards just because. He called just to say "I love you." If I hurt, he was hurting. He also reminded me of how happy I had made his life by bringing him a love that was not selfish, or pretentious. He told me the women he dated in the past simply gravitated to his income. He earned a six-figure salary with bonus amounts many people earned in a full year.

He told me he wasn't sure if it was him or his money they loved.

Although I had to care for my needs in America, it was difficult to ask for help from anyone, including him. He found it unusual that I would not ask him for help and he frequently reminded me to ask him for anything I needed. He at times became frustrated with me about that. Yet, he said it was this very thing which deepened his love for me. He told me repeatedly that I was different and I deserved the best. He ensured I had the best when he bought me something. He cared for me in a loving way. We dined out at some of the finest restaurants in the city. He also made it possible for me to have the financial backing when I needed to have my immigration status extended again to prolong my study status. Through his support and efforts I successfully had my study status extended for several more years.

I loved this man very much and he loved me more than anyone I had or have dated to this point. It was the most beautiful and romantic experience I've shared with anyone. He enjoyed being with me and I enjoyed being with him. Older than me by over a decade, age had not affected him a bit. He looked at least ten years younger. He was young, strong and energetic. We were very attracted to each other, not just physically but in many other ways. I found him to have a brilliant mind. We could talk about anything. The fact that I was a black woman did not bring any embarrassment to the love he felt for me. He took me to the investment banking firm where he held a reputable position for many years and introduced me to his co-workers. I met all his close friends including those who did not approve of his dating a black woman. He treated me as if he had won a pearl of great price. He did not just tell me empty words; he backed it up by his actions.

I met the members of his family who approved of our being together and he kept me away from those who did not. He told me often that love knows no color. Because of the way he loved me, it made it difficult for anyone to frown on our relationship. Our relationship flourished and my heart was now set on marrying him. We had talked about names for our children, amongst other plans people make when they are seeking to establish a future together. Internally I still struggled with loving a man who was non-religious while juggling staying close to God. My romantic feelings had clouded a deep conversation we had in our first few months of dating when he disclosed how he had become agnostic. He shared that he grew up in a religious home but was introduced to the theory of evolution in college. He admitted it made more sense than the concept of creation so he hung on to it from that day. I remember feeling saddened about the disparity in our beliefs, but I was too infatuated in that moment to attempt to end our developing romance. I reasoned that he would change because he loved me. I would learn the hard way that dating evangelism is not an effective way to win people to God. It is the working of God's spirit upon a person's heart that will bring people into an unwavering relationship with Him. In time he did attend a few worship services with me, but later confessed they were the most uncomfortable of experiences for him.

Regardless of how hard I tried, the disparity in our beliefs weighed heavily on my mind. I wanted the relationship to work. It was the best I had to this point. So my hope and expectation were invested in this person. The adventures of travel, golfing, laughing, and loving each other brought such happiness to my heart. We planned a trip to Dominica in November of 1999. I wanted him to meet my extended family and to celebrate Dominica's Twenty-first Independence Celebration. We had a wonderful time together. It was the first time I spent an extended period of time in a home with someone with whom I shared a romantic relationship. We spent five days together in a beautiful house out in the middle of nowhere. We were surrounded by utter darkness and thick forest. The huge four-bedroom concrete house was well furnished. The atmosphere was extremely inviting for a romantic stay. He had great taste and he always aimed to please me. We bonded in ways I never thought imaginable. This took our relationship to a whole new level. Our return to the United States brought an inseparable connection. We needed each other more and more. We spent so much more time together.

We craved each other's presence and companionship. The times when we could not meet due to work commitments or school assignments, he sulked until I felt sorry enough for him to work out a compromise.

Not once was he ever rude or unkind to me. I never heard a disrespectful word escape his lips. He respected me tremendously. He thought I was a very special woman. I felt lucky to have him in my life but he always reminded me that he was the lucky one. This made me feel so special. A day without him felt like a year. A much deeper connection to him and him with me emerged after our romantic getaway in Dominica. He was such a beautiful lover in many, many ways. Loving him was easy because of his overall beauty. He had a laughter which came from deep inside of him; I loved to hear him laugh. He had assimilated into the West Indian Culture in ways which were quite humorous. He had an obsession with our cultural music and dance.

I had an opportunity to accompany him to a few summer events. He became the center of attention when this white boy showed the black folks in view of his performance that he had rhythm; and he did. It was a sight to behold. He had his own issues; he wasn't by any means perfect. I also realized later on that there is much about him to which I wasn't exposed. He did often let me in on some of his internal struggles. One time I found myself getting carried away in an attempt to help him cope. He quickly warned me on not lecturing him.

My desire to comfort those who came to me with their problems had created in me a bad habit of always giving advice. Maybe there are others who wanted to ask me to "shut up" at times. As I matured I learned to listen more than share when someone brings their concerns to me. I am still growing in this area. Overall, this man was a wonderful person. The days we worked and I went to school were tougher. I missed him so much when we were away from each other. I was in love, crazy in love. I soon forgot we differed greatly in our beliefs. I lost sight of the questions and concerns I had. Still one thing lacked; he did not know God and introducing them to each other wasn't something I knew how to do effectively at the time. The more I wanted him, the less I needed and wanted God; he became everything to me. Over time I relieved myself of the responsibilities I had working with the youth at our church. I felt it hypocritical to teach young people in the way of God while I wasn't following in His way myself. This would be the most dangerous decision I had made since being in this relationship. At least when I served, it held me accountable to something in the way of God. Without this responsibility I had nothing for which or no one to whom to be accountable. God saw all the decisions I made concerning Him, however, and it wasn't long before I heard from Him.

God or Man

I tried my best to keep this relationship alive despite its inevitable death. I had lost sight of an intense conversation we had one day when we drove up along the Hudson River. The weather was beautiful. My love looked so handsome in his brown leather jacket and khaki pants. As I admired both him and the beauty of nature, I commented on the power of God displayed in the beautiful scenery of the changing leaves, the still river and the rocky plains beside the highway. He immediately rebutted with a smart look on his face and then asked: "How are you so sure God created these things?" "Creationism" he continued, "has no proof of God in creation but science has countless proof of evolution as the source of life on earth." My heart sank in realization of his agnostic views and sadness filled my heart.

It again became apparent to me that the love of my life and I were worlds apart in our belief concerning God and his existence. Though I had struggled in my own belief, this situation shook me to the core. Determined not to become confrontational, I calmly tried to present a case for creation, but I was too affected to make any sense. Blinded by emotions, I refused to open my heart to see that God kept trying to show me that it is He who had loved me, cared for me and provided for me in unconditional ways my whole life. Since I was infatuated with feelings of passion and desire, I failed to be obedient to God.

By seeking fulfillment in the misguided fantasies of someone who would not even acknowledge Him as Lord, I kept rejecting God's way. It seemed to me that I became willing to throw away years of grooming under the guidance of God's hands, though I did not always know it. I repeatedly ignored the promptings of the Holy Spirit's moving on my heart to come out of this relationship. It was only a matter of time before the Lord showed me a painful lesson of disobedience. By the summer of 2000, I found myself seriously doubting that God existed. I spent much time indulging in agnostic thoughts and views. Although I never told my partner I had been entertaining such thoughts, they had for months begun to preoccupy my mind. Since I settled in my heart to marry this man, I knew something had to give. I was fully aware that he was not at the point of conversion. To make things work, a major compromise would have to take place. Since his influence on me had a stronger effect, though he most certainly did not know it, I wrestled with how we were going to make things work. It is during that moment I seriously began contemplating whether God was really out there. What if I give up this beautiful relationship all because of God and He's not even out there? I pondered. How do I really know for sure He does exist? I pleaded with a girlfriend one day on our way to Connecticut.

My whole life I had waited for a sign from Him that He is out there, and He had presented none. I had no real evidence that the things the church told me were true, factual or whether they were simply myths.

I had no way of knowing for sure. What if my lover was right? This was the most beautiful relationship I had had to that point and I would be giving it up for something I was not one hundred percent sure is real. I wrestled as a battle raged in my mind. I grew angry with my religious upbringing where I learned all these things about God. Then I grew angry with the church for seeking to control how I live my life especially with regard to dating. Then I became filled with regret for ever having known about God. If I did not know about Him, then I would not feel so guilty. I was in turmoil. I tossed and turned all night as those things passed through my mind. I loved this man; I did not want to lose him, but what if God is real. What if the things I learned are true? What's going to happen to my life? I had to choose between God and man, and I didn't know where to begin.

In 2000, I entered a supernatural turning point with my love

ENCOUNTER WITH THE SUPERNATURAL

Chapter 5

Encounter with the Supernatural

In January of 2000, I returned from Brooklyn for a visit with my family. On my way home I stopped in Manhattan to visit my love before making it to Mount Vernon. It was a Monday and the day before he had his annual physical. When I showed up his countenance did not reflect the jovial, free-spirited and lively personality I knew. He was undoubtedly troubled by something. I asked repeatedly if something was wrong, to which he replied, "I am just anxious about my doctor visit tomorrow." Suddenly, he walked over, grabbed me to him and kissed me passionately. He held me tightly against himself, as he kept reassuring me of how much he loved me and the amazing ways in which I had brought such happiness to his life. He had done these things before; they were not unusual. But, something about the way he did it that day spoke to even my naive heart. The anxiety which accompanied his words could not be hidden. He also wanted to know if I loved him and how much I loved him. Was he going to die? Did he have cancer? I wondered. What wasn't he telling me?

I went home that evening with uneasiness in my heart. I fought to hang on to his words that everything was okay, but I knew it wasn't. This had been the first time since knowing him that I felt I could not trust his words. After I called the following day to find out concerning his doctor appointment, he still sounded concerned. The very next morning, Wednesday morning, I got a call that would change the course of our relationship forever. As I picked up the phone, I immediately recognized his voice; I could hear that it did not have the same excitement as it had on other mornings. Frantically, he expressed having bad news. "What is it?" I nervously inquired. I never expected the answer I heard next.

"It's… she's here, in New York." He continued to share that a woman from his past who lived back on the islands, not Dominica, had come here to contend for him. He pleaded with me to understand that he did not approve of her decision and he was not looking to be with her. Puzzled, angry and hurt, I began weeping. Then he started to weep. I then hung up to compose myself. When we first met and over time during our relationship we spoke of prior relationships. He had always been open and sincere concerning a bizarre relationship he shared with this woman who lived back in the Caribbean. They had met while he vacationed there many years ago. He told me he never intended for it to have been a long-term involvement but for some unexplained reason he seemed unable to rid her from his life. He was very clear that this was not someone with whom he ever desired to establish a life.

I knew what he shared to be true because he had friends who knew of this relationship and confirmed what he had shared. When he finally asked me out on an official date, I asked him openly if he was free to be in a relationship, and he said he most certainly was although he admitted they still communicated at times. We began dating on this premise. I never have and never will have a desire to knowingly engage in a relationship with someone who is involved with someone else. I would much later discover he wasn't very open about the frequency of their interactions.

In all the years of his involvement with her and before we ever met, she had never once saw the need to visit the United States, and he never brought her here. It came to my understanding later that he was clear to her about his plans to establish a serious long-term life with me. She and her family grew angry. He told me over the years he had supported their family financially. When he informed me this woman had come to America pleading with him to stay with her, I asked him in very clear terms if that is what he wanted. He told me "No! This is not a relationship I have ever understood why I am in." He strongly stated he does not love this woman, neither has he ever loved her. He said they shared nothing in common and he cannot explain why she is still in his life. He wept and begged me again not to leave him because of her. He seemed very upset about the matter and worked hard at remaining as close to me as possible. I was very disappointed in him and was ready to move on. He purposed to do all he could to "resolve things once and for all." She came determined to ensure this never happened.

With a concerning and troubled tone in his voice, he kept reemphasizing that he did not love her and how much he loved me and did not want to lose me. He wept and begged me again and again not to leave him. Although I felt there was genuineness in his words, I truly struggled with how to proceed. I wasn't feeling the same because of those things, but he seemed determined not to lose me. I also loved him and did not wish to lose him either. So I decided to move forward with him. I made no efforts in the days and weeks ahead to reach him or to get us together. Within days he came to visit me at home. It was an incredibly emotional visit. I didn't know how to react toward him. I had mixed emotions about what to do. I wanted him, but this new discovery had affected my trust. I offered no advice or suggestions; I simply emphasized I would not share in a relationship with anyone who was with someone else. Our first visit since learning of this woman's arrival in America brought me great emotional discomfort. He spent much time assuring me that I had nothing to worry about. He cried much about the situation and appeared genuinely unhappy about it.

This man wasn't the kind of guy to hurt people intentionally. So I could see he was hurting and embarrassed about the whole thing. He was very worried that he would lose me. He also seemed quite angry about her arrival. He informed me how he handled the situation and ensured me that she would not stay in his home. I felt a great sense of discomfort dealing with a situation with him that involved another woman. It unsettled my spirit in extremely deep ways. I wanted no part of it

Her World of Black Magic

By March of 2000, just three months after the news that my love's old flame had returned, things began to take an interesting turn. Something about our interactions was not the same. When we met, I sensed from him a gaze or stare which indicated he wasn't sure who I was anymore. He seemed lost. We had not been fighting, arguing or even talking about the previous events. We had put it to rest. We agreed that we were going to move on together, and we did. We did not talk about the situation, neither did I feel particularly troubled or bothered by it. I took his word to be true. I respected what he revealed. We continued to spend time together but things were never the same. The rest of 2000 we worked hard on holding our relationship together. During this time I had been experiencing some very unusual events in my life. I had no explanation for them but they were very real. My sleep almost immediately began being interrupted around the time he sought to resolve the matter. It was not insomnia; it seemed deeper than that. Since I had for years suffered from insomnia, I knew the difference. When my life began to change, and especially during the time I had been with him, I had enjoyed very good sleep. Now torment accompanied my rest.

I began experiencing particularly unusual dreams which seemed more like visions. They tormented my mind. It was as if they were actually happening. All the dreams were about my partner, where he always presented himself as one who hated and didn't love me. We were like enemies in those dreams. The dreams were often dismal, dark and frightening. One night in what appeared to be a real encounter and not a dream, I saw masses of dead animals including worms and snakes in a pool of disgusting, muddy filth. I found myself trapped right in the middle. I woke up sweating.

In another dream I approached a field only to find my love sitting on one side while I approached him from the opposite side. Between us were hundreds of snakes of all colors and sizes. I also saw many appearances of this woman and her mother, as sinister as one could be, expressing their hatred for me. The dreams were tormenting, daunting, despairing and frequent. In addition to these dreams, I was also experiencing unusual symptoms of severe headaches, and at times I felt that I was losing my mind. I wasn't functioning normally. Something was happening to me and I could not explain it or control it. I did not tell my significant other of the troubles I was experiencing, but on one of our visits, he also shared an interesting dream he had, along with other concerns which involved me. I didn't know what to make of the situation. At the time I sincerely had not connected any of these wild incidences to this woman.

I still did not feel comfortable telling him what I had been experiencing, especially since we were growing more and more estranged from each other since she had arrived. Earlier that year, he bought me a card which brought humor affirming his love. The card, featuring a half-naked Tarzan swinging on some branch to get to a girl, read, "My greatest adventure is loving you." Suddenly he seemed distant, disconnected and out of it. His interactions with me were similar to those you'd have with someone you were just getting to know. It's as if all the things we had shared were erased from his memory. He found himself asking me questions about myself and my family as if he had never heard them before. This was weird, very weird. One day, while things were at their peak in this situation and I was fighting hard to save the relationship, I paid him a visit in his Manhattan apartment. When I entered, a most bizarre welcome awaited me. He almost hid behind the door like a child fearing something. It was the oddest thing I can recall experiencing with an adult, and especially one with whom I had shared such a deep relationship.

All these things made me realize something was significantly wrong. I still did not have the slightest clue that our troubles were supernatural. Exhausted from the turn of events in our lives, I asked for a break from the relationship in the beginning of 2001. It was now almost two years since we began dating. I truly did not want to separate at that time but I was too tired to try to hold things together. I don't fully have an explanation why I requested the separation, since we were not fighting, arguing or fussing with each other. Yet, the relationship had strangely changed and it was draining me.

By April of 2001 he agreed that he, too, was tired and needed a break. We separated with the possibility of reconnecting at some point. It was the last time we ever shared in an official relationship together. The months following this decision grew painful. My troubles intensified. He grew cold and indifferent and my life became more disturbed and troubled. My sleep was even more tormented than before. I was certain that these were not natural occurrences. Depressed by our breakup, I fought hard to stay afloat. Still in my last year of studies, I found it difficult to concentrate and focus on the one thing I had worked so hard to achieve to this point, my education. Confused and bewildered by the shattered dreams connected with this beautiful relationship, I suffered internally. I was ashamed to face my family, since there had been such high hopes in this relationship. I sank into a low place. Though my family knew he did not share my faith, I think we all thought that at some point his love for me would win him over. I also never told them that he was agnostic. They just thought he did not go to church, but that he believed in God. The fact that he was such a loving and caring person, however, had won him their favor.

I truly suffered in the wake of our breakup; I didn't seek God, because I knew I had gone further than He wanted me to in this situation. I felt punished, so I would not call on Him. I felt alone and helpless at this, another failed point in my life. Another failed relationship, another disappointment. I plummeted deep into one of my worst depressions since suffering with the disease. Darkness surrounded me. I took off two weeks' leave from work where I now held a job as a teacher in an after school program. I was called into the office one day where they told me how much they loved having me as a teacher, but that I had changed. My change, they said, was affecting my performance. So I had to decide. I tried to pull it together but I couldn't. A few months later I resigned.

A Shocking Revelation

One day while at home I felt a strong need to call a friend of my ex. We never met in person but we had dialogued a few times by phone. While we spoke, she told me she had been concerned about me and wondered about me. I did not tell her all that I had been going through but told her the pain I felt over how things had turned out for me and her friend, my ex. It is through this conversation that she warned me seriously to stay away from both my ex and this woman, whom I have never met until this day. She then revealed something which almost threw me to the floor. She informed me that since she is also from an island and has been friends with my ex for many, many years she knew much about his life and conquests with women. She informed me that many West Indians in his circle knew that he had not shared in a relationship with this woman because he loved her. Rather, he had been entangled in her world of black magic but he was unaware of it. The world of black magic is a deep secret society in most cultures. Who wants to admit to having any connections to such a practice?

She confirmed that he had tried to walk away from this person, for years, but without success. She then informed me that he had met lovely island women here in America with whom he sought to build a life but, like me, they quickly vanished without a trace or explanation. A non-practicing Christian, she said for him to understand the powers which enslaved him, he first needed to believe in God. Since he had no interest in religion, it would be difficult to interest him in such supernatural matters.

As our conversation ended, she asked me to take care of myself and seek God for help. She felt sure this family sought not only to break up the relationship I had with this man through their witchcraft, but to see my end. I became disturbed and shocked by what I had just heard. I grew tremendously frightened. All the strange occurrences I had been experiencing began to make sense at this point. The days following this news were daunting. Knowing someone would do such evil to have a relationship both shocked and frightened me. Growing up, I had heard many stories of such superstitions. I even heard of people who had been affected by such practices even in my own family. But in the years I lived in America I lost sight of those things. These thoughts no longer came to my mind and somehow I had dismissed the idea that such things were true. It was not something I ever cared to know about or with which I cared to be connected. Neither would I have ever imagined that it would play any role in my own life, particularly in America.

It is my belief that the extent to which this family sought to hurt me with spiritualism in an attempt to keep this man in their family was cushioned by God. I still believe that had I been obedient and ended this relationship, at the times the Holy Spirit pressed me to, I could have saved myself a lot of grief. Juliette, having full knowledge of my ordeal, pleaded for prayers for my healing every Sunday morning at the 6:00 a.m. prayer services in our church. It was not immediate healing but in the following months I felt a gradual change. I sought much counsel on how I could rid myself of these demonic encounters. Herbal teas along with bush baths were recommended for healing. I tried all I could to be well. Still, I failed to call on God, since I knew I had been disobedient to him.

It is my unwavering belief, however, that God in His mercy, never having given up on me, brought me freedom from these demons which hunted me. Satan would never cast himself out of someone. So my healing came from God, since He is the only power who can expel any demonic force. It was after this experience I also had a real epiphany moment that if there is an evil side which so enslaves the mind and controls the behavior of others, then there must be a good side to the supernatural which works to bring about the opposite in human lives. This began a turning point in my understanding of the supernatural. It brought a solid confirmation to me that there is, in fact, a God out there. Realizing this, I reached out to God for help. I cried out to Him to help me heal and promised that I would try to serve Him the best way I could. It would be a long journey to spiritual recovery. I recall that in the spring of 2002, when my deliverance from this demonic stronghold came, it was as if a burden had been lifted from me. Within days my complexion exuded a beautiful healthy glow. I had for months literally changed color and become a few shades darker. The indescribable headaches, which felt like stones packed in my frontal lobe, were gone never to return to this day. Those tormenting dreams which terrified my sleep also left me never to return. My appetite returned and brought with it a deep love and appreciation for food that I am yet to lose. I had lost my appetite for months while I went through this ordeal and had reduced to the size of a twig. My cheek bones were so pronounced that they could have injured someone on impact. I invested in a pair of padded hips and butt to conceal my sickly frame. I wore many layers of clothing to increase my size and even then I looked terrible. I stayed away from church and made my entries and exits very quickly into places where I was forced to be present.

Some months after my healing, I visited a store where I had often bought clothes. When the store owner saw me looking so healthy and glowing, her eyes widened in surprise. As she complimented me on my transformation, she loudly informed me that for a long time when I visited the store she thought I was a Crack addict. I got a glimpse that day into the depth to which I had deteriorated in this ordeal. I had a long way to go emotionally from the trauma I experienced through the loss of this relationship, as well as the damage I suffered from this supernatural encounter. I learned that I would never again doubt the supernatural. I also knew that it was time to trust God fully with finding me a life partner. "Except God builds our house then we will forever labor in vain," should we try to build lives with those who do not know or love Him. (Psalm 127:1). I purposed to renew my mind and spirit by giving them completely to God. I knew that if a man wanted me, he had to go through God. It is close to a decade since making this commitment, and I have held faithfully to it.

The Night I Planned to Die

As the loss of this relationship weighed on me, I cared very little about continuing with life. Since I was prone to depression, thoughts of suicide were never far from my mind. In August of 2001, just a couple of weeks before the September 11 events, I took a trip to Disney World with Juliette and Debbie her sister in an attempt to deal with the hurt I was experiencing. I tried my best to have a good time but inside me suffering controlled everything. I couldn't shake this thing off. Debbie and I returned to New York, but Juliette stayed a bit longer to visit with another of her sisters in Florida. Since Juliette and I had now shared an apartment, I found myself home alone coping with this difficult time. Thoughts of suicide haunted me, and it seemed to offer a sweet relief. A few years earlier my concerns for my mother had kept me from taking my life, but I no longer felt such a restraint. I wanted nothing to hold me back this time from ending this pain. Silencing my conscience to not feel sorry for anyone but myself at this point, I reached for the antidepressants I had been given just weeks before by a psychologist.

A few months earlier, my only friend at the college I attended encouraged me to see a therapist. Though she knew nothing more than the fact I had been having "guy trouble," she recommended that I seek help. Until this point in my adult life, I had never sought therapy for my troubles. When I did not talk to God, I spoke to no one else. Within moments of our visit the therapist concluded I was depressed and prescribed Zoloft, an antidepressant. I never enjoyed taking medication. So I never took any of the pills until my return from Florida. As I found myself alone that night thinking of the best way to take my life, I remembered the pills. As I approached the little trial packs in the cabinets, I contemplated all the reasons why I had to do this. Life until this point had brought only pain. I could not seem to find success in anything I tried. Even while trying my best to foster a loving and caring relationship, something always happened to end it. I had not felt any real joy or happiness for any lengthy period of time before someone or something sought to snatch it from me. My experiences were painful, depressing and exhausting. I didn't wish to have even one more of those episodes. Since I refused to leave a suicide note for the reason I chose to take my life, I wanted someone to know that my body was going to be dead in my apartment. Who would I choose as that someone to know?

As I stood there with this dilemma, I felt a strong desire to call Avis. We had not communicated for a long time. I had not been attending church much, so we did not get to see each other. She is a woman who loves God deeply and she constantly told me God loved me. She reminded me often, "God has a plan for your life and you will be amazed at what He is going to do through you. He is not through working with you yet." I never told her this but I grew quite irritated by those statements. They contradicted the troubles I was having in my life. The fact that God loved me meant nothing to me at that time. So I did not want to hear it. I stayed away. Bruce and Avis had tried really hard to steer me in a good direction through their concern for me. My search for happiness and love in this big world was ongoing, so I could not pause to listen. If God really loved me, He needed to find better ways of showing me.

My experiences up to now had not convinced me of His love. One day Avis drove me to a park. As we sat there, she saw the sadness in my eyes and heard the pain in my voice. She then took my hand like a little child as she assured me, "God is going to do something through you that will blow your mind." She said it with such confidence, I almost laughed at the thought that she would not realize that God just did not love me that way. Maybe he loved others that way but most certainly not me. I asked her, "When. When will it be that He will do those things for me?" As always she had a wise explanation that God would bring His plan to pass in my life in the right time. As we left the park that day, I knew I needed a break from her faith and unfailing certainty that God would do something great in me. Surprisingly, as I planned my suicide that night, her words kept pouring into my mind. "God s a plan and He is not finished with you yet." With several pills already in my system a struggle and wrestling in my spirit emerged to call this very woman who had now been like a spiritual mother to me. I thought, "She's the last person I should call since I know how this conversation will go. I do not want her to change my mind." It was a fierce battle.

I cannot remember exactly how I finally made it to the phone or why I began dialing her number, but she was soon on the other line. I went right into the reason for my call. "I am about to take my life," I announced. For some odd reason she was not startled or alarmed. She remained calm but simply asked, "And then what?" I was not sure what to answer. The line became silent, and then she said, "So the people who have ridiculed you could have victory? Do you think they deserve to live after all they have put you through while you should die? So they could rejoice when you are gone, saying, 'Good riddance?'" Interestingly, she had no knowledge of the depth of pain I experienced in this relationship or the circumstances surrounding its end. I again remained silent. She then asked me, "Where are the rest of the pills?" I told her I held them in my hand. She then instructed me to open the pack and flush the last one down the toilet. I do not fully have an explanation to this very day why her words were so compelling that I did exactly as she commanded. She, at that moment, requested that I call my other cousin, Carmella, who lived next door, to come over. I also had to promise to confirm that she had arrived. She then encouraged me to wait on God as she assigned me to Carmella's care. Carmella did not know she was with me because I had tried to take my life. She just thought I was very ill. By this time the few antidepressants I had taken "kicked in." I began experiencing severe side effects. I vomited several times and shook terribly. Since I vomited the pills I did not have to go to the hospital. God had once again intervened and brought me deliverance in a potentially fatal decision. It is the last time I ever have or ever will attempt to take my life. I have since learned the value of the gift of life. I did not give it to myself, neither should I seek to take it away. March of 2002 was the last time I saw or made contact with my ex until the summer of 2004 when he drove to my home. I had been on errands with my cousin Vanessa when I caught a glimpse of him before making it to my apartment entrance. Still shaken by the whole ordeal and shocked to see him at my address, we turned back and then called him to find out what he wanted.

My best friend and cousin informed me that he had finally discovered his fate with this woman. The wool over his eyes had been removed. She said he looked very sad, hurt and confused. With tears in his eyes he shared what had happened with him since our lives were separated and he involuntarily ended up with this woman. He had now been ostracized by his friends and family. He had been isolated from everyone and she remained the only one in his life. He again confessed that not only did he not love her but he also despised her for the way she had ruined his life. He expressed feeling trapped and pleaded for help to be free. He said he had become aware that her connections to him were not natural but that something greater and more sinister was involved. He literally cried out to my cousin for help asking how he could be finally free from this life. She reminded him that he first needed to believe that God was out there and that the supernatural did, in fact, exist. She suggested he find a church and speak with a spiritual leader, whether pastor or priest, to help him find freedom from this unwanted life. He had been entangled so long, that he needed the right kind of spiritual help. He left his card and asked that she stay in touch with him, but I asked her that we help him through prayer, because I did not wish to have any contact with him at the time. I was still very shaken by the encounter and I know Satan is cunning. I didn't want to re-entangle myself in something so disturbing. The scriptures warn, "Stand fast therefore in the liberty wherewith Christ has made you free, and be not entangled again with the yoke of bondage" (Galatians 5:1-3). There was much repairing to be done on my mind and in my heart. I needed God's forgiveness in huge ways. I had made some choices in seeking to repair this relationship that I wished I had rethought. I also had not been sincere with my family about what really happened concerning our breakup. Still I had to find peace in moving forward in my new life.

I didn't learn all my dating lessons right away. My determination to remain pure was posing some serious challenges in my dating life, but I remained committed to living God's way. I was slow in recovering and rebuilding my spiritual strength, but I pressed forward. In August of 2002 I graduated from college with my undergraduate degree in Business Management. Despite the mental prison I experienced, I found academic success. This milestone in itself was a major accomplishment, given the mental anguish I experienced while going through this relationship ordeal.

Still, I never took a semester off to cope. In my final semester, though, I felt sure I would be overcome by my circumstances, hardships and pain. I was in my apartment at the kitchen table staring at my lunch as tears streamed down my face. It was the morning of what would be my very last exams to end my undergraduate program. I seemed unable to take a bite as I wallowed in self pity. Juliette came into the kitchen and found me crying. She had seen so many of these episodes she showed no surprise. She simply asked what was wrong. I informed her that I was too broken to concentrate or take my exams. She fixed her gaze on me with a firm and determined stare as she instructed me to dry my tears, get up, get dressed and make my way to the exam room. I tried telling her that I did not properly study for my exams since I could not concentrate and that there was no way I would do well. So, it was pointless in taking the exams. It was then she assured me, "Your enemies will not win this war. Not if I have anything to do with it. Get up and go take your exams."

Realizing the seriousness in her tone, I prepared myself and went to take my exams. I passed all my exams with flying colors. I even miraculously graduated with honors from my program. I still do not know how it was all possible. I can only say God had been with me through the influence of human agents like Juliette. Although the intent of this evil over my life was to destroy me, God kept my sanity and He preserved and prospered me. "Though I was cast down, I was not destroyed" (2 Corinthians 4:9).

My Journey Back to God

We all know that if we are ever lost, finding our way can create confusion, anxiety, fear and other emotional discomfort. Well, I had wandered far from God, so finding my way back was not easy. The months following these encounters left me confused and bewildered. I tried to find ways to cope. I found myself plunging into a growing love for dancing again. In some ways it also helped me stay connected to my ex since he loved to dance. My musical interest was not sitting well with the neighbors, and some tenants complained to our landlord. At New Year's Eve 2002, I threw a party. I invited many friends as we decided to usher in the New Year. I did not remember my neighbors wanted to rest peacefully in their homes. While things were at their hottest during the night, there was a clashing bang on my apartment door. At first, I thought it was the police, but it was the tenant living directly below my apartment. She is a nurse and worked long hours. She angrily told me to turn down the music and keep the noise down. I did not appreciate her tone. So, I gracefully closed the door before her face giving her no satisfaction.

The moment the door closed I felt the most horrible feeling in my heart. I cannot ever recall being so rude to someone. Although I tried showing my guest that I was pleased in the way I handled things, I felt very badly. Not too long after this incident the tenant moved and I happened to inherit her new apartment. I had an opportunity to endure the growing years of my godson's jumping and knocking to all kinds of sounds which distracted and disturbed me. It was then I had a better understanding of what this woman endured with my noise. For years I longed to find her to apologize. One day just about a year ago God gave me this opportunity. I was having a pedicure. As I made my way to sit for my treatment, right beside me in another chair was that woman. I greeted her. Then I apologized for my insensitive behavior towards her. She told me she accepted my apology and extended her forgiveness. This lightened my heart.

As I sought to settle in a new life, I focused on getting a good job after graduation. Since I received my work authorization, my ability to work more full-time hours became a huge blessing. I had commenced my professional pursuits working as an intern for an entrepreneur yoga instructor in Pelham, New York. When my time there ended, I obtained a job with Monroe College, now a university, and the college from which I graduated with my undergraduate degree. I enjoyed my two years of study at this college. After I graduated, I worked in the alumni and admissions offices simultaneously. I particularly loved my work in the alumni office where I shared a beautiful relationship with my boss. She was very kind to me and treated me with great trust and respect. She bought me presents and made me feel appreciated. I loved working with and for her. Though I enjoyed what I had been doing at the time, I still felt unsettled with my placement there.

So, I resigned from my jobs with the school. They tried to persuade me to stay, but I just felt deeply convinced that I needed to move on. Since I always enjoyed working with children and I had an extensive background in child care which paid my way through college; I applied for a teaching position. I was granted work as a teacher in an after school program in Port Chester, New York, until 2003. I also still struggled with the effects from the breakup. I truly loved the children but something was still lacking and nagging me. So, I also eventually resigned from my position there. I sincerely could not understand why I had suddenly been unable to settle anywhere in which I worked. While I worked to put myself through college I remained in the positions I held until I was no longer needed. Now that I graduated I couldn't seem to settle anywhere that I sought to work. By this time I had become involved in a multi-level marketing venture to stay afloat financially. This had not helped my income much. I went back to what I knew how to do best, childcare.

I responded to an advertisement in a local newspaper in Pelham, New York, which led me to a lovely couple, the Stein–Fedele family. I started caring for their twins Will and Maria. I have had such a wonderful experience caring for these two children as they grew older. Of all the children I have cared for, I never had more road trips and outdoor fun times as I have had with the twins. We have been to so many fun places together; this allowed us to bond in beautiful ways. I looked forward to our visits. The twins have developed into such a wonderful pair. We share many fun moments and events. I spent more time with them than any other children for whom I have cared. I am still actively involved in their lives and I don't see that ever changing.

With the progression of time, a lovely relationship developed with the entire family which has continued until now. This family has been so generous and kind to me in so many moving ways. They have been used by God to be a good financial support for me. The depth of their generosity toward me would take a lifetime to share. I am so appreciative of their family unit. While working with them, I was also given an opportunity to serve as a substitute teacher at the twins' school until I left for graduate studies. I was enjoying my work with the family. Still a nagging feeling pressed me that it wasn't where I needed to be long term. I was never able to share my internal struggle with them, or anyone else for that matter. Determined to stay with them longer, I decided to pursue further studies in counseling, thinking that maybe this nagging feeling was a nudge to pursue higher education. I applied for the Masters in Social Work program at Lehman College in The Bronx sometime in the fall of 2005 and was accepted into the program. I felt working as a counselor would help me in defining my purpose.

Despite my hardships I often took time to encourage and inspire those like me who were hurting. This gave me the feeling that maybe part of my calling was to be a counselor. Setbacks were a huge aspect of my life journey. So, it wasn't surprising when, after I had been accepted into the college, gotten my class schedule and awaited the beginning of classes, that I discovered my strained finances would not allow me to proceed. Devastated, I cried to God in a way I had not for a long time. "Why is this happening to me?" I sobbed. "What am I supposed to do with my life?" This frustrated me immensely, so I cried until I couldn't anymore. Once again, questions filled my thoughts. In the days ahead I composed myself and continued my work as a nanny and part-time substitute teacher. I still felt most unsure about my purpose in life.

I was confused in that I had worked so hard for the Business Degree, and now it seemed apparent to me that it was not useful in my life. I soon began thinking back on how I had come to choose business as a profession. I realized then it had not been a decision I made. Ever since I was in grade school, whenever I was asked what I wanted to be in life, I always said "A teacher." My desire never changed even when I began college. It so happened that when I applied to that college, I had only two program choices. Education was my first choice and Liberal Arts the second. I soon found out that Education was not offered as a major there, so I enrolled in the Liberal Arts program. When I went to see an advisor, I was instructed to continue with Liberal Arts and then change to Business Administration until I decided to transfer to a university in which Education was offered. By the time I was ready to transfer, I had too many credits invested in Business Administration to switch.

I simply continued on with Business Management. Lacking the opportunity to pursue my childhood dream of becoming a teacher by obtaining an Education degree, interestingly, did not deprive me of coming out of college right into teaching and working again with children. Still, there was a quest to discover what I should to do with the rest of my life. What is my purpose? Why am I here on this earth? More so, if God had in fact kept me here the night I so eagerly sought to take my life because He had a plan, what was that plan? Did it have anything to do with this pursuit? This thought continued to drive me. One day as I made my way home from work, I wept all the way home. Perplexed, I cried out to God for an answer. I asked Him to reveal the plan I was told He had and bring me to that place where I should be in life. Though I was very sure that I loved the people in my life and cared for those whom I worked with and for, I knew deep down inside, this was not where I should be. That night after work I made my way home. I suddenly began to cry like a child from the perplexity I was experiencing. Since I felt trapped, I asked God to help and deliver me. God answered that prayer in October of 2004 not too long after I had so earnestly called on Him.

The end of 2004, I felt a change in my spiritual well-being; I felt God's presence and peace.

THE DAY I MET JESUS FOR MYSELF

Chapter 6

The Day I Met Jesus for Myself

As 2004 entered its fall season I could feel a difference in my overall well-being. I felt a sense of internal strength and peace. Those things I thought I would have died from, in actuality, brought me strength. Time testified to the fact that I could have lived without the person who had become the reason for my existence, my ex. I also wasn't bitter or angry, but I was better as a result of my trials, errors and hardships. The worst was behind me and I needed to press forward this time with God. My journey back to Him was a lingering one. I still needed to trust Him with all aspects of my life, particularly in the area of relationships. Above all, surrender is where I struggled most. I needed to "submit to God so that I could be at peace with him" (Job 21:22).

A few years earlier Juliette had joined a multilevel marketing business. She pressed me to get involved. It appeared that she truly was having fun at those meetings she was attending. I still felt somewhat isolated so I reluctantly began attending the meetings. At the first meeting I attended everyone behaved as if they were on some kind of high energy drug. They were all so energized and excited about life. There appeared a healthy glow on the faces of everyone and they spoke openly about God and how He is the one responsible for their successes, happy marriages and blessings in life. Before long, I felt more like I was at a worship service rather than a business meeting. I truly was hooked. So I kept attending. Within a short time we were going to conventions around the country. I looked forward to those events. I made new friends with normal and successful people. I joined a system of books and started reading many motivational books which began transforming my life.

I read books like *Think Big*, by Ben Carson, and others such as *A Set Back is a Set Up for a Comeback*, and *The Magic is in the Extra Mile*. They reshaped my ideologies about myself, my world view and my God view. I felt a sense of empowerment, not defeat. New purpose and meaning emerged in my heart. Then my hunger for God ignited. I wanted Him, no one else. During this time, I became very familiar with the ministry of the pastor at the Lakewood Church in Dallas, Texas. I watched his televised broadcast every Sunday morning. I also encouraged my cousins to look at his broadcast. His messages brought me great hope in God and confirmed my belief in myself. I purchased his book, *Your Best Life Now*. I loved it. It fired me up in my journey back to God. I also had an opportunity to visit him at Madison Square Garden in New York sometime in the fall of 2005. I was so moved by the experience and felt blessed by his ministry. I thank God for his ministry and for using him to help me get back on track. Through these teachings, I remembered God had a plan for my life and I could now taste its arrival, but I first needed to find Him.

The multi-level marketing business I believe was also used by God to connect my steps back to Him. I had been doing very well in the business, but despite my new found zeal and energy, this reserved calm I possessed had not vanished. I tried at best to be cordial with this new group of people with whom I had now been interacting, but I was still hurting from the fresh pain of my recent experiences. A few of the women there interpreted my reservation as pride. They concluded that because I was attractive I felt myself better than they were so they purposed to let me know I wasn't better. Since I regained a fair amount of weight, I exuded a glow of health and beauty not just from without but from within due to my growing confidence. It's the best I had felt in a long time. The quiet confidence in my demeanor had offended these women. So, one night as I made it into the meeting a large woman twice or more my size and quite a gossip, confronted me as if to fight.

She loudly told me she had been sick and tired of me walking around thinking I was better than everyone else. She wanted me to know, "You are not better than me." She had to be held back by some men from physically attacking me. I did not respond even once to their wayward conduct. If they only knew how happy I was to even be around to take a walk. People only look at the outside of who we are. I thank God He looks deep within to see our hearts. The women also spread some vicious rumors about me involving an illicit relationship with someone's husband. This man was old enough to be my father. I was so disgusted with them. Their accusations made their way to the top officials in the business. A meeting was called with leaders to resolve their unkind and vicious lies. This hurt me deeply, and since I was prone to walking away from any experience or situation which brought me discomfort, I eventually left the business. Its positive impact remained with me, however.

A Divine Intervention

In October of 2004, while still affiliated with this business, I, along with other friends, excitedly planned a birthday party for my cousin who lived in Queens. She and I had not seen each other since she left Dominica many years ago as a very young girl. We were reunited through the multilevel marketing business which I had joined. This was to be a surprise birthday party for her. It was my idea, so the responsibility of its planning rested on me. To lighten my burden I invited different people to contribute by preparing a dish. We agreed we would leave from Westchester for Queens at a certain time. Someone had been assigned to keep her occupied and out of the house until we arrived. Everyone was dressed and waited a while for one of our designated drivers to arrive with our mutual friend who had cooked the rice and beans. Although she had a history of lateness, I never anticipated that she would be late to a surprise party.

The time for our departure had long passed with no word on where the driver was with our friend. By this time I became upset and shocked by the sudden turn of events. My personality is such that, when I set a time for something, it's that time. I also can get a bit carried away once involved in planning an event. This is due to the perfectionist trait in my temperament. It's something I have been working hard to yield over to the Lord. I've gotten better, but I am not all there yet. Once they arrived, they had barely put the car in park when I began addressing our friend in a very strong tone. I was very upset. I found her behavior to be highly insensitive. So was mine in the way I rebuked her like a child. Once I finished my address, I felt horrible.

It wasn't in my nature to be unkind or rude to others. I would be honest and direct but not rude or condescending. I did not feel good about what happened. Besides, our friend the driver verbally lashed out at me for speaking to her that way. Shocked by his defense, I became very quiet as I fought to choke back tears. The party started off wrong. We all got in the car with these two friends with whom I had just fought, since the show must go on. In the back of the car I choked back tears. The ride to Queens, though not usually a long one, seemed like an eternity that day. In the back seat of the car my life flashed before me. A deep reflection on the major events which had taken place until this point arrested my attention. Spellbound by the things I had endured and overcome in recent months, I craved peace and happiness. Soon a voice which seemed to come from outside my head, but not an audible one, pressed me: "You are looking for love and happiness in all the wrong places." I knew I was the only one in the back seat so I wondered about this internal, compelling voice. I gave no reaction. I remained seated with my head rested on the back seat. I kept my eyes closed as I paid close attention and waited for the remaining aspects of the conversation. The words only resounded in the same manner, "You are looking for love and happiness in all the wrong places." This soon arrested my attention in a remarkable way for the entire ride.

I had been looking for love and happiness for a long time. I had searched for it in many ways and through a variety of means. Regardless of what I tried, my feelings of emptiness continued to envelop me. Nothing filled me and no one could satisfy me. I continued to hunger and thirst. All the wells in life from which I drank eventually ran dry, causing me to thirst all over again. I wanted my hunger to be satisfied and my thirst to be quenched, but I failed to turn to God. My experiences through the church and religion had not given me a good impression of Him and His love. I had already been with Him. I thought, "What new experience could He offer that is different from what I have had with Him since I was a child?" My search was ongoing but I could not find what I was looking for. Where would I find love and happiness, since I had not found it in relationships, friends, education, business, or anywhere else that I searched? It seemed obvious that it had to be in God, but how could I get this peace, love and happiness from Him? It seemed I had been searching for it my whole life and could not obtain it.

We arrived at the party. Though the same in body, something new had been happening in my heart. As master of ceremonies, I painstakingly took care of all that was needed so that things would run smoothly, but my heart wasn't in it. Somewhere between ten and eleven p.m. or a little thereafter, I felt held by my two arms and transported to a couch resting against the wall in the room. I saw no hands but I had been drawn by a compelling force which felt like hands moving me from one location to the next. While in the couch I leaned my head back and drifted into what seemed like a state of sleep yet consciousness. As I lay there, I felt that the same compelling thought which had pressed me in the car returned, echoing the same words. "You are looking for love and happiness in all the wrong places."

My life again passed before me. The choices and errors I made in recent years, my straying and wanderings, highlighted by all the times I deliberately disobeyed God, pressed in on me. My spirit felt heavy. Weighted, I remained where I was. Though I wasn't given any specific instructions to do anything or go anywhere, it was understood that my next step would be to find a church. A softening rested on my heart as I was awakened from this encounter by one of my cousins. She called my name a few times before I sat up and opened my eyes. "Are you okay?" she asked. I nodded my head. I asked that we go home. So we packed up and left. I failed to speak on our way home. I simply craved to be at church. A peace filled my spirit while a hunger for God overwhelmed my heart and mind. It was as if I fully understood, that night, that there was nowhere in the world, neither was there in anyone on earth the peace and contentment I had sought for so long. It was in one being and He was God. The only place I had known to find God was in church. I did not know what awaited me when I arrived that would be different from all the other times I had gone since I was a child, but it was clear that what I sought, I would find in church.

Since this encounter took place on a Saturday night, I had to wait until the next week to go to church. The wait was painful and long. For as long as I lived life as a Christian, never did I yearn so much for a Sabbath to come. Still not having said a word to anyone concerning my encounter that night, I kept my heart's content to myself. The internal wrestling I had so long experienced did not weigh on me anymore as the days passed. I felt calm and at peace. It had been months since I attended church, and I did not miss church. Yet, there I was sick from being unable to wait for the next Sabbath to come. Feeling starved and spiritually malnourished, I needed to be fed. Having forsaken assembling with the people of God (Hebrews 10:25), the time came for my return.

My Turning Point

I remember the beautiful fall morning that welcomed this particular Sabbath day. The trees gave up their colorful leaves to welcome the new season. It was cool and bright. I woke up knowing this day was special. I felt like a bride the morning of her wedding, and wore a lovely dress indicating I was prepared for a very special occasion. My outward calm didn't reveal the anticipation and excitement which flooded my heart. I had a meeting with God at church. As I made my way up the stairs and through the main entrance door, my heart raced. It had been a while since my last visit. Our first elder greeted me with surprise. He welcomed me and inquired of my long disappearance. I glided by before pausing too long to give an explanation. As I took my seat, I felt strangely at home. I noticed nothing unique in our worship service that morning which was different from anything we had done in the past.

Interestingly, inside me something beautiful was taking place. The songs sung by the congregation were the same we had sung all my life, but this time they brought new meaning accompanied by a sense of wonderful healing. I remember distinctly "I Surrender All" as one of the hymns of choice that day. I sang it with my whole heart. Then I knew I had found what I had been looking for and the reason God led me to church that morning. I needed to surrender. For years I had refused to sing that song because I had not lived a life fully surrendered to God. Once I sang it, I meant it. I knew at that moment that Jesus was the answer to my problems. He alone could fill my void. He alone held the happiness, joy, and peace I had sought for so long. I fell in love that day with Jesus Christ and I have wanted Him in my life ever since. I felt a freedom in worship that morning; I lifted my hands before God in praise. This is especially uncharacteristic for me. I am not expressive that way. I had actually found people who so publicly displayed their spirituality to be a distraction. I realize now this is judgmental since I truly do not know the reason for their methods of praise. I only know, "If the Son makes you free, you are free indeed" (John 8:36).

I belonged to God and this time my soul knew it well. The year 2005 met a brand new me. Peace lodged deep in my heart in ways I had never felt since I first believed. I spent much time in confession and prayer for forgiveness. I needed God's forgiveness desperately. I opened up my heart in prayer through confession, spilling all I could remember in offense against Him. Besides confession, I needed to repent, which meant turning away from the mind set which had so often kept me running from God. The more I prayed, the closer I felt to God. The more I shared with Him, the lighter and freer I felt. I embraced "The peace of God which surpasses all human understanding" (Philippians 4:7). As my relationship with God grew, my faith in God increased. I stuck to prayer because I saw a direct correlation between talking with God and growing close to Him. I fed on His word, the Bible. A joy filled my heart – "Real Joy, wonderful Joy." Truly, "in the presence of God, there is fullness of joy and pleasures ever more" (Psalm 16:11). My life in Christ was now the purpose for my existence. He is the reason why I live, literally.

The Devil Gone Mad

When any person loses someone they love, they put up a fight. When my relationship ended with this wonderful man I loved, I put up a fight. Although I never met in person the woman who sought my demise, I tried hard to find ways to repair the relationship I had with this man. I knew what he meant to me and what he had done for my life. I did not want to lose him. When God led me back to Himself that beautiful

131

Sabbath morning, Satan was angry that his hold on my life had disappeared. For years, I believed his lies that God did not love me; he plagued me with depression, fears and anxiety. Even before I was born he tried to take my life. Despite his rage and determination to destroy me, God continued to rescue me. My surrendering to God was a major blow to Satan, and the hold he previously had over me he wasn't willing to give up without a fight. There was no telling what I could become in the hands of God. I started seeing clear evidences of a spiritual battle when certain members of my own family rose up against me. Certain at this point that "We do not wrestle against flesh and blood" (Ephesians 6:12), I turned to God on my knees to help me fight the enemy. It all started when I received a disturbing phone call one night from the only aunt I have here in the United States. She called to confront me on a damaging letter she received just a few days earlier in the mail. She seemed obviously upset but cautious in her approach toward me. Until this date she and I had never once in all the years we knew one another had a conflict or confrontation. My aunt had practically become a mother to me after my mother left Dominica. She treated me like her very own as I grew up. I am the closest to her of all my aunts even though I love all my aunts. If my aunts and uncles are sincere, they will confess that, though I will be truthful in my approach with them, I have never been disrespectful, unkind or rude to any of them at any time in my life.

This explains why she had been so careful in bringing to my attention the letter she received which she was told came from me. The letter was written to reflect my verbiage and handwriting. So, whoever wrote it did so with the intention of framing me. The contents of the letter were damaging. My aunt's character was attacked and her integrity questioned. The letter highlighted a religious tone as if whoever wrote it meant to rebuke her life in some way. Since I had now been very involved in church life, I appeared to be the only fanatic who would take such an approach with someone. She told me that earlier in the week someone assured her that I am the only likely person who would write such a letter.

132

As she challenged me on why I would send her such a letter, I questioned its content. As we discussed its contents she realized that there were some details in the letter she had never discussed with me. I would have no knowledge of them. It was then that she discovered whoever wrote the letter did it with the intentions of framing me. As I wept at the thought of the evil perpetrated against me, she apologized to me. Then she comforted me by saying, "I should have known you would not do such things to hurt others."

This was only the beginning of my sorrows. In the months ahead, I battled a string of accusations that left me some enemies to this day. I was verbally assaulted on the phone by the daughter of a relative who said I had been spreading vicious rumors about her. These are things I would never consider doing. Having had my own character attacked so many times throughout my life, I have always had a great regard for preserving people's reputation. I am not a perfect person but I would never do those things I was being accused of and they knew it. Soon I received a letter in the mail burned at all four edges. something that is considered a major insult in West Indian culture. Not too long after this, I was confronted by the mother of this same relative as I sat with a cousin in the lobby of a hospital in Brooklyn while we visited another sick relative. She also claimed I had been spreading rumors about her. I did not have a clue what these individuals were talking about. I had never mentioned their names to a single living soul on God's earth. I did not utter a word in response to the confrontation. Neither did I ever address any of the accusations made against me. I knew they were demonically fueled and I failed to add fuel to the evil. I knew that I had never once been rude or unkind to her at any point in our lives. And at the time of her accusation, we had not been in a single disagreement or fight. I was completely bewildered by these situations. So I just purposed to resist the devil working through them so he would flee. (James 4:7).

I also pleaded with God to trouble the consciences of those who sought to do harm until they couldn't live with themselves and turned their lives around. This has always been my prayer for my enemies. One of them later confessed to some relatives how deeply affected and terrible she felt when she saw that despite all the things she had done to me I never once responded in kind. She acknowledged that her behavior toward me was unjustified. I do not hold those things against her. I prayed intently during those times that God would work on her heart and open her eyes to the fact that she was being used by a demonic influence. I asked for a spirit of conversion so that she and others involved could experience what I had found in God. I knew that if they allowed God to change their hearts they would understand me better.

After my graduation from Seminary in May of 2010, she surprised me with a visit at a church where I preached in August. I was somewhat surprised to see her. She told me it was clear God was present in my life. She asked if I would consider giving her Bible studies in preparation for baptism. God be praised! She has given many indications that she is sorry and has tried hard to foster a relationship with me. I have not denied her that opportunity. Being able to forgive is a true indication that God is present in one's life although we all have to be wise in our forgiving process.

These were not my only trials in a string of vicious accusations and lies which challenged my growing faith and brought me much pain in the months of my new walk with God. Having entered such a peaceful place with God, I knew I did not need to fight in these battles. "I needed to stand still and see the salvation of the Lord" (2 Chronicles 20:15-17). During these moments of crisis, rather than fall apart as I did in times past, I fell on my knees before God and pleaded with Him to intervene. My prayers were answered. After a couple months of harassment, without ever a response from me on any of the allegations made, these demons were quieted. I resisted the devil so he fled (James 4:7). I remained calm and silent; "For I shall be quiet from the fear of evil" (Proverbs 1:33).

My Purpose Identified

By the fall of 2005, just one year after my conversion experience, new inspirations which I recognized to be from the Holy Spirit filled my mind. In spite of my new relationship with God, I still wanted to know my purpose for being, the reason for my existence. Though it no longer consumed me to the point of despair, it mattered to me. I wanted to know the purpose for which I was in this world. Since that night in Queens when God arrested my attention through a very strong and compelling impression on my mind, it became His way of reaching me. Each visit met me its own way. One thing was clear. This wasn't my mind playing tricks on me. They were clear communications that had nothing to do with any prior thought that I had. Regardless of where I was or in what I was engaged when one came, it solidly arrested my attention. It was never long, but its impact was always severe.

Sometime in the summer of 2005 I kept feeling strongly that I should begin a speaking ministry. For months I ignored these thoughts, since I had no desire to be involved in any public role. While I was studying in college for my undergraduate degree, one of my teachers, Mr. D, felt convinced that I should be a motivational speaker. I found it odd given my issues. I asked him why he felt this way. He said, "Often in conversation I find your words inspiring." I did not know my words were inspirational. I do recall many times throughout my life encouraging others in their own struggles regardless of the complexity of my circumstances. For almost all of 2005 nagging thoughts that I should engage in motivational speaking haunted me. I dismissed these thoughts until October of 2005, while in the lobby of my church at Mount Vernon. I was about to climb the stairs into the sanctuary, when I felt arrested by this compelling thought pressed upon my mind with the words, "If you do not respond to my request to speak publicly, I will never ask you again," held my attention. Frightened by the occurrence, I ran to Robert, a friend and one of our youth leaders at the time, who stood at the top of the stairs of our church. I urgently said, "I think I want to start a speaking ministry."

While my heart was still palpitating from this bizarre occurrence, he responded, "And you need an agent?" I stuttered, "I just want someone to help me find places where I may speak." "What's your platform?" he asked. "What will you speak about so I can tell those asking?" I had nothing in mind so I quickly responded. "Well, God is changing me and I'm now feeling better about myself. Maybe I can speak about self-esteem? Yea, self-esteem," I reiterated. I reminded him to only find me Sabbath afternoon programs for youths at local churches in the area. I knew that few people attend afternoon programs. I couldn't envision speaking before a large crowd; that would kill me.

I walked away from this conversation not expecting anything to come out of it. I only wanted to do what I felt inspired to do. To my amazement, just a few weeks later Robert came back with the news he had found me a speaking engagement at a youth rally convention in Stamford, Connecticut with the North Eastern Conference of Seventh-day Adventists. As he excitedly shared the news, I panicked. I reminded him that I only wanted afternoon programs at local churches. "I can't speak at a conference convention where hundreds of people will be present," I told him, falling immediately into frightened mode. In the middle of my reasoning, he interrupted me and said, "Go put a PowerPoint presentation together." Petrified, I walked away intending to do my best.

The convention was set for January 13, 2006. I barely slept in the months leading up to it. This appointment consumed my thoughts day and night. I took Rob's advice. I designed a wonderful PowerPoint presentation. The Friday morning of the weekend convention I joined the many attendees at a Stamford hotel, but my nerves threatened to take over. As I spoke that day, the audience seemed quite engaged with my presentation. I longed for its completion, however. My listeners could not suspect my concerns and fears, though, considering I spoke with such authority and confidence. When the session ended, many expressed their satisfaction with the presentation. Mothers requested that I meet with their children for spiritual counsel, prayer and guidance. I had expected rocks to be thrown at me, but a great blessing poured out. Out of this engagement came many speaking appointments around New York all through 2006.

Satan tried to discourage the movement, when I was asked just a couple of weeks after the Connecticut success, to do a presentation at my church. I was so afraid to speak before a known group of people. My fears were confirmed when, after my presentation, two ladies sitting next to each other, called me to them to tell me the PowerPoint slides were filled with grammatical errors. They expressed that they barely were able to concentrate on my words because my slides were so poorly written. They each reminded me of their strength of the English language which qualified them to address me on the matter. They spoke to me as if they were offended that I had the audacity to address people on any matters. I was quite crushed, but I did not show it. I remembered, "You never let them see you sweat." I fought hard for weeks to shake off the things they said. I then took time to look over all twenty-one slides but the errors spoken of were undetected. As time passed and I became more involved in church roles, I was asked to lead in a particular lesson study group.

One Sabbath, as we celebrated our Community Guest Day, I led in the lesson study. One of these young ladies made a great effort to humiliate me before the class. I tried hard to ignore the open rebukes to every comment or point that I raised that morning. The class was filled with visitors from the community, but she paid no attention to the fact that she needed to represent Christ. She simply centered her focus on trying to remind me that I had no business teaching anyone. I was very hurt, but I failed to respond to her hurtful behavior. Shortly after our study was over many of our members came and apologized to me for the public attempt to humiliate me.

While at Seminary I experienced a similar incident. In my final semester one of our classes ended with five-minute presentations by all students. Our teacher was out that particular day. She asked her Administrative Assistant to oversee our presentations. On the day of the presentations four other students spoke before me. During their presentations you could hear a pin drop as they spoke. They had everyone's undivided attention. No sooner did I make my way to the front, greet the class and begin my presentation, than two of my female colleagues who sat together decided to face each other and begin to converse loudly enough that I became very distracted. Although our eyes met, and they were being stopped by other students, they proceeded to interrupt my presentation through its entirety until I was officially finished.

I never once stopped to address their rudeness as it was evident they intended to embarrass and humiliate me. As we ended our class a few students came to me to tell me how sorry they were for the way I was treated. One woman with tears in her eyes expressed her discontent to me regarding their behavior, but expressed her satisfaction about how I handled myself. She asked me why I did not defend myself. I reminded her that these two women worked hard to humiliate me, but what they did in essence was reveal to everyone whose spirit was actually at work in them. I could sense Satan working through them, so I extended my forgiveness. It is my observation that Satan succeeds at accomplishing his greatest exploits through supposed followers of God.

Despite the harsh criticism, a public speaking ministry was birthed from this one Connecticut appointment. My success in public ministry was so rapid that I had already established a name in many churches in the New York area. Soon the pressures of public life started weighing on me. My involvements were an immense drain on my energy. With each appointment I fell in too deep. It's exactly what I had feared, a life in the public. I began contemplating how to get out, but I now had connections. It would be difficult to escape. I needed out immediately. Giving up speaking and staying in the area would not work. I thought I would have to relocate. That's exactly what I set my heart on doing. I called my uncle who had recently purchased a home in Georgia and asked him if he would be willing to be a partner with me in a day care. I did not tell him why, and he agreed. I contacted the state of Georgia to ask for a package on such a business to be sent to me. The package arrived within a couple of weeks. I began my own plans for my life. I had asked God to reveal my life purpose to me, but I wasn't ready for what He was showing me. It seemed unnatural that the thing I dreaded most (public life) is where He would lead me. I could not tolerate spending the rest of my life speaking before audiences. This is contrary to my natural need to be isolated, reserved and private. I could not do it. I decided that the best thing to do was to run away to a place where no one knew me and start over. Plans were underway when my attention was once again arrested in a remarkable way.

*2006 met me actively making
plans to leave town.*

SIGNS OF MY
PASTORAL CALLING

Chapter 7

Signs of My Pastoral Calling

The remainder of 2006 met me actively making plans to leave town, but God kept working behind the scenes to bring His purpose to pass. Sometime in the middle of 2006, the church board voted me as their Personal Ministries secretary. It wasn't a position I welcomed, although I never verbalized it. I saw this as another duty tying me down. I had been asked many times before I agreed to accept the role. Sometime toward the early fall, while serving as secretary of this department, a very tall, lean African-American man entered the church's foyer. He held in his hand a small cardboard box. I approached him to find out how I could be of help. He told me he lived in the neighborhood. "I am getting rid of some books and I thought that your church could use them," he said. I thanked him, and took the box into the church's office where I began to remove the contents from it.

As I unpacked the box it appeared to be prepared for someone going on a journey. In it was a black journal, a woman's devotional Bible and a study Bible still in its case. I had not owned a study Bible to this point. There was also a Strong's Concordance and Strong's Bible Dictionary with Greek and Hebrew sections. I proceeded to shelve the items hoping they would be of use to someone, when a quiet yet clear, prompting pressed me, "They are for you." I couldn't see what use I would have for a Hebrew and Greek concordance but I took all the items home that night except for the journal and the woman's devotional Bible. They would become my first study materials in my seminary studies. I also had no idea I would have to study a year of Hebrew and Greek each at Seminary. I do not recall ever seeing the man who gave me the items before that day. Neither have I seen him again since. I continued to speak while still entertaining plans to leave town.

In October of 2006 I was given my first Saturday morning speaking appointment at the Mamaroneck Seventh-day Adventist Church in Mamaroneck, New York. I tried hard to cancel the appointment but the pastor, who is now my dear friend, would not take no for an answer. I tried telling him I was only a speaker, not a preacher, but he would not hear me. He reminded me that he had an opportunity to evaluate the youth seminars I conducted at his church. He told me he felt sure God wanted me to deliver His word that Sabbath morning. The appointment was set for February 3, 2007. During the months prior to the appointment, I was deeply troubled. I reminisced on the days when no one knew me or cared to know me. I didn't want this life.

By the beginning of 2007 while at a church board meeting, I was voted Director of the Personal Ministries Department. This department is responsible for the evangelistic and soul winning efforts of our church. Ours is a large congregation, so this was a huge responsibility. Before I could object, everyone started endorsing me for the position. It would seem odd to object at that point. So, I accepted to serve in the role. Just a couple of weeks later, my Pastor, Dr. Abraham Jules, called me before going into another board meeting. He said he felt a strong desire that I should serve as an Elder at our church. He felt sure God was leading him to do so. I almost had to be scooped up from the floor. "What is going on?" I thought. I tried negotiating with him to not make me an Elder, but he remained firm in his decision to follow what God had laid on his heart.

I was frustrated, confused and overwhelmed with all these sudden changes plunging me deeper in church responsibilities. Just a few months earlier, I also had been placed in the role of Prayer Coordinator for our church. Our Prayer Coordinator had suffered a mild stroke. Unable to continue in her function, she called me to say she felt strongly I should replace her. After discussing it with leaders, I became her replacement. This also seemed odd since there were so many I felt who were better suited for the role at the time. Now, with the Elder position added to my responsibilities, and all the speaking engagements popping up, I thought "How could I possibly leave town?"

I'm a Preacher?

I never thought I would survive the morning of February 3, 2007. I would be the preacher for the Sabbath's Black History Month Awareness. The small church in Mamaroneck received me well. My nervousness soared. I spoke on "The Miracle of The Five Loaves of Bread and Two Fish" found in Mark Chapter 6, in which Jesus took a little boy's lunch, blessed it and fed over 5,000 people. I wanted the people of God to know that if we shared the little we had with God, He could do great miracles through us. It dawned on me I really needed to practice what I preached. Until this point I had spent the past two years resisting God, by not wanting to share myself for use in His vineyard. In retrospect, though, I did not see my unwillingness to be in public life as resisting God. I had my own hang-ups about women in ministry or in any kind of upfront role, as a matter of fact. After I finished preaching, I stood at the door to greet the members. One of the members asked to speak with me privately afterward. He told me he is a pastor who responded to his call to ministry quite late in life. He said he was a former engineer. When I ended my greetings, we met to talk. Very calm and gentle in spirit, he shared with me a firm conviction. "I believe you should consider becoming a pastor. There is a calling on your life." I was taken aback by his words.

One woman at my church had previously called me a preacher, but it bothered me greatly. No one had articulated it so clearly until that time. I respectfully said, "No! I don't want to do that." Surprised by my stern response, he encouraged me to pray about it. I left Mamaroneck that day determined to leave New York. I spent much time wondering how I would resign from all my church roles. I thought of individuals who could be suitable replacements.

Frustration set in. How did I get to this point? When did all these things happen, so unplanned and so fast? Why is this happening to me? Now people think I should be a pastor. I am a woman and women are not to be pastors. Until this time I had only met one female pastor. It was in the summer of 1997 at my Mount Vernon Church. I quickly concluded the world was coming to an end.

In the spring of 2010, I discovered this pastor was Dr. Hyveth Williams, a powerful pastor in our denomination with whom I now share a wonderful friendship. I had been willing to speak, even tolerate serving in all these different roles in the church, but I wasn't willing to become a preacher or a pastor. I thought myself too feminine for such a masculine task. I had already been involved much deeper than I anticipated. I would proceed no further, or so I thought. I soon learned that it wasn't the humans I encountered who asked this thing of me, but God Himself. About a week and a half after my encounter in Mamaroneck, I called my church treasurer, who is also one of our elders, to request funds for an evangelistic effort. He seemed delighted to hear my voice.

Our treasurer and I now share in a very nice Christian friendship, but we had barely interacted personally at the time of this call. I didn't know him on a personal level at all. He immediately caught my attention by expressing an urgency to share something with me. I gave him my undivided attention thinking it related to funds for our department. What he told me next, both troubled and somewhat angered me, though he didn't know it. Calm yet convincing, he appealed seriously to me stating,

"I believe the Lord is calling you to go to Andrews University to become a pastor. I believe that this is where you will meet your husband."

Shocked and bewildered, my heart began to race as I kept myself from drooping to the floor. I quickly and sharply responded, "I have not sensed that calling at all on my life. It is neither a thought nor a consideration." He pleaded with me to pray about it on the basis that in recent months he had had an opportunity to evaluate my work in the areas in which I was serving at our church, particularly as Prayer Coordinator. He then reminded me, "Every time you open your mouth, the things you say reach me deep in my heart. I am in my 70s and have heard a lot in my life, but the things you say pierce the heart. This is the Spirit of God." He also offered to help in whatever way he could financially. I felt flattered and my heart may have softened a little, but I was not going to become a pastor.

As we hung up, I was deeply frustrated and irritated that all these people thought they knew what I needed and what was good for my life. I wondered, "If God wants me to do this, why is He not telling me Himself. Why is it that only people were suggesting I go into pastoral ministry? Where is God in all of this?" Already in my 30s, the last thing I wanted to do was start over. The very thought of going to Andrews seemed impossible to me. Besides, becoming a pastor is not something I wanted at all. The days following these conversations brought me to tears. I thought about the insensitive requests of these men who would not consider I had an established life here in New York.

God Got My Attention

On February 15, 2007, exactly twelve days after my first preaching appointment and less than two weeks after my conversation with our church elder concerning going to Andrews University Theological Seminary, God finally got my attention. It was about 7:30 in the morning when one of my relatives in Brooklyn called my cousin Vanessa and me to report that there had been a terrible accident in Dominica involving two of my uncles. We knew that at least one of my uncles had been killed. Since my cousin and I now shared an apartment, and we called home together to confirm the report. We then learned that both my uncles died from the accident. My cousin and I looked at each other in disbelief. Unable to console each other, we individually found our mourning spots in the apartment. I fell to the floor and wept uncontrollably. I cannot fully describe the depth of pain I experienced that day.

This ordeal had unquestionably topped any of my pains until this point in my life. When we were able to compose ourselves, we informed our places of employment of our loss. Then we joined the rest of our family in Brooklyn. News of the deaths of Pastor Mozart and Peter Serrant (Malachi) swept through our little island of Dominica. These are the same two uncles my mother said saw me walk for the first time and proclaimed a miracle had taken place. They were also the two uncles who introduced the Bible Sabbath into our large family. Their lives amazingly seemed to have remained closely connected except for their walk with God. Malachi struggled for years to stay on the straight and narrow, but Uncle Mozart went on to become a Pastor. He served faithfully as a pastor for twenty-three years. Interestingly, they were also the only two of their fifteen siblings who had their homes built right next to each other. The morning of their deaths we understood that Uncle Mozart was outside in front of their homes pleading with Malachi to give his life to God. It is the final conversation they would ever have.

A vehicle heading in the complete opposite direction from where they were standing lost control and ran into them, killing Malachi immediately. Uncle Mozart died moments later on his way to the hospital after praying his final prayer. They had witnessed the miracle of me walking, and another miracle was about to take place in my life as a result

147

of their deaths. As my life had begun to change, Uncle Mozart felt pleased that I had been walking in the ways of God again. He sensed something in my life was different. I was saddened that I did not get a chance to tell him of all the changes I had made. When I preached at the church in Mamaroneck on February 3, I recall feeling a strong desire to call my Uncle Pastor Serrant.

I put it off for almost two weeks, and finally decided I would call him on Friday, February 16. Sadly, he died on Thursday, the 15th of February. I experienced so much guilt. He called me not long before he died telling me he wanted me to come to St. Lucia to speak to the young people there. Since I had only become an Elder in January, and just preached a sermon a few days before his death, I hoped to share those things with him. I am uncertain how he would have dealt with those two issues, since I know our denomination, particularly in the Caribbean, still struggles with women in ministry on even deeper levels. Fortunately, a close friend of his and our family, who attended the church where I preached that day, called him and told him the Lord used me to deliver His word. When we met in Brooklyn after the deaths, she told me, "I called a first time and we spoke long until I forgot to tell him about your preaching appointment at our church that day. After hanging up I called back to share with him the good news." "What did he say?" I asked. She told me that he was elated. He said that he would call to express how proud he felt. Unfortunately that call never came. My heart broke even more, but I was happy that God found a person who was more willing to respond and act more quickly than I did.

When we arrived in Brooklyn, we found that my Aunt Maria and other relatives were present. No one could console the other. We were all broken by the news of the deaths. The sound of sobbing filled the room for several hours until we had no more tears left to cry. Unable to cry anymore, we joined in remembering the lives of our loved ones. There were moments of laughter as we traveled memory lane. Since I felt somewhat baffled by the whole ordeal, I felt the need to go into a room alone to talk with God. Upon entering the room I knelt by the bed where I wept some more. For a little while I could not find words to communicate with God. I just knew I wanted to talk with Him about why this terrible thing had happened. I also wanted to know the purpose of their deaths.

God, who sees all, knew the reason why this happened. I hoped He would help me find reasons so I could peacefully move forward. With my Bible in my hands and tears running down my face, I prayed, "Father, I don't know why this happened. I don't understand why you allowed this terrible accident to take the lives of these two people, especially Pastor Serrant, your servant who loved your work so much. I ask you to please tell me why you have allowed this to happen, and I promise I will not grieve these deaths so deeply anymore."

With my Bible in hand, and my eyes closed I said, "Speak Lord, for I am listening." With my eyes still closed I opened my Bible. It opened to Joshua chapter one. I immediately centered my focus on reading verses one through nine. It read, "My servant Moses is dead. Now arise, go over the Jordan...." Verse nine emphasized "Be strong and of a good courage. Do not be terrified; do not be discouraged, for the Lord your God is with you wherever you go." The words, "My servant Moses is dead" impacted me greatly. Realizing God heard me, I quickly shut the book in fear. I left the bedroom abruptly, and returned to the living room where I could no longer shed a tear. Later that afternoon, Vanessa called me to the computer to see a photograph which Uncle Mozart's son had posted on line. Above the photograph were the words "This is me and my father Moses."

As I read it, I felt the confirmation that the death of God's servant Moses in Joshua chapter one had been shown to me as a reminder that now his servant, Mozart was dead; someone needed to "Arise." I did not have the faintest idea on how I would do this. With all prior discussions concerning ministry far from my memory in the weeks preceding the deaths, not once did it dawn on me that I should be a pastor like my uncle. The thought sincerely did not cross my mind during this time. I wondered about what I would do to help His work. Conducting myself as a better Church Elder and Prayer Intercessor came to mind, but never did I remember the encouragements to become a pastor. The thought had been so far removed from me, it left my subconscious.

That same afternoon, my aunt reflected on my uncles' lives. She particularly spoke of Pastor Serrant's ministry. She wondered about its continuation and then appealed to me to carry on his work. She said I appeared to be the only one in the family whose life was moving in a more serious, committed, spiritual direction. She said "It seems natural that you keep the work going that your uncle started." Though I gave no response to her prophetic proclamation, I could not help but notice these three incidents were tied into each other. Plans were now under way for the funeral arrangements in Dominica. The family members here who were unable to travel would view the services via satellite. We were shopping in downtown Brooklyn one afternoon in preparation for travel, when I stopped to use a public rest room.

While there, a compelling voice spoke not audibly yet clearly and strongly to me. The words "Andrews University, Andrews University, Andrews University" three times pressed my subconscious. Immediately the words of our treasurer and Elder, "I believe you should go to Andrews University to become a pastor" raced back to memory. I leaped from the bathroom stall with my heart pounding out of my chest. At that very moment, my life purpose had been defined and revealed. I understood my part in the death of my uncles and I now knew what I was to do with the rest of my life. Not once did I feel inclined to share any of these encounters with anyone. I am not sure if anyone would have concluded that I was either prideful or crazy. So I said nothing. After the funeral services on February 25, 2007, I returned to Mount Vernon destined to find Andrews University.

Although I had now lived in America for many years, I knew nothing about Andrews University. The first time I heard the name was in 1995. Then again, in 2005, I met two pastors who were graduates of the University. I knew nothing of its history. I also had no knowledge there was a seminary there. I looked up the University online where I obtained an 800 number. When I called, I asked, "Is there a place here where you make pastors?" After sharing the reason for my inquiry, the director seemed quite impressed with my story. He encouraged me to be on campus as soon as possible. An application package was mailed out to me. I answered every question authentically and sincerely. I provided all requested documentation, and submitted my application. Then I was told it would be at least a month or two before I received a response. The response arrived by e-mail in less than a week. The hard copy of my letter of acceptance was sent later in the mail. My call to pastoral ministry was now official. What I resisted for months and feared most had come upon me. God revealed His purpose for my life which I had so earnestly asked Him to show me. I not only knew, but I then understood clearly my purpose in life. I was about to begin a brand new journey with God.

My uncles' deaths devastated our family. But it is how God got my attention.

CONFIRMATION OF MY CALL

Chapter 8

Confirmation of My Call

The deaths of my uncles undeniably devastated our family. Each person dealt with the loss differently. For me, however, it remains the way by which God was able to get my attention. This has shown me that, in fact, "All things will work together for good to them that love God" (Romans 8:28). I continued to remain quiet about the events which had led to this point in my calling. I also protected myself from the opinions of others, especially those people who have their concepts and beliefs about women in ministry. I knew this was not a path I personally chose. I wouldn't have. So, the last thing I needed was the theological discourse of those who oppose this issue.

When God gives an assignment, it cannot and should not be overruled by culture, tradition and personal opinion. Nothing or no one supersedes the word of God. The apostle Paul confirmed this when he said, "But when God who set me apart from my mother's womb and called me by His grace, was pleased to reveal His son in me so that I might preach Him among the Gentiles, my immediate response was not to

154

consult any human" (Galatians 1:15-16). God has the last word. I had His word that this is what I had to do with my life to satisfy the quest I had been on. I couldn't ask family and friends what they thought, after hearing from God.

Answering the call did not take away the struggle involved with my journey into Pastoral Ministry. The months of preparation brought new pressures. Flashbacks of my life, the choices I made, moments of disobedience to God, failures and pain all haunted me. I felt unworthy. Though my spiritual life had soared to amazing heights by this time, I still could not reconcile becoming a minister. It troubled me greatly. I asked God if He would confirm for me that it is really He who wants me to do this. As I came home from work one day, I went to my mail box and there, to my surprise, were several other application packets from Andrews University. My answer came that day.

Now that it was clear God wanted me to be a pastor, I wanted to know why? I am especially feminine and love being a woman. My sometimes reserved and conservative demeanor mingled with such feminine characteristics made it difficult to accept my new vocation. I felt sure pastoring is a masculine role. I just could not envision serving in this capacity for a lifetime. I also knew that, once I became a pastor, I would always be a pastor. This frightened me. I also did not welcome the thought that people would have to look to me for their spiritual guidance and nurturing. I felt it too great a responsibility. Frequent involvement in any public role brought me great distress. I loved being unseen, and unheard and enjoyed keeping a low profile. I do not mind serving as long as it's not visible. Those things troubled me deeply. When I am with friends, family and people I know, I can be sociable enough, but in general, I really prefer to be obscure and away from the limelight. People who have interacted with me in moments when I am a bit more vocal and open have interpreted this as me, the social butterfly. Nothing is further

Josian Frampton

from correct.

Until this date, the way I feel about placement in public life has not changed. I still do all I can to be in the background. I love the People of God. When I am with them, I am certain that I feel God's love by the way they interact with me. I set aside my personal preferences and comfort so that their spiritual needs are met. Yet, I am happy when I am able to find places to retreat and recharge. Otherwise, my life in public service would kill me. Knowing my internal struggles with public life, I wrestled with the thought that God would do this to me. He knows me in depth. How could He ask me to do the very thing I dislike? I could not understand it. It was a few months prior to my departure that I got the answer to this question. One day, I sat at my computer desk feeling very sad about leaving New York to begin a new life away from my friends and family. I called a very dear friend who serves at the Philadelphia church in Bronx, New York, and shared my struggles. As I shared with him my decision to accept the call to be a pastor, he excitedly affirmed my calling. I then told him the emotional struggle which accompanied my decision.

I shared with him all the reasons why I felt it wasn't something I could do or wanted to do. I told him about my understanding concerning women in ministry while growing up. As a young girl in the church I always heard that women are to be submissive and "remain silent in the church." I recounted my own shock when I first heard a female pastor preach at my church in Mount Vernon in 1997. I didn't hear a word she said that day as I quickly concluded that the church had gone contrary to scripture, and the world was truly coming to an end. Today I know this is in fact true, that the proclamation of the gospel being preached by women across the world is an indication that the world is coming to its end. This is confirmed in Joel 2:28-29 which states: "And it shall come to pass afterward, that I will pour out my spirit upon all flesh; and your sons and your daughters shall prophesy...and upon the handmaids in those days will I pour out my spirit." In my last semester at Seminary I met Dr. Williams, a powerful preacher of the word of God and one of the forerunners for women in ministry in the Seventh-day Adventist denomination.

Our paths providentially crossed in the spring of 2010, while I was in my last semester at Seminary. She asked me home for lunch one day. I didn't recall who she was at that moment and I knew nothing of her life in ministry. She also didn't know who I was except that I was a student leader. As we had lunch in her home in Berrien Springs in February, 2010, exactly thirteen years after her preaching encounter at my church, I felt strongly that it was necessary to inquire if she preached in Mount Vernon in the summer of 1997. She said, "Yes I did." I felt chills travel down my spine. It dawned on me I had met the woman whom I concluded would bring the world to its end because she was a pastor.

In that moment, a beautiful God-led friendship was born. We continue to share in a wonderful friendship today and have even ministered together as I conducted interviews with her to promote her autobiography, *Will I Ever Learn?* I truly respect and greatly admire this woman. It is true that men and women will bring the gospel into the entire world so that the end will come.

As I continued to share my woes with my pastor friend, of my inability to sleep or properly function since accepting the call to ministry, he took me to the scriptures to see the many leaders whom God had chosen who also felt unworthy and incompetent. He particularly focused on Moses and Jeremiah. He helped me to understand that my calling had been confirmed by the community of faith since so many had already endorsed the work I was doing on behalf of God. He concluded our conversation by sharing some life-altering words. "You don't have to go, but you will never be happy doing anything else." I then understood why I could not find peace in any of the professions I had pursued over the years.

After this conversation I went to bed, covered my head with a pillow and sobbed. I thought I was going to lose my mind. I felt angry with God for calling me to do something I did not wish to do. Feeling powerless in the matter, because I now knew that I must go since I didn't want to be unhappy all my life, I surrendered. Shortly before I officially left town, I had a dream. I take my dreams seriously only because, since I was a child, whenever I dreamt something, it often came to pass, not all the time but frequently.

An Unexpected Affirmation

In that dream I saw a stairway descending from heaven to earth. I sat at the very bottom of the stairway facing a huge mirror with thick, gold-plated rims all around it. My face was buried in my hands as I sat facing the mirror. I looked a wreck from weeping. Sadness covered my countenance; I was grieving because I was going into pastoral ministry. Suddenly, I looked up to see someone descending from the very top of the stairway at the part which connected heaven to earth. It was my uncle Pastor Mozart who died just a few months earlier in the accident. In the dream, I was startled to see him alive. He was casually dressed and looked just the way I remembered him when he was alive. He confidently came down the stairs and paused halfway in the middle of the steps; he looked me square in the eyes, and with caution and warning said, "You have to go. It's going to be okay. This is what you were meant to do."

He headed back up the stairs as if indicating that he did what he had come to do. I woke up from the dream fully convinced that this is now my life. On that day, a peace enveloped me. Somewhere in my subconscious, I still wrestled with the thought that my uncle would not have endorsed my life as a pastor because of our denominational teachings on the issue. I believe this is why that dream came to me that night. I am aware that the dead are dead and I may never fully know the significance of this dream, except it felt like the final piece in the puzzle to be connected, before beginning my new life. Pastoral ministry is the best and sweetest decision I have ever made since my birth. I love my life as a pastor. It is the most peaceful my life has ever been, despite continued adversities.

This does not mean I am free of hardships and struggles that threaten my peace at times. Yet, I cannot envision doing anything else in life. It encompasses the professions I always desired, teaching and counseling. It is the one thing I never chose for myself. Yet, it is the best thing that has happened to me. Through it, I have reaped manifold blessings. I have gone to places I would never have otherwise gone. I have met people I would never have otherwise met, and I have received gifts and care I would not have otherwise received. I understand and see that the blessings of God are intricately tied into our trust and obedience to Him. I am so glad I obeyed God. Preparations were tedious and uprooting wasn't fun. The packing process drained me and brought me much fatigue physically and otherwise. I crashed one night on my couch. I felt inclined to indulge myself in some television.

As I retreated on the sofa that evening surfing the channels, an image caught my attention. A little boy became the subject of a study because of his rare deformity. I generally do not enjoy medical shows. I never had the heart for such things. I picked up the remote to change the channel, when I felt stopped in my mind. Lingering to discover what the show is about I caught a glimpse of the toddler's leg stuck somewhat toward his back. Immediately, my birth defect came to mind. Arrested by the sight of what I had just seen, I indulged in the story. The documentary featured the amputation of this young child's leg. He was born with this deformity which could not be corrected medically. Early amputation allowed him to familiarize himself early in life with a prosthetic leg. While sitting there, it dawned on me that even in today's age of advanced science; it still wasn't possible to correct this medical problem. I then realized that having had the use of my leg without surgery and amputation is proof that a miracle took place in my life. It is the first time that I faced this reality.

There are different times during my growing up years that my mother tried to talk about my birth deformity. Since I carried so much shame from my childhood, I didn't want to be brought back to that place in my life. Consequently, I always dismissed it. I eventually asked that she never bring it up. I intended to never talk about it or ever share it with anyone. I found it embarrassing that I had been born this way. When I saw this documentary that summer day as I got ready for Andrews, something awakened in me. I recognized that what transpired in my life that day over thirty years ago truly had been a miracle. The world needed to know. My shame left at that moment and I knew the time had come that I should share with others the amazing miracle God had performed in my life.

My first opportunity to share this miracle came at Andrews in October 2007. It was my first semester. My Spiritual Formation teacher asked a few students to share their testimonies of something God had done in their lives. I remember wrestling with what I should share. I battled back and forth between the details of my call to ministry and the miracle of my healing at birth. I finally decided my story of the miracle at birth happened too long ago to have any significance or impact today. So I settled on sharing the events which led to my call to ministry. I was extremely nervous. We gathered in the classroom as each student shared their stories. My heart moved at the way God works in the lives of his people. As it approached my turn, I felt the struggle again between my birth miracle and my calling.

Even as I made my way up-front the battle raged. Still convinced no one would care to know something which happened over thirty years ago, I opened my mouth to speak of my call to pastoral ministry. To my great surprise out of my mouth came, "I was born crippled." You could have heard a pin dropped. Forced to continue, I shared the whole story the way I knew it. By the time the class ended, news of this miracle had spread all over the Seminary. Students were calling students, even their families, to share the news that they had actually met someone whom God had miraculously healed. Many students' faith was strengthened as a result of my sharing. No one cared how long ago it happened. It only mattered that it did happen and I stood before them as proof. God has a purpose in the things He asks us to do. We must always obey Him.

While I settled arrangements in New York, there were many more arrangements to be made for my relocation to Berrien Springs. My package from Andrews University contained information helpful for my transition. I called the housing and registration offices, since these were the most pressing to my arrival. I needed a place to stay as well as to confirm registration for my classes. In retrospect, it never dawned on me that I needed to visit the University before officially relocating. I did not take a trip at any time to see the state, the school or even the apartment I would live in. It would not have mattered at this point since nothing would have altered the decision already sealed in my mind. Where I lived or what the school was like mattered not. Since it was God who chose, I believed all would be well. August 19, 2007 is the day I was to leave New York. My pastor Dr. Jules, who has been a strong support of my work in ministry, asked me to preach my last Sabbath in town. He also encouraged the members to show their support to me in whatever ways they could.

It was also the night I drove into my new journey with God. I hadn't anticipated it would be such an emotional time for me. My church family, and even visiting members, showered me with gifts and cash which lasted me for months. When I counted how much I received. I was amazed at the amount. After I preached, a woman whom I never met before took me by hand into our mother's room. She handed me an envelope with $1000.00. She said that while I was preaching, she was so moved by my testimony that she felt compelled to leave the service and go to the bank to get me the money. She said, "I have to contribute to this ministry." I could not believe my eyes or ears.

Many, many people lined up to share their hugs as they placed envelopes and gift bags into my hands. I could not believe this was happening to me. I became overwhelmed with emotion. Their support continued right on through my almost three years of schooling. I also felt God's love pour out amongst my friends in Pelham. The Steins threw me a wonderful going away party, where I also received beautiful gifts of love. Many of the children I babysat along with their parents were present for this occasion to show their love and support. I felt so loved and blessed. I met many other friends and acquaintances individually who also poured out their support for my work and life in ministry. I didn't realize how much I was loved by so many until my final departing moments from New York. My heart melted at the vast network and circle of friends I had developed. From a life that had been so hopeless, now right before my eyes were the visible blessings God had bestowed upon me. I cried tears of joy. News of my call to ministry transcended my religious affiliation and I received cards from community members endorsing and confirming my calling. These things amazed me. Never did I realize that so many people had paid attention to me.

A Tough Goodbye

Leaving my family and friends was difficult. I worked hard on concealing my obvious difficulty with the situation. My cousins met in my apartment to help me load the van the night of my departure. I could see in their faces that they, too, were saddened by my departure. I guess it seemed surreal to all of us that I was actually doing this. We had had so many fun times together. We fought and became angry with each other at times, but we had a deep bond. In some ways I guess I kind of glued us together. In recent years, as my life began to change, I became the spokesperson for the group. I decided on most of the things we did. I established a book club where we often met together to learn the things of God. As a result of this book club, Carmella's conversion journey went from being a devout Catholic to a Sabbath-keeping Christian. As they helped me pack that night, all these memories flooded back to mind. I did not want to leave them, but I had to obey God. I especially hated leaving my cousin Vanessa. We are a lot more like sisters than cousins. We had now lived together since 2004. I had in many ways mothered her. I cared about her successes and I wanted to see her advance, particularly in her education. I was determined to also see her advance in her spiritual growth. We had many enjoyable times together and stayed up many nights into the early hours of the morning talking and bonding.

We share much in common and so we had a fairly nice relationship living together. I enjoyed my time with Vee. I now wondered what was going to happen with me being gone. I left her in good hands as I parted, but my heart was breaking as I realized how much I would miss my cousins. I knew they understood my life at this point. They were fully aware that I had been sold to my commitment to the gospel mission. Jesus

Josian Frampton

was now my true love.

 Saying goodbye was not an easy thing to do. Leaving them brought me no joy but around midnight on August 19, 2007, I drove into the unknown to embark on a faith journey with God. My former teacher from undergraduate school Mr. D, and Rema, a dear friend and prayer partner at our church, accompanied me on this journey. We drove all through the early hours of the morning only stopping for bathroom breaks. We took turns driving. All through the ride flashbacks of my life passed before me. Some brought joy, others tears and sadness. Everything seemed surreal at this point. Avis had been right. "God had a plan for my life, a 'good' plan (Jeremiah 29:11-12).

The drive to Michigan lasted fifteen hours. My life reflections were painfully impactful.

MIRACLES AT ANDREWS UNIVERSITY

Chapter 9

Miracles at Andrews University

The drive to Michigan lasted about fifteen hours. We arrived a little after 3:00 pm. The housing office warned us that we should arrive before the office closed. I picked up my keys and internet package as I approached my Garland apartment. It somewhat reminded me of my old apartment building in New York. The environment spoke of peace and tranquility, just as I like it. The weather was gorgeous, the big bright sun spreading its light over the well-manicured grass, beautiful trees and flowers. As we made our way up the stairs to my apartment, I nervously wondered how the inside would look. Having suffered with depression for years, including seasonal depression, proper lighting in a room meant everything to me. Whenever I felt depressed over the years, I often isolated myself to enclosed, dark areas. When I received healing from this demonic stronghold, I became deliberate about being in very open, lighted environments.

I did not visit the University to see where I would stay, as I trusted God to choose a suitable place for me. When I turned the key in the lock and step inside the door, my jaw dropped as I saw the large living room window and very large kitchen window which brought brilliant sunlight into the rooms. I went into the bedroom to find the windows. They were even larger than the ones I had in my New York apartment. I could not have been more pleased. I loved that little, one bedroom suite-like apartment at first sight. It became my home until I graduated in May of 2010. My prayer partner and friend stayed one week with me, but my former teacher and friend left that same day after resting a few hours.

The next morning I visited the students' financial services office to confirm my loans and payments. While in New York, I worked on securing loans sufficient to carry me through my three years of study. Before I left town, it was brought to my attention that there was a document I needed to proceed with the disbursements. I informed the loan company that I did not have what they requested. The loan department agreed to disburse payments anyway because I had a cosigner. I suffered so much while obtaining my undergraduate degree without loans, that I truly did not want to experience similar hardships in another state where I knew I couldn't hustle the way I did in New York. I met with my financial advisor who confirmed my loans were approved for $33,000 since about 80% of my tuition would be covered by the Master's of Divinity Program. He also informed me that the school had already received payments for my first semester. I excitedly proceeded with my orientation process.

I really enjoyed orientation as a new student on campus. I felt like a teenager all over again. I remember once in New York, sometime in the fall of 2005, I sat at my kitchen window fantasizing about what it would feel like to live on campus. I was saddened by the thought that I missed an opportunity to ever live on a college campus. Yet here I was being given a second chance to live on a college campus as a seminary student. It was such a wonderful experience to attend orientation for campus life. I enjoyed the process. As the week ended, it came time for my friend to say goodbye. I was saddened. I missed her. With her gone, a deep loneliness set in. The reality of my journey rested heavily on me. I knew no one in this new environment. The thought of starting over made me tired, yet, in some ways, it freed me, since no one knew me. I knew that the fatigue of public life would fade during my three years of study and I could now rest from life in the public eye, or so I thought. On September 22, 2007, I returned to New York for a prescheduled preaching assignment. I looked forward to seeing my family and friends again. (This would mark the beginning of many other preaching engagements all throughout my seminary journey. Throughout my entire three years at Seminary, I traveled to different states teaching and preaching.) When I returned to school from New York, I entered a storm which changed my seminary life and challenged my faith till the day I graduated.

Faith Survival

My test of faith began when I went to my mail box after my New York trip to find a bill from the University requesting my first semester payment. Confused, I called my financial advisor to inquire into the matter. He appeared just as confused as I was. He asked that I call my loan company and inquire as to why my payments were revoked or not disbursed. I will never forget the day the loan advisor told me they had decided against sending me payments until the required items were submitted. I knew I would not be able to provide these items at any point during my studies. I attempted to negotiate but they were not budging. While in the middle of our conversation, I felt a strong desire to end the call.

I immediately ended the call and fell to the floor like a wounded bird. With my legs folded behind me and my face buried in my hands, I knelt with my face to the floor and wept until my stomach hurt. Thoughts

169

of defeat swept through my mind. How could I possibly survive full time enrollment in a program with rent expenses, in addition to other educational costs and daily living expenses? Faced by these obstacles, I didn't foresee how I could successfully make it through seminary. After crying uncontrollably for a long time, I felt deeply inspired to "Rise."

As I wondered whether I had made the right decision or if I had interpreted God correctly, I felt supported to the edge of my bed. "Get up," the deep prompting on my mind beckoned me. "I want to talk to you." I knew now to go to the Bible to hear from God. So I wiped my tear-streaked face with the back of my hand so I could see the pages of scripture through my puffy eyes. With huge drops of tears still falling on the words, I fought to see what God wanted to say to me. I closed my eyes and did what I had done before when I invited God to speak to me through His word. I closed my eyes and the Bible then I said, "Speak, Lord, I am listening." I later learned at seminary this is not an appropriate way to communicate with God. I know He has spoken to me this way and I have not changed my method.

As I opened the Bible, my gaze centered on Jeremiah chapter thirty-one. Immediately my attention drew to verse fifteen which read, "A voice was heard in Ramah, lamentation and bitter weeping, Rachel was weeping for her children, refusing to be comforted. . . . Cease from weeping, dry your eyes from your tears for your works will be rewarded . . . there is hope in your future."

Immediately strength returned to my body. I knew in that moment that God was with me in this situation and that He was going to see me through. I responded to the words I read by following them distinctly. I got up, ceased from crying, dried my eyes and purposed to trust God. I felt confident that God would take care of me. The next school day I got up, got dressed and went to school like every other student. I knew not what the future held for me, but I was certain that the One holding my future would not lie. If He said there was hope in my future, then there would be hope. In the days ahead, I went back to my financial advisor, paid my first semester with the funds which I received from going away and then waited on what God would show me to do next. It's in waiting on God that I knew I would see His hand move.

Surviving at Andrews University without employment, loans or savings would require a miracle. Confident that I would not look back by returning to New York, I knew I had to put my whole trust in the Invisible God. The first evidence I saw that God designed this journey for me was when I entered my Berrien Springs apartment. I had fallen in love with my Mount Vernon apartment particularly for its lighting. As the days passed in my new home, I welcomed the sun each morning as it rose in the eastern skies. Like a huge ball of fire, I saw it in the evenings cascading down the Michigan horizon. My apartment had also been freshly renovated. I inherited new furniture and appliances. The only thing which looked like it could use a new look was my bedroom lamp. One day when I called to have something repaired in my bathroom, the worker brought me a new lamp that I did not ask for.

Early in my first semester I requested a program change from the Masters in Youth Ministry to the Masters of Divinity. Divinity had always been my ultimate objective, but since I did not have a theology background, I would not be able to begin seminary in the fall of 2007 except I enrolled in the Youth Ministry program. Non-theology majors begin their program in May of each year to catch up with their prerequisites. This meant that the next time I would be able to enter the divinity program would be in May the following year, except by a miracle. The Masters in Youth Ministry is more costly than the Masters of Divinity. Already having serious financial challenges, I could not wait until May. I needed to begin in January. Having relied on prayer, I began to pray and then went to the one responsible for handling such transitions in programs, the Director. I presented my case to bring my petition before the Dean's council. The personnel in this department had worked in this area for a long time. He tried to help guide me, knowing my non-theology background could pose some challenges. He appeared understandably reserved in bringing the matter to the council. I kept returning to him, however, to plead my cause on the basis of faith.

I encouraged him in stating, "If God only had my folder before the council, He would have something with which to work, and I would possibly find favor. This man was a man of faith himself. He simply wanted to respect the Seminary's policies and I guess avoid acting partial to anyone. I respected this. Still, I had a financial crisis and I grew desperate. After much probing he eventually provided my folder for review. God answered the prayer. The council, not really knowing who I was at the time, voted unanimously in my favor. I was allowed to make the transition. This man shared his amazement with me concerning my persistence and the remarkable answer to prayer. This experience resulted in a wonderful interaction and many prayers together whenever I visited his office.

At the beginning of my first semester I had paid my rent for the first four months of school. My next rent payment would be due in December. My monthly payments were then only $520.00. This included all my utilities, cable and internet, but I only had about $400.00 left over from the monies I received when I left New York. My human tendencies began to kick in. My concerns grew as I wondered not just about December, but all the other months after that for the next three years. I was scheduled to leave for New York on the thirteenth for the Christmas break. I knew that when I reached New York I would be able to work out finances. I went to the office to work out a deal. I intended to give a down payment of the money I had with the intentions of sending the balance in once I returned home. The prorated fees accumulated to $618.00. The office personnel pulled up my account for review only to discover that my rent had been paid in full. We both tried figuring out where the payment came from but she saw no evidence of a check, money order or bank transfer to my account. She proceeded to ask me, "Did your loans arrive or did a relative pay?"

No one besides the wonderful earthly angel who had co-signed my loans knew that I had no funds for school. On the day I went in to pay my last month's rent to the housing office, I discovered $300.00 of the $618.00 came from my security deposit. The office had no record of how it had been removed from my security saving to my rent that December. They still had no record of where the other $318.00 came from. My account still reflected a full payment for rent in December of 2007. I heartily believe a miracle happened that day.

I Saw a Great and Unsearchable Thing

My faith soared in the wake of this rent encounter. Seeing this clear manifestation of God at work encouraged me to trust even deeper in Him. I left for New York on December 13, 2007. As I prepared for the trip to the airport, I received a phone call from home reporting bad weather expected in the Northeast. I had a connecting flight in Detroit out of South Bend, Indiana. When I arrived in Detroit, my 3:00 p.m. flight to LaGuardia Airport was cancelled because of the weather in New York. A standby opportunity opened up for JFK Airport at 5:00 p.m., but soon it was cancelled as well. My concerns grew when passengers were told it would be at least two days before we could leave Detroit if we did not make it into New York that night. Knowing my financial restraints I began to pray, "Lord, please do not let me sleep here tonight or any other night. I do not wish to pay for hotels or put any money on my credit

173

cards." When another flight opened up for JFK at 7:00 p.m. I prayed even harder. I asked God to still the storms in New York, as He stilled storms in the Bible.

I was confident that He can do these things and I trusted Him to help me. I pleaded with God silently to not let me sleep in Detroit. I then opened my Bible to a familiar Bible promise found in Jeremiah 33:3 which reads: "Call on me and I will answer you and show you great and unsearchable things that you do not know." I needed a great and unsearchable thing in this situation. I really needed a miracle. As soon as I had finished claiming this Bible promise, a thought came to mind to inquire concerning a very small airport in White Plains, New York. I didn't even know it existed until 2006, and I flew out of the airport only once since discovering it. This airport is about a 20-minute drive from my home.

It wasn't logical that the major airports would be closed and this very small airport would remain open in a snow storm. Yet, I obeyed the prompting upon my heart and proceeded to ask the flight staff. Sure enough the little airport was open. I asked that my reservation be transferred to the White Plains airport. We boarded the flight at 9:00 p.m. on a nonstop flight to White Plains. After flying for what seemed like a few hours, the pilot announced we were unable to land at the airport in White Plains due to de-icing issues. This announcement had been made only after we were already headed back to Detroit. Passengers were furious. Many people were swearing, murmuring and complaining, understandably so given the circumstances. I wanted to complain and be angry, too, but I knew I could not pray and worry at the same time. I chose to pray. I said "Lord, I don't know what You are doing, but I know it is in my best interest. I would rather be safe, but I beg you, please don't let me sleep in Detroit." It seemed ridiculous to pray that prayer considering we were already headed back to Detroit. Thinking of my low budget and my inability to afford a night in a hotel, I knew I would have to sleep on an airport bench for two days. My prayers became desperate and ridiculous.

As we were about to land again in Detroit, and people were still fuming from the previous announcement, hope came through the intercom. The pilot announced that if they could have us switch planes quickly, we could make it back to New York that night. I sighed at this ray of hope. It was now after 11:00 p.m. I was exhausted since my journey began about 6:00 a.m. that same day. Within moments we were on another plane headed back to New York. I thanked God for hearing me as I rested back to reflect on his faithfulness. What happened next revealed the unsearchable thing I read from Jeremiah 33:3 earlier in the evening.

For what seemed like more than two hours we flew, only to hear another announcement from the pilot. "The airport is closed and we do not have a place to land." Are you kidding me? How can a plane fly to a closed airport? I leaned forward in despair and almost cried out aloud, "Lord please don't let me go back to Detroit." Shortly after praying this, the pilot announced, "Since the White Plains Airport is a privately owned airport, the CEO has been contacted and they are dispatching a crew to open the airport to receive us." To this day, I have no explanation why an aircraft would leave a major airport and fly toward another airport, not knowing its operating schedule times. We circled for a while in the air, as we waited for the crew to arrive. By this time it was almost 2:30 in the morning. We finally landed. Despite the drama, I made it home about 3:00 a.m. and I did sleep in my own bed in New York. These things brought new meaning and strength to my faith. I felt a security and confidence in prayer and the word of God in ways I had never felt before.

I saw God's supplying power at work in remarkable ways.

GOD SUPPLIES ALL MY NEEDS

Chapter 10

God Supplies All My Needs

In January 2008 I returned to Michigan to begin the new semester. The Lord blessed me tremendously and I received funds to start this new semester. I told no one of my financial hardships and I requested help of no one including my family.

I purposed to ask God only. After paying my tuition with the funds, I still had a balance of $1073.00 towards my new semester expenses. Having witnessed the miraculous workings of God in the previous months, I turned to Him for help. I took the bill one night, opened it on my table and prayed over the balance. I reminded God of all the wealthy children in the world who lived off the wealth of their fathers. I even mentioned a few celebrity children who enjoyed the privilege of living wherever they wanted and attending the best universities in the country. Realizing this, I shared with God that I know He is my Daddy and I know He owns the wealth of the world's wealthy. They borrowed from Him to give to their children because, "The earth is His and everything in it" (Psalm 24:1-2). I remembered that "The cattle on a thousand hills belong to Him" (Psalm 50:10). I asked that He sell some cows to cover my tuition debt.

After less than one week of praying this prayer, a check came in my mail box for $1,000. Knowing I had only spoken to God privately, I felt sure that He heard me. I still needed the $73 towards the rest of the bill. I thanked God for what I received. Then I asked Him to help me with the $73 balance. Within days I received a call to babysit. I only babysat for about three hours but I received exactly $75. When I saw the amount given, I told my colleague for whom I babysat that I received too much. He said "I know. We'll work it out some other time." Whenever I babysat in Michigan, the most I made an hour was $10.00. So this $75 payment for the three hours of work was highly unusual. He also did not know of my immediate need. For several semesters after this my tuition was paid in ways which I still cannot trace. I registered each semester in faith. Not once was I unable to attend a semester, and I do not recall ever having my classes dropped. I had discovered the secret to surviving at Andrews University. Prayer, claiming God's promises, and putting my whole trust in Him. Often I also added works to my faith. Sometimes I had to do more than just pray. "Faith without works is dead" (James 2:17).

My journey at Andrews taught me many lessons. Since migrating to the United States, I had to supply my needs, and quickly became independent and self-sufficient. In the process of having to work so hard to provide for my needs, I stopped asking God for things. I thanked Him for the things I had, but I lost track of coming to Him for help. This level of independence had robbed me of an opportunity to exercise faith. I seldom went to God to ask for food, clothing or shelter when I had a job and salary which provided me with all those things. While I was at

Andrews, caught between a rock and a very hard place, I had to relearn total reliance upon God. Asking others for help challenged me in some amazing ways as well. I never asked anyone for help with anything. If I had something, I was grateful. If I did not have it, I learned to live without it. As my hardships increased, I learned new lessons in meeting each challenge. Though my cupboards were never bare, I didn't always have the things I really liked to eat. Sometimes I found no pleasure preparing food for myself alone. Most Sabbaths I did not cook, because I was invited home with a friend or acquaintance for lunch.

Andrews has a rich potluck culture. While at service one Sabbath morning, I realized I had made no lunch plans that day with anyone. Neither did I make meal preparations at home. Since I would not invite myself to someone's home, I worried that I would not have lunch that Sabbath. Since I learned to pray for just about everything, I prayed a simple prayer, "Lord, let someone ask me home with them for lunch today." I silently prayed this a few times throughout the service.

As the service ended I greeted friends hoping someone would extend an invitation. Since I always looked composed, happy and having my act together, I truly did not appear to be needy or destitute. I do not blame anyone for not asking me to have lunch that day. Andrews is a warm and friendly environment where people thrive on fellowship. I had many opportunities to dine in the homes of many friends. I also took time to entertain occasionally. God simply meant to teach me lessons of faith and dependence upon Him through these experiences. As the crowd gradually dispersed, a handful of us remained for a brief meeting. None of the people present at the meeting were individuals I had eaten with before, so I concluded that God had not answered my prayer for lunch. I felt disappointed with the thought of returning home to nothing.

As we concluded the meeting, one of my colleagues asked,

"Would you like to join our family for lunch today?" I felt right away my prayer had been answered. The interesting thing about this family's invitation was that they also had not prepared a Sabbath meal that day. It was not until after informing his wife that I had been invited home for lunch, that she told us someone had actually invited their family to lunch and it was okay for me to join them. I shared in a beautiful Sabbath meal with the families that day.

The winter of 2008 dropped snow on Michigan unlike anything I had ever seen since I had come to the United States. Once the snow season begins, it snows until the season is over. I developed an appreciation for the snow. It seemed constant. I learned to live with it. In the winter months, many days would find me looking out my large windows in admiration of the lush, thick flakes trapped in the tree branches. They comfortably rested there as if a part of the branches. The snow fell nonstop sometimes, with a beauty covering everything in sight. While in a busy state like New York, I was caught in the rat race, running from one place to the next. I never took time to appreciate nature. Life in Michigan gave me a brand new appreciation for the simple things in life, even snow. I used to detest snow days in my earlier years in New York. I found it such an inconvenience. Snow had now become a big part of my life.

As the brutal frigid temperatures of the Midwest greeted me, I realized my winter jackets were not suitable for the weather. My best jacket was a long white down jacket. I didn't want to wear a long white jacket everyday trailing through snow up to my knees. I had another pink jacket, but it wasn't warm enough. When "lake effect" snow poured on Berrien Springs one day in the winter of 2008, I knew I needed to change my winter gear. I came home wondering how I would replace my winter jackets. As I hung my pink jacket in the coat closet, I paused for a while fantasizing about a medium length black down jacket. Not having money,

I knew affording a jacket would not be possible any time soon. I could have easily called home and said I needed a jacket. Determined to remain in this faith walk with God, I purposed to ask Him first for everything. This time, I truly did not pray an actual prayer. I simply said, "I wish I had a black down jacket." This is the honest, sincere truth. Just days after this statement, I received a call from a very dear friend in Pelham, New York. The mother of a set of triplets and a little boy, with whom I share a birthday on May 13, called me for the first time since my relocation to Michigan. In a voice message left on my cell phone she said to me, "I have been online doing some shopping for the children and I came across some beautiful warm down winter jackets from Lord and Taylor. I thought of you in Michigan facing those frigid temperatures and wondered if you could use one. Please call me back and leave me your size and color."

Amazed, I quickly responded with my size, a medium and a black. In less than a week I received a medium length, black down winter jacket expressed to my door. I loved the jacket. It became my most worn jacket until I left Michigan. God promises to "Give us the desires of our heart" (Psalm 84:12). For the first time in my life, I understood what it meant to "Give me this day my daily bread" (Matthew 6:11). Well, I needed daily bread, and many other daily and monthly things. As the Christmas holidays approached in 2008, I had not a penny to make my way home to New York. I had no desire to spend the holidays in Berrien Springs away from my friends and family. My policy to not ask anyone but God for help still had not changed. I prayed and asked God to help me find a plane ticket back home. I prayed for several weeks before getting an e-mail from a dear friend inquiring concerning my plans to return home for the holidays. In the e-mail she said "I will pay your way home." Within a month I had a plane ticket to return home to New York. She was not aware that I had such surmounting financial challenges. There was also the time that I was running behind in my rent by $200. I had done some braiding and babysitting, but the hours were so few that it did not add up to my rent for the month. Nervous that the months would pile up on me and make it more difficult to pay, I cried to God for help. I asked specifically for the $200.

A few days past and I saw no sign of any money. My anxiety was starting to increase when I received a call from Bruce, my spiritual dad. He said he had been doing some sorting out at his sister's house and found a stack of sermons that could be useful to my sermon preparations for ministry. He informed me that they would be with me as soon as he could get them out. I did not inform him that I needed financial help for rent. Before he ended the phone call, he said, "When you get the material look through the pages."

I interpreted this to mean, read the sermons. I had way too many projects for the semester so I decided they would be read at a later time. I received an express package within days. I wondered what the urgency was in expressing the package but did not mention it. When Bruce did not hear from me, he called me to inquire concerning my receiving the package. I told him I had received it but did not have the time to read it. "I did not ask you to read it," he said. "I told you to look through the pages." I quickly paged through the large file to find hidden in its pages, two hundred dollar notes. This was exactly the amount needed to sum up my rent. My jaw almost dropped at how precise God can be.

The summer semesters at seminary can be mandatory for some students. I knew that attending them, however, would not be possible without a miracle. I could barely afford to make it through the regular year. In May of 2008, just days before the first summer session began, I went to negotiate a deal with student financial services. It is the first time I had been back since I learned that my loans were cancelled. I did not understand why that morning I woke up compelled to meet someone there. When I got there I found out the individual with whom I had worked before was gone, replaced by someone else. Although I carried a substantial balance from my previous semester, I still wanted to register for the summer session. I tried to negotiate making a later payment, but the person in charge was not able to assist me since the requirements did not allow for a previous balance in order to qualify for any assistance. I needed yet another miracle.

He told me repeatedly he could not help me. I somehow felt compelled to stay until I received a positive answer. I did not really know why I stayed when it seemed clear there was nothing he could do for me. When he saw my persistence in sitting before him refusing to leave, he said he would find his superior. He assured me there was nothing she would be able to do for me either, since they do not provide any assistance if you carry a large balance. My balance was a substantial amount according to the school's requirements. I am not sure why, but something caused me to stay despite the discouraging news. I am uncertain what he said to her but he returned and told me she asked to see me. When I sat with her, she looked at me with compassion. She then told me there was a University scholarship for which I might qualify. After verifying the qualifying requirements she assisted me in obtaining the scholarship for that summer and the following summer. I was elated for the opportunity to be able to attend classes that summer.

One of my greatest financial miracles since my seminary journey began came in June of 2009, when I preached at my home church for the first time since going to Andrews University. I had never disclosed my hardships and financial struggles to my church family until that day when I preached for our Women's Ministry celebration. I felt strongly it was time to inspire them by sharing what God had been doing for me. That Sabbath morning I poured out my heart to share, not my need for help, but what God had been doing for me. God blessed the testimony in a remarkable way. My church family, along with the countless visitors who were present, poured their love to me in a tremendous manner. By the time I was finished shaking hands at the door I received about $2000.00. I was able to meet all my upcoming semester expenses and demands.

Saving wasn't an option, however, surviving on such a stringent budget. With each passing month I needed various basic necessities. The month came when I ran out of my last bath product. I had many bath products on reserve for a while. I love showers, so, my bath supplies ran out quickly. I became nervous when I saw my bath supplies diminish to the last item before I was able to replace them. With no funds available on hand to replenish my supplies, I once again looked to God for help. I remembered He promised to "supply all my needs" (Philippians 4:19). I prayed that He would help me find some bath supplies before my last ran out. Praying is okay, but God does not support laziness. He wants to know that we also try to assist in improving our lives. To add some works to my faith, I posted a flyer for hair braiding and child care. This would also help me to manage my own hours and not overwork myself, since I was enrolled in six or seven classes most semesters.

One day someone came to have her hair braided. It was not possible for me to complete the task in one sitting. I asked that she return the next day. During our time together, I felt comfortable sharing with her how the Lord had been carrying me through school. Not once did I mention to her any particular need. When she came by the next day so that I could finish braiding her hair, she brought with her a lovely gift bag. Almost embarrassed, she shared with me that she didn't mean to offend me by giving me bath products as a gift, but that, as she left home to come to my place, she said she felt strongly that she should bring me a gift. She had nothing in her house that she could give as a gift except the unopened bath products in her bathroom. She placed them in a gift bag for me. The bath products lasted me until I was able to afford more of my own.

Josian Frampton

The more evidence I saw of God working on my behalf, the stronger my faith became in Him. There are other miracles involving wonderful Christian brothers and sisters, too numerous to mention, who opened their hearts to me. There was also a time I needed to have my own hair braided. I was too tired to do it myself, but I did not have the money to get it done. It was overdue for grooming. I did not know anyone at that time who could braid. I asked around and received a referral. She was also a student. As we made plans, we discussed pricing, and to my recollection she said $95. We set a date for my braiding. It took everything from me to pay this much to get my hair done at school. This $95 felt like $9,500 to me. I literally pleaded with God to help me not to have to pay for getting my hair done. This seemed like a ridiculous prayer, since everyone in this environment is also trying to find ways to make ends meet. After my hair was braided I gratefully thanked, then paid the young lady for her services. It was then she informed me that the price she gave me was not $95 but $120. I almost dropped to the floor. It took a great deal to come up with what I had. Now it had increased by a whopping $30. I tried apologizing to her.

I proceeded to explain that I would not have used her services if I knew she would cost so much, since I wasn't in a position to pay this much for my hair on campus. She seemed very dissatisfied with my reasoning and walked away. This bothered me. I went out for a short while. When I returned she had come back to my house and put all the money I gave her under my door in an envelope. I called to seek her understanding in the oversight but she would not answer or return my calls. As I ended my final phone call, a still small voice reminded me, "You told me you did not want to pay to get your hair done. Now your hair is braided and you did not spend a penny. Give thanks and put it to rest." I did just that.

When we pray, there is no telling how God is going to answer our prayers. He can use even conflicts to bring about His purpose. Within a short time, this student and I were relating quite amicably again. We never again mentioned this incident; it's as if it never happened. As the close of my seminary journey approached, the weight of my almost three years of pastoral ministry training weighed heavily on me. Like any runner in a marathon, my mind and body were feeling the strain of my journey. My energy in petitioning God, though still strong, grew strenuous. In March 2010, just two months away from graduation, I faced two months of back rent, eviction notices and a letter summoning me to the courts if I didn't act speedily. I felt too tired to fight.

Still holding to my rule of not calling on anyone but God, I faintly reached out to Him one night. Drained from seven classes including the challenging pressures of Greek, a presidency term to wrap up and other personal concerns, I had a huge meltdown. All night I sobbed more in frustration and exhaustion than anything else. The next morning I wore my favorite Andrews cap deep over my eyes to conceal the puffiness in my eyes, hoping to get by without anybody questioning me about it. I then checked my phone for messages, and found three calls from Avis, my spiritual mom, telling me that she was worried about me and that I had rested heavily on her heart that same night of my meltdown. She said she felt sure something was wrong. We had not spoken for a few weeks by then. After calling her back, she further expressed how I had weighed so heavily on her mind. I confirmed her concerns and shared my frustrations. She made an immediate deposit to my account and settled the matter that very day. God, yet again, showed me that I may be silent in reaching out if I choose, but He will always speak in my behalf and bring me the help that I need.

Josian Frampton

A Test of Faith

It's easy to talk faith when we are not tried. My faith was tested one semester when I returned home for the holidays. I earned some money to help with expenses for the new semester. In my financial situation every penny counted. I paid tithe over the years when I was gainfully employed. Now that things were so strained, giving back to God did not come so easy. As they called for the collection of the offering that day, I felt obliged to give $250. I had collected a substantial earning by then. I intended to tithe but not so much. At this point, $250 to me, felt like $2500. As the deacons approached me, I felt the internal struggle as I sat there with my check book and pen in my hand.

Finally, I sensed the ungratefulness in my heart. God had given so much to me by this time, what was $250 if I really felt He owned the world's wealth? I prayed in my heart over the envelope. I quickly said I was sorry. Then I dropped the tithe into the plate. I reflected on God's promise concerning tithing in Malachi chapter three which said "Prove me in this if I will not open for you the windows of heaven and pour out a blessing, you will not have room enough to receive it." By the time the worship service ended that Sabbath around 1:30 p.m., various members came to hug and welcome me home. As they said their hellos, checks and cash were placed in my hand. When I counted the funds I took home, I had received $480, double the funds I put in that day. I continue to maintain that the blessings of God are tied into complete trust and obedience to Him.

Set Up for President

By spring of 2008, despite my attempts not to become involved in seminary life, I kept getting roped in. It all began when the Dean's secretary told me she thought I would be a suitable candidate for the role as Religious Affairs Leader of the Student Government. I had started a prayer ministry with a few students in October 2007, but my interest in taking on any additional roles was low. As elections approached, no one filled forms to run for that office. I finally, reluctantly, decided to try after a bit of good-natured pressure from supporters. Not too long after I decided to run for the office, another student also signed up for that same one. After we had been introduced to each other one night when he and his wife offered me a ride, we agreed that since we were the only two people running for that office, we would commit to assisting whoever won in their leadership tenure.

Since I never wanted to participate in the elections to begin with, I started praying that I would not win. I had never participated in any elections before, and I did not feel at all comfortable running. The election of new student officers took place in April and the young man won by nine votes. I was very pleased with the news. As promised, I committed to work with him only if he would assign me to behind the scenes roles. Since I already had the prayer ministry established, he asked that I remain responsible for the prayerful atmosphere of the Seminary. This worked well for me. The behind the scenes arrangement did not last very long, however. The official start date for the new officers to begin their term in service took effect in May. By July my partner had to leave for six weeks of Field School out of state. This left me in charge of the planning for convocations and worship arrangements for the Seminary chapel services. I became accountable to the Seminary Student Forum Sponsor and the Director of Worship for the Seminary. This seriously interrupted my plans not to get involved in seminary life. I served to the best of my ability, going beyond the call of duty to ensure the spiritual needs of the Seminary community were met. I made a special effort to interact in the lives of the students the best I could regardless of their race, culture, or ambitions. I took time to assist those who struggled in their studies, particularly with the writing of papers. We wrote a lot of papers at school. While I gave serving my all, I longed for the return of the elected officer. I spent much time pondering how I lost the election but still involuntarily became the serving officer.

To my surprise, when he returned in September, he asked if I would retain the position a bit longer since he had to catch up with intensives. This frustrated me, though I did not allow it to show. I reluctantly agreed to hold on to the position, and remained actively involved until December. I had now served in the role more than the elected leader. Though God answered my prayer to not allow me to win the election, he most certainly ignored my request to not get involved in seminary life. Nominations began again in the winter of 2009 for a new student government at the Seminary. This time I knew with certainty that I was not interested. I waited too long to leave public service to just return so quickly. It seemed that the more I tried to avoid the idea the stronger the prompting on my mind that I should run for President.

Given my past experiences with God, I had now learned not to disobey Him because He always wins. Since I am not one to ever volunteer information concerning my life or the things I am experiencing, I kept my thoughts and feelings to myself. As the election temperature heated up, possibly fueled by the nation's own election with the historic win of the United States' first Black President, my colleagues intensified their endorsement for my nomination without my consent. There were varying positions on where they felt I would best serve on the student government. Many gave their endorsement for Religious Affairs Leader since I had already functioned in the role. I also felt it made sense since I became very familiar with the functions of that office. Yet, I tried to keep an open mind. Despite my own desire to run as Religious Affairs Leader, if I did decide to do so, coupled with the support from many other students, the very clear response from God was for me to run for Student President. The Seminary Student Forum comprises a team of eight officers including a President and Vice President. The President is the one who sets the tone for the rest of the team and the overall seminary student community. Serving in such a position would be more public press than I ever wanted. Such a person would be the Seminary representative before the entire University. The President also represented the students at the Dean's council and any other area in which they were called to serve. The answer was unquestionably "No!" An internal struggle began. I prayed earnestly and intently. I told the Lord that I did not wish to be President but, if He really wanted me to do it, He must have a purpose in mind, so I would consider running for the role only on one condition – I did not want to nominate myself for the role.

In times past and just as I had done the year before when I ran for Religious Affairs Leader, a person signed up on a list next to the positions, indicating where he or she thought they would serve best. I always felt that this option challenged one's humility. So, I did not want to say I would serve best as President. As I prayed and pondered those things in my heart, some weeks into the election process the current administration announced they were doing things somewhat differently that year. They would allow the student body of the Seminary to nominate students for office. My prayer was answered. To be certain that I did not have to be the one to determine where I served, the Lord also placed it on the heart of a colleague, whom I was just getting to know at the time, to motivate others to nominate me. I met him when I heard of his wife's illness, but we really were not close enough that he should have assisted me the way he did in helping me to be nominated for President.

He came to me one day and said he felt sure I would make a great President for the Seminary. He felt so committed to his conviction that without my consent he ran his own campaign to have me nominated. In the weeks before the elections I never asked anyone to nominate me and I also never asked a single soul to vote for me including my personal friends. I did not even talk about the elections; it was as if they weren't even happening. One day while in the Seminary Commons, a hang out spot for students, just a month before the elections, a friend overheard me in a conversation regarding the elections. I had been sharing with someone where I felt the Lord was leading me to participate. When I arrived home that night, I received a call from this friend telling me that he also felt convinced that the Lord wanted him to run for President. He asked if I would consider running as Vice President as it would give us an opportunity to work together on the team. We had worked well together on things before, so this wasn't particularly an odd thing to ask. I felt it was a genuine request.

Though he is someone I respect, I should have learned by then that when God asks me to do something, I never confer with someone else to do something different. Without giving the matter to prayer, I quickly said, "Yes." The moment that the phone call ended I completely lost my peace. I knew I had gone contrary to the will of God. I felt so unsettled and troubled internally I almost could not function. As I went to class the following day, a mutual friend met with me to ask if I would consider running in another area of office. It appeared they were concerned that since we are both effective leaders, if we ran in the same area of office one of us would obviously not make the team at all since there is only one President. The only odd thing about the request was that we had not even been on associating terms for a lengthy period. So, I did not understand why our working together became of such value.

Once I realigned my priorities and purposed to obey God above anyone else, I informed them that he should run where he thought the Lord was leading him and I was going to do the same. Regardless of the outcome, we would each continue to give of ourselves in service to God. I did just that and my peace immediately returned to me. When nomination day arrived, I received an e-mail informing me of the three areas where I had received most nominations. I needed to respond to the area I felt most called to serve. Having already settled in my mind where I felt God wanted to place me, I responded to the office of President by first asking someone on the team in which of the three offices did I receive the most nominations. He told me an overwhelming response came for President. With that confirmation I pressed forward to follow God's leading.

One day while in the Seminary Commons someone asked me, "So, my sister, are you running for Religious Affairs? I think you'd be great in that role." "I feel the same way," I responded. "Except it's not where I feel the Lord is leading me to serve." "Where do you think He's leading you to serve?" he asked. "For President," I responded. His eyes popped open. He looked at me with somewhat of a half grin on his face, which almost reflected a pity look for my overly ambitious mind set then said, "Huh, interesting." I immediately sensed that he felt I was being overly ambitious in undertaking this venture. His sarcasm had a certain logic in that I was black, female and a reserved enough personality despite my involvements. For a while, there were also uncertainties whether there had ever been a female who served as President. The Seminary is obviously a male-dominated environment. About the time I graduated there was confirmation that at least one other female had served in that role, but I would be the first black female to serve as President, should I win. The odds were most definitely not in my favor. In my grandmother's island dialect, this young man must have felt "A donkey has no right in a horse race." Yet, I felt a humbling confidence that if God asked me to do this, He had a plan in place.

Just weeks before the elections I felt a deep anxiety about the whole thing. I wanted out. I went to my greatest supporter, Paul, to tell him that I was struggling with the decision. I told him I was going to pull out altogether. He seemed frustrated with me and in a strong tone cautioned me: "Has God not commanded you to be strong and of good courage? Why are you allowing others to sway you from what God is calling you to do? God is with you. Do not back out of this!" His words were piercing. At the moment the words left his mouth, I was taken back to Joshua chapter 1:9. "Have I not commanded you? Be strong and courageous. Do not be terrified; do not be discouraged, for the LORD your God will be with you wherever you go." This is the passage of scripture through which the Lord spoke to me the day of my uncle's death, which actually led me to the Seminary. Immediately, I sensed God speaking through Paul. I told him right then, "I will do it. I will follow God." On the day of elections seven candidates contested for the role of President. There were three women, including me, and four men.

One of the candidates enlivened the elections, and voting turnout was strong as a result. Many said it was the most exciting and involved seminary elections ever held. On election day all respective offices had a winner except the role of President. There was a tie between me and the most popular candidate for the presidency. The serving leaders of the Student Government met with University leaders on how to approach the matter. The Seminary constitution did not cover such a situation. Based on the University's election policy, a runoff was the best way to decide such an issue.

I resolved in my heart that whether I lost or won I would willingly continue to volunteer myself in service anywhere God called me to serve at seminary. It wasn't really about winning, but about giving myself to God's service. Although winning wasn't necessarily a major priority, it would have been nice since I had come this far. On the day of the runoff, I won the position by a clear margin. After I took office, the Vice President of the Seminary Student Forum and I met with seminary officials towards the close of our term to clearly state runoff policies in our seminary constitution. I sat in the Seminary Commons on the day of the elections when the current student government came to share the news. The gentleman who had before indicated my over-ambition in running for President was there as I was being congratulated. He looked at me almost in disbelief and said, "My sister, this has been providential."

God revealed His purpose in this endeavor when I became the very first black female to serve the Seminary as President since its inception. It came to my attention that certain of my female colleagues spent much time looking into the election history of the Seminary, determined to ensure that I wasn't the first female to hold the title as President. It was quite shameful, witnessing their determination. Once again, I was glad I obeyed God.

Post-election days confirmed all my fears and concerns. I had almost overnight become a celebrity. I was applauded in classes, saluted in hallways, bowed to at entrances. Many of these things were done in fun and support. Still, the attention weighed heavily on me. News of my presidency transcended the Seminary community. Many offered their support and encouragement: teachers, students and staff alike rallied behind me. I felt so blessed.

Leader Shaping

Our team commenced their new term in office as the new leaders of the Seminary Student Forum in May of 2009. I was very nervous about my new role though no one would ever know it if I did not mention it. There was much I needed to learn about leading a team in such a capacity. Though I was a member of our Church Board for about a year before leaving for seminary, I did not pay much attention to its method of operation. Not enough to have internalized the things I learned. So I would be starting fresh. I obviously made errors, I asked many questions of Paul and our sponsor, I read and I observed. My first leader shaping test came when some serious challenges arose on the team with one of our leaders. This individual had some questionable behavior patterns which I believe he felt went un-detected.

I sensed an attitude by this individual to discredit my performance and credibility with other team leaders and students. There were obvious deceptive actions which in my estimation arose possibly from envy due to the attention I was receiving in my new role. I found interacting with this individual to be quite daunting. I sincerely did not feel that I could trust someone who worked so hard to discredit my performance. To be fair, there were some positive aspects to this individual's ministry contribution on the team. Wonderful creative ideas had been proposed, since this person is knowledgeable and experienced. There was truly no need for the insecurities. We each had been assigned our individual tasks and my objective was to serve, not as a competitor, but as a servant determined to fulfill God's will in everything which he had assigned me to.

I tried my best to encourage and support my colleague's endeavors in the most impartial way I knew how, but this individual made my objective almost impossible. Soon I began receiving feedback that I was unsupportive of this person's endeavors on the team and that I had been unkind. I try never to be deliberately unkind to others, but I also do not relate well to insincere interactions and friendships. So, I did not care very much to foster any deep relational bond with someone I knew, without a doubt, worked behind the scenes to prove my service a failure and to tarnish my reputation amongst my peers and fellow students. One Wednesday morning I walked down a flight of stairs in the Seminary making my way into the Commons. As I slowly made my way down the stairs I saw this individual's back turned toward the stairs while conversing with someone. Neither of them saw me coming until I was upon them.

I heard my partner on the team making some negative remarks about me. As I came nearer the other person became startled and alerted my partner that I was upon them, but it was too late. My teammate stood up with pushed out chest in my direction, fixed his gaze straight at me as if in arrogance and pride to indicate a "So what" attitude, and walked away from me. God allowed me to know for myself what I was up against. Even through all of this, I sought to the best of my ability and in spite of my human weaknesses and tendencies, to maintain a cordial team spirit. When things intensified in our inability to work effectively together, I was forced to call for a meeting with one of our leaders. I wanted to positively move forward. All wrongdoings were denied and I was labeled "A liar."

I don't think I am always successful in approaching my conflicts in the best ways. But I would not seek help in dealing with any situation if I did not feel a sincere conviction that I faced a crisis. Interestingly, I saw significant adjustments in this person's behavior in the days following the meeting. Once I had addressed my concerns I purposed to move forward and I did. Since my overall relationship with the rest of the team was a pleasant one, I tried to focus on the positive and pressed onward. There was much I also needed to learn from this encounter, as it taught me better how to effectively deal with all personality types. Generally and overall, we worked wonderfully together as a team and accomplished much for God and His people. We gave our best at everything we did on behalf of the student body. We enjoyed many great times together. In the process my own character was being molded for my future work as a pastor. These challenges in service as President came to groom me. Becoming a pastor meant more than enrolling in classes and completing assignments.

While I had experienced much change since my new walk with God, I had a lot of growing left. Throughout my life I always avoided conflict. I often ignored things or let them build up to a point of great frustration. It was also difficult for me to become engaged in certain types of activities. The overwhelming interactions would at times drain me. The more I engaged in these activities, the more I realized that I was gaining comfort in my social interactions. But God meant to assist me in conflict resolution, and the best way to discover how to resolve a conflict is to have one.

I had grown much in dealing with conflict, from not addressing anything to addressing almost everything even in my personal relationships. I felt like years of suppressed issues were emerging. Finding balance became my next objective. Another huge challenge I faced was explaining myself so frequently. This frustrated me greatly. Serving as President afforded me many opportunities to practice explaining things. Over time I saw that my discomfort greatly diminished, though it has not completely vanished. "Leader Shaping" truly brought new perspectives to my personal growth. In some ways, I can be impatient and at times intolerant of pressuring situations. I have a tendency to quickly dismiss anyone or anything that brings me discomfort or pain. I am still learning, growing and maturing in these areas. My role as President helped to shape and refine me in remarkable ways.

My demonic attacks while studying were frequent and severe.

TRYING AND
TEMPTING TIMES

Chapter 11

Trying and Tempting Times

My decision to respond to the call to pastoral ministry was unquestionably a devastating blow to Satan's kingdom. It confirmed the decision I made to follow God in an unwavering commitment. Satan's ability to entice me into a wrong direction as he did in times past would no longer be possible, though I am not immune to sin. The revelation of his fury came when I tried to take a nap one afternoon in October 2007. I was exhausted from a full day of classes. I curled up on my couch for an afternoon siesta. Moments into my rest, I had a frightening dream. I am aware that not all dreams have significance or prophetic connotation or meanings, so I exercise discernment on when to take them seriously.

For instance, one time, after moving to the United States, I had a dream that my mother in Dominica sat before a prison cell facing iron bars and weeping. On the other side of the cell was my brother. My mother seemed very distressed as she tried to visit my brother behind bars. Concerned about my mother's health, since she suffers with high blood pressure, I called home just to check on her. My brother had never been in trouble with the law, so I did not take his being behind bars in the dream seriously, especially since no one called to report anything. No sooner did

I call my mother than she informed me of the stress she was under because my brother and his girlfriend got into a fight. She called the cops and he had been arrested. He was placed in a cell at the precinct and she was left with the burden of posting bail for him. I knew absolutely nothing of this incident until the dream. Not all my dreams come true or carry meaning, but a vast majority do. Consequently, I don't take them lightly.

In October 2007 while I rested that beautiful sunny afternoon, in a dream a hand almost the size of my living room wall gestured me to come to it. I felt its significance. In the dream I felt frightened by the size of the hand. I tried pulling away, but its gestures persisted accompanied by a deep, thundery voice which seductively beckoned me to "Come, Come, Come." I fought not to be caught in its snare, but the voice pressed more aggressively to reel me into its quarter. Deeply afraid, I could feel my body almost responding as I sought a way to escape. Then a gentle voice interrupted the demonic invitation and appealed to me, "Call for Jesus." I cried out, "Jesus come, Jesus come, Jesus come." Immediately, I became frightened from my sleep and sat up sweating and shaken by the experience.

Later that same month, while I peacefully slept, I had yet another dream. In it I looked in the distance and saw a fertile, well-cultivated piece of land stretching many miles. The land seemed extremely rich and well plowed. As I made my way across this piece of land, I came to what looked like a dividing line. The line separated the fertile soil from an ocean on which a terrible, terrible storm raged. The winds were amazingly strong and the rain fell with a fury. Together, they struck the large body of water with unspeakable force. I seemed determined to press forward into the storm despite its visible aggression. I pushed hard against the gale, but it beat my body and pushed me back. I pressed even harder as the strong winds and rain hit my face and body with undeniable impact. Suddenly, in a final push of the wind, the storm appeared to win and I was sent flying back onto the fertile soil which I had just left. Despite the storm's fury, I was unharmed. But as I made it to the soil, I landed right in front of a farmer accompanied by a dwarf bull. The bull's face spoke of anger, hatred and aggression toward me. It seemed determined to gore me with its very sharp and pointed horns. Buried in its eyes was an intense hatred as it pawed the ground in preparation to charge. The farmer tried hardtop keep it restrained but within its little body was unspeakable strength. I awoke from my sleep with the lingering thought of this bull's anger toward me.

The dreams stayed with me for a while as I tried to understand their meanings. I felt strongly that they may have been associated with my seminary experience and new spiritual journey; I waited for the unfolding. One day, as I meditated on them, I felt the answer come to me. I understood the hand on the wall to be an invitation from Satan to come to him. The cry for help to Jesus told me that only God could keep me from the continued snares of the enemy. The bull in the other dream was also Satan. I understood the fertile land to be New York where I had left behind a more comfortable life. I wasn't entirely sure of the interpretations but there appeared to be many manifestations of these dreams through the storms I encountered in my life while on my seminary journey.

One such storm came as I prepared for a preaching assignment at the Broadview Seventh-day Adventist Church in Chicago one Friday evening in July of 2009. I felt fine all day and even when I sat to review the scriptural passage for my sermon that evening. Within moments, however, I began feeling an unusual weakness threatening my very ability to rise from the chair. I felt no pain in any particular area of my body, but it was clear that something was significantly wrong. In a short while my condition had worsened and I feared I would die in the chair. I wasn't sure what the medical problem was, whether it was my heart or something else. To this point in my life I suffered from no known physical illnesses. Yet, I just grew worse and worse in this sudden, bizarre illness. I asked God for strength to drag myself to my phone to call 911. I managed to make it to the phone. As I held the phone in my hand, I could feel a strong probing tugging on my mind not to go to the hospital. I obeyed the prompting on my heart as I proceeded to make my way to my bedroom.

I made my way to my bedroom where I collapsed on my bed with the phone still in my hand. I remember that I was conscious enough to ask God that if I died, to please let me see His face when I woke up again, whenever that was. Then I went to sleep until the next morning. I was exceedingly grateful to be alive. I did not feel as sick as I was the night before but some effects lingered. The pastor of the church picked me up about nine that morning. I did not share with him what I had experienced through the night. I didn't want to alarm him.

I arrived at church without ever having fully looked at my passage for the day. This was not particularly unusual. Since my preaching journey began, I found it impossible to preach from a manuscript. Whenever I receive the call to preach at a church, a passage of scripture will immediately come to mind. No matter how much I try to focus on other passages to preach on for that day, I can never sway from it. At times I would not know what my entire sermon would be until I stand in the pulpit holding the microphone. I often became nervous sitting on the platform, since I did not know how my sermon would ultimately end. It dawned on me that it was in that moment of preaching that my words and thoughts were being developed.

I preached my heart out that Sabbath morning nonetheless, and my symptoms disappeared the moment I took up the microphone, never to return. I cannot recall ever before feeling this ill and I have never again felt that way. When I returned home from this preaching assignment, I fell into deep despair over my preaching life. Since my ministry had begun, I had always felt this kind of despair after any preaching time. I became especially depressed each time I spoke. Part of it was because my life mistakes and errors often rushed back to mind while preaching and almost interrupted my flow of thoughts.

Often, after my sermons, people would comment on how powerful a preacher I am. I frequently felt saddened by their remarks. This sadness often resulted from deep feelings of unworthiness. I also could not reconcile the physical change which took place once I began preaching. It appeared that I took on another personality and exuded a strength which made me uncomfortable. I would often come home and try to play back in my mind how I went from my usual reserved nature to this out-of-character extrovert who dominated the pulpit. I found it unfeminine and it severely bothered me. I never once verbalized my concern to anyone, but Satan used this to play with my mind. I often spoke to God about it.

That day, I fell into one of my most despairing moments concerning a preaching encounter. I felt it was time to call a trusted prayer partner and ask for prayer. I called Olga, a lovely lady whom I met at the All Nations Seventh-day Adventist Church in Berrien Springs. She prayed with and for me. She rebuked Satan and encouraged me to press forward in the work God had called me to do. She strongly affirmed my calling and encouraged me to "Proceed in Jesus' name." It is the last time I felt so despairing about this. I still have my moments when preaching weighs on me, but never as it did in times past. I am confident in my calling and feel blessed to be a part of this precious and humbling spiritual vocation.

A Supernatural Visit

One of my favorite classes in seminary was Pastoral Counseling. One of my textbooks for this class was an exceptionally compelling book by author Ellen White, called *Mind, Character and Personality*. She highlighted many deceptions of Satan. In one of the chapters she stated, "If Satan has sent an imp (one of his demonic angels) to antagonize a follower of God and they are unsuccessful, he comes himself to do the work in destroying that person."

In the spring of 2008, as if my plate had not already been filled to capacity with adversity in the early stages of my studies, I had an encounter one morning around 2:00 am, which I knew was an out-of-this-world visit. It all began when I felt held down by a presence in my sleep. I did not feel any physical contact but something kept me immobilized for what seemed like forever, although the encounter only seemed to have lasted a short while. I struggled to sit up in bed but to no avail. I tried to yell or scream, but no words came from my mouth even though I could sense that I was blurting things out. After what seemed like an eternal struggle, I flew upright in bed and reached for my Bible. Knowing there was not a physical presence in my room, I identified this visit as a supernatural one. I quickly turned to Psalms to find a scripture on God's protection and deliverance. I then placed the opened Bible under my pillow and went right back to sleep. I slept well until morning, and carried on with the day, but the experience rested heavily on my mind.

I soon dismissed it as something unusual, not expecting to have a repeat of the situation. To my amazement it happened again the next night and almost every night for almost seven months. The weeks and months ahead found me dozing off in classes since my sleep had been frequently interrupted during so many nights. I was totally exhausted. Though it did not show on my face or in my interactions with others right away, I grew highly frustrated and concerned. I observed that when I visited New York in the summer of 2008 I never once had an occurrence for the entire four or more weeks I remained there. I mentioned the problem to a few close prayer partners and asked that they help me pray about it. The very day I returned to Berrien Springs, the attacks started all over again. They also intensified. I had less and less sleep. I failed to discuss the matter with any classmates because I know people tend to be leery about such supernatural encounters. Although I prayed much about the situation, I saw no visible change in my sleep pattern or in the attacks. I reached out to someone on campus who had been involved in deliverance ministries. We prayed about it but nothing changed. My concerns grew that maybe God no longer heard my prayers or maybe He left me. Fear began to set in.

A few students remarked on my stressed demeanor and fatigued look in the early weeks of the encounters. In the later months, though, I learned how to cope so my concerns did not show so much. When I realized that I was not victorious in the matter no matter how much I prayed, I knew I needed to reach outside myself in seeking help and an understanding about my situation. It was then I reached out to a prayer giant on campus, Dan. We met in October of 2007 at the Coloma Church in Michigan. He has a powerful prayer ministry. I called him in desperation one night to share the encounters I was having. I had cried for nights in frustration from a lack of sleep. My body became exhausted from the lack of rest and I wasn't concentrating well in my courses. As I reached out to him, he encouraged and prayed with me. He assured me that the enemy (Satan) was trying to intimidate and distract me and that he had been dealing with similar concerns from other Christians around the world as he traveled.

While in conversation with him, I felt a strong desire to write Bible promises on deliverance and hang them up around my bedroom. It seemed clear to me at that moment that just reading them was not sufficient. I had to make them come alive in my situation. When I ended my call, I did exactly that. I went on my computer and for hours typed as many scriptures as I could possibly find on the power of God. Promises such as Luke 10:19, "I give you power to trample on serpents and scorpions." Psalm 91, "He who dwells in the secret place of the Most High God, shall abide under the shadow of the Almighty…" Psalm 46, "God is my refuge and strength, a very present help in my time of trouble…" Psalm 27, "God is my light and my salvation, whom shall I fear…" Proverbs 3:24, "When you lie down you will not be afraid; your sleep will be sweet." Colossians 1:16, "For by Him all things were created: things in heaven and on earth, visible and invisible, whether thrones or rulers or authorities. All things were created by Him." These and other Bible passages were written and ready for posting all over my apartment.

That night, I stayed up for hours pasting the promises all over my walls, around my bed, closet and bedroom doors, both on the inside and outside. I also placed them on my living room and kitchen walls. Before retiring for the night, I prayed those scriptures back to God as prayers. I reminded Him that I knew He was able to do as He promised in the Bible to deliver me from evil. After praying, I went to bed, closed my eyes and slept like a baby. I slept beautifully that night and every other night after that until this day. I have ignored any of Satan's attempts to revisit me in that way. From this day forward I developed a brand new appreciation for the promises of God found in his holy word, the Bible. I read my Bible before, but never with the intentionality, confidence and meaning as since this incident. I am prepared to live life "by every word which proceeds out of the mouth of God" (Luke 4:4). Dan suggested that he place my story of how God intervened in my situation on his prayer website as an encouragement to those who were dealing with similar situations.

How Can I Do This Wickedness?

The unfolding of the dreams I had also came through some interesting relationship situations. My first few weeks in Berrien Springs were lonely. I missed New York terribly. When the frigid temperatures of Michigan welcomed me in the fall of 2007, I prayed more earnestly for companionship than I ever had in times past. I would not have turned down a premature marriage proposal if I was sure it truly came from God and awarded me a handsome pair of strong arms to wrap around my goose-bumped arms during the cold season. My desire for companionship, however, would not surpass my obedience or loyalty to God.

My need for companionship remained a need, not a desperation. I was willing to wait on God in this area of my life. So when, within my very first semester at seminary, I began receiving some questionable, immoral relationship solicitations, I knew Satan was on the prowl. My first invitation to engage in an inappropriate relationship came within my first few weeks of school when I began receiving a series of letters from a brother in Christ back in New York.

This was someone I knew quite well and respected. I am not sure what possessed him to take the approach with me that he did, but I knew it was not of God. He is married with a lovely family. He expressed how much he has been in love with me and misses me when I am away. Not too long afterward, he wrote again expressing a desire to help me get dressed for the frigid Michigan weathers. I informed him that God was doing a wonderful job keeping me warm with his care during those times and that I would never be in need of his help in this area. It's the last correspondence I received from him along those lines before our interactions died off. Another brother tried hard to get my attention. I wasn't interested, but I also did not wish to be unkind. For a while he took it upon himself to call me at some decidedly inappropriate hours. I spoke to him about it, but he made no changes. Trying not to be harsh, I tolerated his immature and insensitive behavior. Things finally reached a boiling point one night when he called to tell me he had just gotten back from grocery shopping and dropped all he was wearing to the floor. As he painted the mental picture that he stood in his living room window in the nude the way he was born, it became clear to me that he wasn't the person for whom I had been praying. I asked God for a life partner, not a sex partner.

In the fall of 2007, I attended an event on campus. As I head out at the end of the program, a young lady approached me to give me a flyer. When I took it and walked away, I was stopped by a man who said he wanted to speak with me concerning the material I had just received. He was not a student at the Seminary, but seemed familiar with its functions. Since I had seen this man before at worship services and we had exchanged good hellos, I showed no reservation in hearing him talk on the matter. I guess I exercised less caution in my interactions, being in a Christian environment. He asked for my number and I gave it to him. The very next night he called me around ten. He expected me to know who he was, although I never before had a phone conversation with him. Within moments of my picking up the phone, he abruptly blurted out, "I am not going to beat around the bush. I want to have a relationship with you."

I was quite taken aback by his approach. In spite of my coming from a city like New York where people are bold and daring, this was too strong an approach for me. I still extended respect to him when I expressed that I felt sure that I wasn't the one for whom he was looking. He tried convincing me that he would be a good fit for my life and that he would be a great person to help me as I journeyed to becoming a pastor. I reminded him that I did not know who he was and I did not feel comfortable with the conversation. I maintained my lack of interest in his offer as I informed him that I was going to end our conversation. It is then that he informed me that he had been part of a group of guys who had been discussing who would go out with me first.

He told me men do not respect the women who come to the

Seminary, as they are sure they are not there for ministry but to find men. I quickly told him I am not so ambitious in finding men that I would allow it to cost me such headaches and several thousands of dollars in tuition. Before we ended the call, he cautioned me that there were others coming my way to try to involve me with them. I ended the conversation, thanking God that He'd found a way to alert me to this concept of women in ministry that could obviously hurt me. I tried to be "wise as a serpent and harmless as a dove" (Matthew 10:16). This dialogue followed a string of unwelcome relationship solicitations.

Spiritual Wickedness in High Places

My most severe attack came from an unexpected person, someone I had given my respect even before having known him on a more personal level. My student involvement allowed me to work with many different individuals in various leadership positions around the University. I was humbled by the respect I received from the Seminary community. I felt a sincere love from my fellow students, the teachers and staff. My journey with this particular person began my very first week on campus. Although I would not have connected this piece of the puzzle to the many inappropriate encounters I had with this man for a long time, it all came back to me that his deceptions began my first week on campus when he sought out a friend with whom he saw me and asked her to bring me to meet with him. In a Christian environment, one can be naive and let one's guard down.

From the moment we were introduced, I later realized, none of our encounters until the day I left the University were incidental but deliberate and deceptive. My first observation that something was unusual was when he tried telling me the people I should and should not trust. Before long, I was called constantly asking if I needed rides to various

211

places. Transportation in Berrien Springs is a major challenge, with no available taxis or buses. Without one's own vehicle, it is almost impossible to get around. I did not own a car, so I was in great need of help in this matter. Because he so openly extended his assistance, I occasionally allowed him to take me places. Since he was, of course, of the opposite sex, and had a family, I minimized the number of times I accepted a ride from him. I felt grateful, however, that I had someone who could help me.

Over time a fairly cordial friendship was formed, not just with him but also with his family. This helped with my transitioning. As the weeks of school progressed, it became evident to me this individual had a vested interest in my care and needs. He called several times day, day and night. There were always reasons for his calls. I valued this in the beginning. My first inappropriate contact with him was when he informed me he had read my personal diary. My laptop computer had shut down just a couple of months into classes. I needed to have it checked at a computer repair store as soon as possible. Since he was the one taking it in for the repairs, he asked that I leave the computer with him, so I did. Some time had passed and it turned out I had to make a trip to New York in the spring of 2008 for a preaching assignment. I asked him if he'd drive me to the airport.

As we drove to the airport, there was a bit of silence for a while. Then he abruptly asked if I was married. Surprised by the question, I gave him a puzzled look, as I said, "No, where did that idea come from?" He paused as if to think of his response, then told me that when I left my computer with him, I had my diary halfway open on the inside of my computer bag. He told me that on the open page he saw where I documented I had a husband. I knew it wasn't possible to have a book open while inside a bag. I learned something about him that day; he was not honest. In my diary I often wrote my prayers and my desires about things including a future spouse. He would have had to read a lot to come

212

up to those pages.

This left me with a disconcerting feeling, but I still maintained my association with him on the basis that he is a pastor. This situation began a series of encounters which left me many discomforts over the duration of my studies. I discovered that he is someone who is extremely manipulative and deceptive. He is obviously skilled at what he does and leaves not a trace of evidence behind. Every encounter in the weeks ahead came with subtle questions concerning any male interest at seminary. He appeared to have kept track of my male interests and interactions.

One night I attended a prayer meeting and he was present. I sat next to a male colleague. As I interacted with the gentleman throughout the service, I could see that he studied my behavior the entire time and was visibly upset. Since he is a husband and father, I could not reconcile that he could possibly be upset that, as a single woman, I was talking with a single man. After the service ended and I went over to greet friends, I tried to greet him but he turned his back and would not speak to me. He was visibly upset. I felt greatly confused, and for a while I wondered whether I was reading something into his actions that did not exist.

Yet, there were simply too many coincidences for this to be overlooked. I still continued to observe to make sure that I was not judging this person wrongly or misunderstanding his actions. Sometime in the spring of 2008 I received a call from him to meet for an important meeting. He gave me a list of a few other people who would also be present. It was already after 7:00 p.m. and the meeting was scheduled to begin around 7:30 or 8:00. I met him at our designated church location and waited for a few hours, but not one other person came. I found it unusual and asked if he would at least call to inform the people that we were waiting. He said he was tired of reminding people of meetings and would not call anyone. He was going to give them some more time and, if they were not there, he would leave. It turned out no one ever showed up. For hours I sat there answering his questions and enduring his lustful stares.

Amidst all these encounters I continued to give this person the benefit of the doubt that, as a supposed "man of God," his actions may be sincere. In time I learned the hard way. Some people are excellent at masking themselves in Christianity. Clothed in piety, they give a semblance of godliness. All the while they are engaged in performing exploits for Satan. I unquestionably see this individual as one such person. There is not a doubt in my mind that I had stumbled upon a smooth Casanova, who knew well how to work the pulpit. Gradually my eyes were opened to the fact that there were too many isolated incidents to conclude that I was just imagining things. On the contrary, I was dealing with deliberate tactics, schemes and strategies to reel me into an illicit adulterous relationship.

As May 13, 2008 rolled in, I welcomed another birthday. For years, since I was a young child, my mother had always been the first person to call to wish me a Happy Birthday. For the first time since I can remember, someone beat her to it. It was this man. My phone rang at almost 8:00 a.m. as I hurried to go to class. I rushed to the ringing phone, not paying attention to the caller's ID. I felt sure it was my mother. But there was his deep, seductive voice telling me to note that he had not forgotten my birthday. The same thing happened May 13, 2009. This time I stood right by the phone and listened to him leaving his message. I did not answer or respond to it. No sooner did I make it out to classes that morning but he was awaiting me to inform me he left me a message for my birthday. I quickly dismissed him and went my way.

I had an active Prayer Ministry on campus, praying with many people and encouraging them in their faith walk with God. No one utilized my prayer services more than this interested patron. As the summer passed I received more and more calls to pray for all kinds of nonsensical things. For instance, one night at almost midnight I got a call that he was driving back from Indiana and it was so foggy that he could not see his way. He said that since he knew my prayers "went through," he was asking me to call on God to take him home safely. Well, it had been foggy all day in the Michigan, Indiana area, but his call came in near midnight. Despite these distractions, I kept focused on my studies.

When I returned from New York at the end of the summer that year, I encountered him after a worship service. I extended my hand to greet him when he quickly grabbed me by my waist, pulled me to him, and kissed me by my face exclaiming, "I missed you, Sweetheart." Startled by his unwelcome display of affection, I walked away, uncomfortably upset. I have wonderful male and female colleagues in ministry whom I love and respect deeply. I welcome their endearments and extend mine with no reservation because we share such a bond. Among these are married men, but we share in respectable Christian friendships. He could have been numbered among those if he had given me the respect of a genuine Christ-centered friendship. Sadly, I did not sense the comfort to have such a relationship with this individual. Since I not once confronted any of these situations directly, I believe he thought I had been ignorant of his manipulations.

I felt strongly that it was time to begin slowly severing my ties. Since I was aware of his deceptive nature I knew I had to be cautious in my approach. He has an unassuming but, in my estimation, vindictive and retaliating streak. Since I never verbalized my decision to separate myself from him, but rather made it more and more impossible for there to be any contact between us, he grew desperate in his attempts to keep in contact with me. Gradually, I became more and more distant. My unavailability both frustrated and angered him. He possessed an inflated ego that gave me the impression he expected me to move at his beck and call. I grew uncomfortable about his unwavering and relentless interest in me and found it necessary to seek counsel on how to approach and deal with the situation. I took the counsel I received to heart as they taught me how to safeguard myself.

Sometime in the spring of 2009 I received a call from him on a Thursday afternoon asking if I would accompany him to a hospital visit in a neighboring town three hours away. A mother and son in our local community were to go through organ transplant surgery. He expressed that the surgeries were scheduled early the next morning and he wanted to be present to pray for them as they awoke from their operation. I found it an interesting reason but did not comment on it. He asked if I would make the overnight trip with him. I quickly turned down the offer, knowing it would be highly inappropriate to make an overnight trip with someone of the opposite sex and most certainly not someone else's spouse. I dismissed his request and quickly ended the conversation. The family had their surgery and came back home. Not once during their recovery did I receive a call from him to pray for them in their home which was in the same community I lived in. It further dawned on me at that moment that prayer was being used to ensnare me.

With each turn down of a request came new manipulative ways to engage me in his company. Sometime before this encounter, I received a call from him to pray for a friend who is also a minister but is planning on leaving his wife and family for another woman after several years of marriage. He said the friend is mostly torn about the children. He asked me to pray for the matter so I said I would. I prayed earnestly about it and left it with the Lord. The next few days I kept receiving calls stating emergencies to pray harder because he thought his friend was going through some puppy love phase, but he's now realizing his friend has it really bad for this woman. He often would tell me of guys in the Seminary

216

he knew who "had it really bad" for me. In frustration, I expressed my strong dissatisfaction for this person, who professes to be a minister, yet he is willing to destroy his family for another woman. Since he realized my position on the matter, he dismissed me, quickly saying, "Okay, Okay, Okay!"

This happened during the spring of 2008 in my second semester. I never heard another word concerning the situation. I soon realized he spoke of me and his distorted interests in me. In the fall of that same year, a pastor who was visiting the Seminary from out of town offered me a ride home after our Friday night service. It was during our annual week of prayer. As I made my way to leave for home, this same man came and tried offering me a ride also. I told him I had already made provisions to get home. We went our separate ways that night. He was nowhere in sight as I left the parking lot with the pastor. At around eight the Sunday morning of that weekend, as I hurried to a babysitting assignment, my cell phone rang. There he was on the other line asking me if I would join him for breakfast. He then informed me that he had also invited the pastor who took me home to join us. My heart sunk. I quickly contacted the pastor to confirm if he had, in fact, received an invitation from him. He told me "Yes." Then he told me, "But I am not available." I also planned on being available.

After confirming we were, in fact, both invited to breakfast with this individual, I felt weak in my stomach. I knew he was not present or at least not in view when I left with my friend that night. I also did not inform him who had offered me a ride home. I further realized that he kept track of me. This troubled me immensely. He always tried to get me to be alone with him and manipulated many instances to make this possible. In my earlier months of study he called me late at night asking that I accompany him on private walks as he walked the tracks at school. He also tried to get me away from the University environment for

217

sporting activities. He said if we played on the campus and people saw us, they would talk. It was evident this man was carrying on a relationship with me in his mind. These things just unsettled my spirit in deep ways.

Disturbed by these occurrences, I confronted him. I asked him how he knew the pastor and what was the purpose of the breakfast to which we both needed to be present? He informed me he did not know the man but that since we were both single he thought he would get us together. Feeling disturbed, I prepared to leave his presence that morning. I asked to pray with him. In the prayer I asked God to preserve his marriage, to bless and keep his wife and family, to strengthen the bonds of their union and not to let the enemy destroy the years they have built together. I wanted him to be reminded that he had a wife and family, since it appeared that he had obviously forgotten his commitment to them. As I opened my eyes from the prayer, his face wore a dry, dissatisfied expression.

As I got ready to leave he announced, "You look like you are a sadist." Barely making eye contact with me he awaited my response. Since I had never heard the term before, I asked him "What or who is a sadist?" He failed to give me a definition to the term he had just used to describe me. Rather, he reached for a dictionary as he exclaimed he also needed to verify the meaning. As he grabbed the book I wondered why anyone would use a term to describe someone if they themselves did not know the meaning? It seemed senseless, but I waited to hear what he had in mind. He barely turned one page of the large dictionary and without looking for a second he found the word then proceeded to read: "Someone who enjoys sexual gratification by inflicting physical and mental pain." He looked up at me as if shocked by what he discovered. Then he insisted on apologizing. Disgusted with his trickery, I said, "This does not in the least bit describe me" as I left his presence. I purposed to cut all contact with him.

During the months between these encounters, he subtly tried to manipulate my mind by telling me I would never find a spouse because I am in my thirties. He said that the men my age are all married with families. I believe he intended to paint such a bleak picture of my romantic future that I would have no choice but to settle for him. He also showed no respect or support for my work in ministry. Regardless of all ministry endeavors I pursued or engaged in, even the ones involving him, he never commented on it except it suited his manipulative purpose. He reminded me often that no man would sit in a congregation and listen to his wife preach to him. He concluded I will have a huge problem finding a spouse. With a calm courage I stared straight in his face once and said, "God is never stuck between a rock and a hard place. Neither is He ever in a corner biting His fingernails not knowing what to do with a problem." He often told me, "No one could truly be as spiritual as you are. They have to be hiding something."

With all of these frequent incidents and occurrences by this same man, my mind began to reflect on some bizarre experiences I was having in my initial stages of school. In the first few months of my seminary experience, I began receiving some obscene calls. The calls came in periodically for a couple of weeks. Since I was new to the area and I know that campuses tend to be targets for pranksters and outright criminals, I concluded they were isolated incidents. When the calls persisted approximately the same time, at around midnight to one in the morning, with someone making strong sexual groans on the phone, I realized that these could not be coincidental calls. I began to grow concerned. I had planned on reporting the incidents to the housing office as well as to the police. That very weekend I was picked up for a ride to church by this man, and he kept asking me if I was okay and I insisted I was fine. He probed harder, asking me if I was really sure.

Finally I shared the strange encounters with him. He quickly

219

informed me if it ever happened again let him know because he would know exactly what to do about them. I said "No! I think it would be best to call the police and have them trace the calls." He became very quiet and said nothing further on the matter to this very day. Never again did he ask me concerning those calls or how I had dealt with them. I also did not ever again receive another one of those calls.

He returned from a trip during my first year of studies. As he spoke to me of his travels, he told me that he brought something back for me. I shared gifts with colleagues before. I also had students who returned from tours to the Mid-East and brought me souvenirs. This was also still in my early stages of knowing him. He handed me a bottle of what I thought was special cooking oil. I mentioned in our earlier dialogues that I cooked my own meals to save on cost. As I glanced one more time at the orange oil in the bottle, I could not interpret the language in which it was written. So, I asked what kind of cooking oil it was. I quickly shared I would ask one of my teachers from that country for the interpretation. Realizing my naivety and the possibility that someone else would be involved, he quickly told me that it was not cooking, but body oil. For a moment time stopped. I dismissed myself from his presence still holding the bottle in hand. I had insight into his plans for me that day.

One night while on a prayer walk, there he came driving past me, supposedly a coincidence. I walked often to rest from my study challenges. It was very therapeutic for me to culminate my school day while talking to God. As I walked in the neighborhood at approximately nine at night, on a back road nowhere near this man's residence, he came supposedly coincidentally driving by. He pulled alongside me to tell me that he happened to be in the neighborhood "praying for someone." In the same way, he so happened to be in the same grocery aisle with me one night close to eleven. We had just met at a prayer meeting. As I left I went to a local supermarket for some water and produce before the supermarket closed for the night. There he was with two bananas and a bottle of gummy candy in a basket almost eleven at night. I asked him why he selected these shopping items. He said that the candy was for me when I visited him. He proceeded to ask me to keep him in serious prayer, as he had some crucial work matters the next day which required urgent intervention. All of his prayer requests appeared to have needed urgent intervention. I knew he was lying but I interacted with caution.

With all these scenarios playing back in my mind, coupled with the most recent incidents, I concluded it was time to seriously separate from this person. When I met with him that day to share my thoughts on not associating in any endeavors with him, he was visibly upset. He no longer could contain the supposed calm that had so long masked his devious conduct. He realized he had become unsuccessful in any of his manipulative schemes to ensnare me. So, he tried hurting me with words. He made some derogatory comments, telling me I was "cheap and loose and simply wanted to have my own way." I was very upset but contained myself. I did not wish to engage him any further. I simply maintained my decision was sealed.

He treated me as someone in a relationship who wasn't handling a break up very well. As I proceeded to leave, he lashed out at me. Pointing to my chest area he said, "Is that a hickey on your neck? I dismissed his question knowing I would never again allow him another opportunity to address me on any matter. I confidently reminded him, "My commitment to God is the same privately as it is publicly." I had concerns that he would manipulate situations to hurt my reputation. His anger toward me was apparent from our last visit. In the later months he tried infiltrating the lives of my friends to inquire about my whereabouts. It troubled me greatly. Still, I could not tell them at that time what was really happening for fear word would go out and I would further endanger myself. Since he portrays the semblance of a clean image, this would serve as a perfect alibi for him. It is my belief that he knew very well he could get away with such behaviors because of the impression he gave others of a humble and pious "man of God."

When I was first getting to know him, he gave me the impression he lived a life above reproach. I have often sat in pain and wondered about the many young women who embarked on this journey to become a pastor, and may have fallen to his demonic traps. I continue to pray that Satan, manifested through this man, will someday soon be exposed. It is my belief that this man feels confident that he has many people fooled about who he really is. This experience became a very pressuring aspect of graduate studies. Prior to becoming a pastor, I would never knowingly engage in a relationship with married men. Why would I choose, at this stage in my life while becoming a minister, to openly and willingly engage in an adulterous affair with another minister? The thought of it unsettles my spirit in deep ways.

A Painful Stand

I knew that my decision not to engage in an adulterous affair with this man angered him greatly. He knew that I was deeply committed to my spirituality and faith. He seemed determined to destroy my ministry and walk with God. It was obvious that he could not accomplish this by any open invitation. So, throughout my almost three years of study, he stopped at nothing to devise manipulative schemes to ensnare me in an adulterous affair. When he realized that I actually completed my studies and he did not have my body, it is my belief that his anger and fury followed me even after my graduation. I always felt he would try to destroy my reputation in order to protect his image and ministry reputation.

During the months following my graduation from seminary, I suffered immensely as rumors circulated regarding some serious and damaging accusations about me. I realized the depth of the evil toward me when I received word from leaders within our denomination questioning me concerning these serious accusations. Most certainly, those things said cast doubt on my character and integrity. Throughout my studies he had exercised great skill in manipulating his way into the life of anyone he knew I was connected to. This made it possible for him to spread his venomous lies. But I saw God's favor shining brightly in my defense. Still, only God knew the depth of pain I experienced in this process.

As I recall my dialogues with this deceiver while studying, one thing is clear, he needed to disarm me. He told me often, "No one could be as spiritual as you; you must be hiding some sin." My unwavering faith in God made it impossible for him to penetrate my mind with his demonic deceptions. I believe he despised me for my faith in God. He often tried to discourage my confidence in Pastoral Ministry. One of the ways he attempted to do this was to tell me that he did not think people took my spirituality seriously because I was "atractive and fashionable."

He told me often I would not find work as a pastor because I was female and I needed to face the fact that only one percent of females ever get hired as pastors in our denomination. It is my belief he intended to tell me that I would have to do a bit more than just pray and trust in God in order to secure a position. I reminded him of the confidence I had in God that He would help me, and even if He did not help me, I would still serve Him wherever His hands led me. It became apparent to me that my faith both angered and frustrated this man.

Based on my experiences with this man, I am of the firm conviction that he does not believe in the true existence, realness and authority of a monotheistic God, even though he serves as a minister of the gospel. Many of my encounters with him spoke loudly of someone who sees his role as any regular paying career. It is void of any relationship with God. This shocked me into the harsh reality of the spiritual wickedness perpetrated by some in religious leadership positions. I failed to focus on his negatives, however. I knew I could trust God, since it is He who guided me into pastoral life. It is true this man's hatred for me has brought me deep pain. But one thing is certain. I stand for God and I believe God is standing with and for me. I continue to pray for the exposing and conversion of this person.

The Journey to Hire

As graduation drew close, I began petitioning God to reveal to me His will for me in pastoral ministry. I did not wish to be presumptuous in thinking I belonged in a pulpit. In March 2010, God heard my prayer and I was presented with an opportunity to pastor with a Conference within our denomination. After deliberations by their Executive Committee I received a call in April informing me they were interested in offering me a position. I was both shocked and excited. It all happened very quickly without any effort of my own. The leaders felt confident in their decision to make me a part of their team. I looked forward to the opportunity of joining them. For a while I was unsure of where I felt I would serve in ministry. One thing remained clear in my mind. I did not wish to pastor a congregation. Since my journey in ministry began five years before, I had truly enjoyed the freedom of traveling to many different places and ministering to so many different people. I truly, deeply enjoyed ministering this way. This offer to serve as pastor seems to have given me clarity into where I would be placed in ministry.

In 2007, just days before I left New York for seminary, I met with a friend from our church who also wanted to celebrate my departure. He still tried to obtain complete understanding why I chose pastoral ministry and a location so far away for study. I tried helping him understand that I sincerely did not choose any of those two things. Concerned, he said, "You may never be hired within our denomination and you may never be ordained as a female pastor, so why are you doing this?" I again reminded him that I had not accepted the call to ministry to be hired or to be ordained. I responded to the undeniable call in obedience to the living God. What He would do when I was finished with seminary remained unknown to me. I was simply acting in obedience to His call.

For a long time throughout my seminary preparation for ministry, I did not sense a calling to pastor a church congregation. This confused me because I felt uncertain as to what my ministry vocation would be once I finished seminary. When I learned of the Chaplaincy Program at seminary, I felt sure this aspect of ministry fitted my life since I always had an interest in caring for others' needs. Sometime in February of 2010, I heard from my home pastor. I am aware of his very busy schedule, so I was both happy and pleasantly surprised to hear from him. He inquired concerning my plans for ministry after I graduated. I informed him of my conviction not to pastor a church but rather to go into chaplaincy. He encouraged me to consider parish and pulpit ministry because of his observation of my work in this area. He seemed deeply convinced about the matter.

One month after my discussion with him, while at the school's library, I received an e-mail from another very close colleague in New York. He asked me the same question concerning my plans for ministry. I responded with at least six reasons why I did not feel I was called to pastor a church. He was shocked. He responded by asking me to pray and let the Lord lead since he was sure I belonged in pastoral ministry. While I was in the middle of trading e-mails with him that day at the library, my cell phone rang. I saw that it was another colleague from out of state. We did

225

not communicate often, so I was surprised by her call. I was unable to take the call since I was at the library so I decided to call back later. Within moments, however, she called back. There appeared urgency in her voice beckoning me to send my résumé to conferences as I prepared for graduation. She then pleaded with me to consider pastoring a church and to open my heart to all possibilities.

In a conversation we shared in the summer of 2009, I told her that I was uncertain as to whether or not I was being led to pastor a congregation. I remember her feeling puzzled by my decision. I began to feel strange about the connection of these three encounters. As a result, I decided to open my heart to their advice. My convictions to not pastor a congregation still had not changed. Due to the experience that I encountered with God in the past when He tried to speak to me through others, I became determined to listen. I had also been pleading with God in previous weeks to clarify my call for me. These encounters prompted me to attend the Seminary's Annual Ministry Fair in March.

God's Plan Revealed

It all began when, as the President of the Seminary Student Forum, I discussed with our team the need to have a forum address to review our year in service. As the time for re-election approached, I thought it was wise to share with the Seminary community the things which the current Seminary Student Forum had done on their behalf. We intended to hold the event in the Seminary Commons on March 11, the day following the Annual Ministry Fair. Since such events had never been held in the chapel in previous years, I did not think of asking to hold it there, but God had a plan. I met with our new worship chair a few days later to inform him of the SSF's desire to implement some changes made to the constitution. According to the constitution, all constitutional changes are to be addressed to the student body at large. The only time the entire student body is present in the same place and at the same time is at our chapel services. Our worship leader is a spiritual and gracious man.

He reminded me that the Seminary does not allow for such addresses right now but is open to visiting the possibilities in the future. He did allow for a few minutes to be granted for promoting the constitutional changes. I left his office very grateful for the opportunity. The Executive Committee of the SSF continued its planning for the March 11 event. Just one week before the Vice President and I were to go before the student body I received an e-mail from our Worship Director informing me I could use the entire chapel hour for the Seminary Student Forum address. I immediately wrote back to him to see if I understood him correctly. Sure enough, he was willing to set aside his own worship plans by rescheduling his already set program to accommodate ours. I was amazed and grateful. I began plans to shift the event to its new location. We had a bit of fun with the day by asking our military chaplains at seminary to dress in full uniform to escort our platform personnel. It was a spiritually charged occasion. The Executive Committee of the Seminary Student Forum recognized and acknowledged those who had given years of service to our seminary community. The SSF team also acknowledged me for my service to the team. I felt humbled by this gesture, and I had no idea the team was doing this. I believe it is also the first time I was publicly recognized for any work I accomplished related to ministry. We also highlighted the major accomplishments during our time in service.

The morning concluded with my seven-minute President's Address in which I encouraged my colleagues to run their race of faith with a purpose. I ended on my grandmother's signature note. "Though 'donkeys have no right in horse races', they should run not allowing anyone to steal their eternal crowns." Our scheduled forum address was held on March 9. The next day was the Annual Ministry Fair in which officers from many conferences in North America and Canada attended. The representatives at the conference were seeking prospective pastors to fill ministry positions. A leader of a conference, in town for the Ministry Fair, happened to attend our chapel service that morning and heard my address.

God Knows My Name

The next day I awoke to prepare for classes and the Ministry Fair. I still struggled with attending but I adhered to my desire to be obedient, and prepared to attend. Since I had never attended any of the other ministry fairs in the past, I reluctantly made my way to the event. I lingered for a while before making it to only two of the thirteen Conferences. Then, I gave up my pursuit and began to make my way home. As I strolled across the Seminary Commons toward the exit at approximately 3:30 in the afternoon, a gentleman whom I had never met called me by name; he said, "Josie! I'd like to speak with you." I immediately turned to inquire who he was. He introduced himself as one of the leaders of a Conference at the fair. He informed me he and his associate had waited all morning in hopes of finding me. He confidently told me that he had also inquired of many of my male colleagues in seminary who unanimously agreed I would fit well into the role as female pastor. This Conference had never employed a female pastor before. I would be their first should I be chosen.

I felt extremely humbled by the possibility. He quickly introduced me to another leader of that Conference with whom I would interview. I had concerns about being interviewed in an open setting. The interviews were held in the Commons to accommodate all the Conferences and students. Though I did not share my concerns with the leaders, I was immediately informed that my interview would be conducted privately. I sensed the Lord at work. I felt the interview to be an open, sincere and pleasant one. My service as the first black female President of the Seminary Student Forum appeared to have resonated quite well with the leaders. I waited with calm anticipation at what the final result of my interview would be. Within a month I received word that I was considered for the position to serve as pastor within that conference. Planning began to bring me in for an official interview. During this time my pursuer, that same man who would stop at nothing to engage me in an adulterous affair, confronted me about his knowledge of my hire.

He was not enthused for me, but rather appeared disappointed and dissatisfied. He spoke in a low, dry tone without looking at me, while he played with his fingernails in deep contemplation. He never once congratulated me or said he was glad for me. As I made my way to leave he said, "If you go down there and stick your foot in your mouth, they won't give you the position." I did not take his words lightly. Somewhere deep inside I knew he meant to tell me that regardless of how my interview went, if they decided against me, it would be my fault. It was a very uncomfortable encounter.

Since he often told me that I would not find placement in ministry, he did not welcome this news of my hire. It meant defeat for him, and I believe he decided in his heart to prove me wrong. He truly had not understood my concept of ministry. I never saw ministry as a business venture or another career move. To me it is a way of life. It is who I am every day and not something that I do on a given day. With or without hire I would still serve God anywhere and in any place with all my heart. God has taught me to survive on little and to live by faith. I have been called to this work of pastoring not to climb any ministerial ladder or to become successful. I have one burning desire and it is to share the love of Jesus Christ with a dying and lost world.

Josian Framton

Interestingly, my interview was scheduled on my birthday, May 13. They were totally unaware of my birth date at the time. In an interesting turn of events I was no longer assigned to the position. They were graceful in informing me that I would be considered for any future openings. Human that I am, I felt hurt, perplexed and confused. But I believed God had a plan for my life. So, I prayed to Him earnestly in the days following these events and I continued to keep my trust anchored in Him. I asked Him to help me find peace in the matter and to intervene to bring about His purpose and will for my future in ministry. I relied on scripture and prayer to help me cope. I kept ever present in my mind, "All things work together for good to them that love God and are called according to his purpose" (Romans 8:28).

I remained confident that God was going to work things out in my favor and He did. Less than two weeks later I received another call from the Conference office informing me that "their Executive Committee was convinced there is a calling on my life and they wanted to again offer me a position." I gracefully accepted the position with the understanding that God heard my prayer and He was working and leading in these matters. I was brought in for a second interview. After my return from my interview, while finalizing some post-graduation work, my pursuer again sent someone to summon me from my class while it was in session. I was informed that he eagerly needed to see me to discuss my interview. I sent word back to him that I was busy and would be for a very long time. I owed him no explanation on the details of my interview. I went on this interview on God's mission not his.

My acceptance of the new position, however, took me down a strenuous and emotional spiritual journey I never thought imaginable. The weeks following this offer brought strange occurrences and puzzling events which almost cost me my sanity. I entered a mental prison in the months following this decision. There became an uphill battle in the months ahead to have me fully instated in the Conference. I awaited renewal of my working status and had disclosed this to the leaders within moments of our first meeting. I saw avenues where the enemy sought to make simple matters highly complicated and to portray me as one who was not trustworthy. Although my attorney said the renewal process would only take 30-90 days, months passed with no word on the progression of things. I saw clear evidences where Satan sought to portray me as a liar and deceiver. This brought me deep pain. Although those involved were doing their best to approach the matter carefully, still, it became one of the most mentally draining and painful experiences I can recall having since my ministry journey began. I felt the spiritual battle. It was fierce. And though the magnitude of this situation cannot fully be comprehended or stated here right now, only God knows how I remained sane during these times.

Confusion and perplexity enveloped me as I dealt with the daily interactions concerning my employment. As I responded to the questions and concerns regarding my joining their staff, I felt overwhelmed and mentally exhausted. Many questions daily occupied my thoughts regarding the nature of their concerns. Yet I knew they intended to make this work for everyone. As my friends and family inquired about why I was still in town, I could not openly share with them the delay in my process. It was often difficult to find answers. I felt certain this battle was not of the flesh. "We do not wrestle with flesh and blood but with spiritual wickedness in high places" (Ephesians 6:12). I remained constant in prayer to deal with the situation. My mental pressures began taking a severe physical and emotional toll on me.

One night in July of 2010, while in Atlanta, I became overwhelmed with the matters concerning my situation. Feeling powerless I labored all night in prayer and cried out to God for help. I knew He is the only one who could deliver me from the mental prison into which

Satan had thrown me. While I prayed I felt drawn to Job 24:22-24. It read. "But God drags away the mighty by his power; though they become established, they have no assurance of life. He may let them rest in a feeling of security, but his eyes are on their ways. For a little while they are exalted, and then they are gone." Satan had found a way to work hard at blocking my path to assuming my position as a pastor, but God had the power to override his roadblocks. I pleaded with the Lord to let His promise come true in my situation. When I woke up that morning, I went to my uncle's garage. I sat facing the street. It was a hot, humid summer day. I felt heavy in my spirit and hurt by the things I was experiencing. As I looked around, I saw one of the neighbors loading his van with work materials. I did not know him well but he always said hello. He and his family are friends of my family. I turned to carry on with my duties when I saw him busily crossing the street and coming towards me. In the short time that I observed his interactions with my uncle, he seemed like a deeply spiritual man. He stood in the entrance of the garage where he greeted me. Then he said, "Young lady, can I sing you a song?" It seemed an odd request, but I said "Yes." He then stared me straight in my face and with a strong conviction sang, "God and God alone created all these things we call our own, from the mighty to the small. The glory in them all is God's and God's alone." He then paused, looked at me with a firm stare and said, "Now pay attention to this. The best and worst of man can't change the master's plan for He is God and God alone."

His words pierced my heart. I asked the man what propelled him to come and speak to me. He said, "I was about to enter my van for work when I felt an urgency pressed on my heart to go over and sing this very song to you." As he left, I felt renewed. Strength entered my body. I felt a renewed confidence that no one would change the plan God set for me. God "set before me an open door that no man could shut" (Revelation 3:7-8). Though my troubles and pain would drag on for months, I

232

purposed to keep my faith and trust in God.

God Is in Control

As the weight of the process pressed, my memory carried me back to how this all began. In February of 2010, as I made preparations for graduation, the continued processing of my status renewal weighed heavily on me. Early in the morning, as I communed with God in devotion, I asked Him for a miracle in the matter. As the burden of the wait rested on me, I opened my devotional guide for a word from God. In Oswald Chambers' *My Utmost for His Highest* I read, "God's people come to Him with a problem as if it is impossible to Him." He reminded his readers, God is a God of the impossible. This encouragement fired up my faith as I went forward in the hope that God would intervene. Within less than two weeks, the Conference Executive Committee offered me a position and became instrumental in working with me in resolving the matter. I felt sure that the position came in answer to my prayers.

God opened my eyes to the fact that the circumstances surrounding the situation were not accidental. He has a plan that will be revealed in His perfect timing. God showed me that He is the One who is in control of this entire situation. This was revealed to me when I realized that, from the time of my first interview on May 13 until September 13, something major took place on the 13th of each month in between. I felt sure it could not be coincidental that on exactly that date something significant took place regarding the processing of my status. God showed me through this that it is He who had begun this good work of having my status renewed and He is faithful enough to bring it to its very end. Since He has never failed me, I kept my trust in Him. The knowledge of this restored my peace.

Josian Framton

Valley Faith

The most empowering object lesson I have learned on this journey of faith with God is that, "The just shall live by faith..." (Hebrews 10:38). Despite the overwhelming discomfort I experienced in the process of assuming this pastoral position, I had to remain and endure. I remembered that I did not want to pastor a congregation. I loved ministering in different places and to different people for the past five years since my ministry began. I felt a sense of freedom that I did not wish to give up. I recalled that I only accepted the position to pastor because of my deep conviction that God was leading and I wanted to be obedient to Him. As I reflected on the pain in the process toward being hired, I could not help but feel deep confusion about my decision to accept God's will. During my toughest moments, when I reached out to Him, it seemed as if He had abandoned me. My prayers concerning the situation appeared to be unanswered. Many days and nights I cried intensely asking God for a resolution. Yet, it seemed the more I prayed the worse things got. I felt a silence from God that was challenging my faith to its core.

I cannot ever recall a time in my life that I felt so helpless and powerless to do anything about a crisis I faced. I suffered deeply in the initial months of this experience. I grew impatient, irritable and at times angry with myself and God. I felt angry with God for placing me in the situation. It's as if someone had literally tied my hands. I could not move forward but I seemed unable to go back. I wanted to be removed from this situation so badly but somewhere deep inside I knew I could not interfere with the process because it was a supernatural battle. This was not easy for me. It is actually contrary to the way I have dealt with my life's challenges, difficulties and conflicts. I always totally avoided any avenue of conflict throughout my life. I am exceedingly prone to walk away from anything or anyone who creates such discomforts in my life. I never really dealt with my situations by confronting them or those who caused them.

My inability to confront my issues made it increasingly difficult to be successful when I did try to resolve a conflict. Things often came out wrong due to my mounting frustrations and my unwillingness to have to explain myself. These were deep personality flaws that God greatly needed to help me overcome. I am deeply convinced that the process of renewing my status and taking this pastoral position was designed to assist me in my endurance, perseverance and tolerance growth. It literally pushed me to my limit. This hiring process appeared to top my painful life experiences.

Often, I could feel God reminding me of all the ways He had led me since my ministry journey with Him began. Flashbacks of how I miraculously made it through almost three years of seminary studies comforted me. It's as if God kept trying to ask me to hold on because He was still working in and through me. Yet, the battle I faced was, in my estimation, the worst of any spiritual battle in which I have ever been caught. I marveled at the wickedness of Satan. Its documentation here does no justice to the depth of my experience in the situation. The enemy seemed determined to cost me my sanity. Since this journey began in March, I worked hard to remain positive regardless of how discouraging things seemed. It wasn't easy keeping my head up in the face of such adversity.

Great perplexities continued to envelop me. I caught a glimpse into the situation, yet I knew its magnitude was beyond me. I was being encouraged by leaders within the Conference as they themselves felt their own confusion about the situation. I am not sure they have experienced such chaos having someone join their team. It was quite a disconcerting situation, to say the least. Things turned messy and my privacy disappeared. This was unbearable for me. I am a deeply private person. Satan knows this. He sought hard to publicly embarrass and humiliate me.

As I continued to minister in New York where my ministry practically exploded since seminary, without any effort on my part, it took much prayer and all the strength I could find to stand before God's people. There were times I did not want to preach, but I knew this was exactly what the enemy wanted, to shut me up. It is the very reason I knew I had been placed in the deadlock I was in. I knew that God was counting on me to fight back, and I could not disappoint Him. I felt a sure confidence that "My redeemer lives" (Job 19:25). I needed to make Him proud.

Satan needed to know through my determination that in spite of my pain and hardships, I was going to trust God even though He "slay me" (Job 13:15). I had to fight an internal battle to preach messages of hope and inspiration concerning the power of God while I wrestled with His providential working in my own life. I did not turn down any preaching engagements during that time. I believed every word I spoke to God's people, since it is He who fueled me for each preaching assignment. I was being encouraged by my own sermons. I could not have done this in my own strength. There are days I felt too low in my spirit to even get out of bed, and some nights I literally cried to God all night until the morning. Some days I felt strong in the Lord and in the power of His might. Other days I found myself having some severe saddening moments. One such moment came for me on November 9, 2010.

My day started with a visit to Avis, my spiritual mom's, new office in the Bronx. What should have been a one hour trip by bus and train turned out to be a three hour trip. As I walked into her office, tears filled my eyes. By the time I arrived, I felt wasted, irritated and frustrated. I tried composing my emotions, but I was losing this battle. After meeting with her, I had another meeting with someone nearby. As I met with this individual, she found herself confirming for me something I felt the Lord was instructing me to wait upon. The idea of waiting was killing me because I had now been waiting on things for months to no result.

I grew so irritated with this person that I abruptly ended our meeting and left. If I had stayed another moment in her presence, I would have broken down before her. I felt isolated, alone, saddened and grieved in my spirit. I made it home and headed to The Bronx where I was attending a revival series at the Philadelphia Church. On our way to the church I began sharing with Bruce, my spiritual dad, how my day went. I started calm, but I soon became emotional. I felt the pressure in my frontal lobe begin to build and my head felt like it was going to explode.

From the way I was feeling mentally, I felt certain I was having a nervous breakdown. Suddenly, as Bruce began telling me how much he was hurting because of all that I was experiencing in this situation, I broke down in the car and bawled as if I was going to die. I suffered some things during this time in my life which are too painful and shameful to share. When Bruce realized the magnitude of my pain he pulled the car over to comfort me. After I cried for a while, he assured me that my suffering was not in vain and that God was going to vindicate me. I composed myself enough to make it into the sanctuary. My spirit was heavy, but I received a blessing. I thank God for tears. I felt so much better after I cried. This was the worst of my mental pressures, exhaustion and frustration since dealing with the situation.

The following day I felt a strong desire to spend the day in fasting and prayer. I pleaded with God to restore my joy. He did. Through consistent and persistent prayer I was able to break the mental chains. That burden was lifted and a great peace surrounded me. As my mind cleared I began remembering how God has been with me throughout this journey. For instance, in May 2010, a dear friend threw me a surprise birthday lunch in the home of a mutual friend. We had a blessed time. As I made my way to leave, one of the hosts encouraged me on my

237

spirituality and connection to God. She reminded me of how much my life had inspired hers. She then hugged me and said; "Follow the Lord and you'll be okay." I felt inspired by her words since I was feeling very down from the previous day's event. I thanked everyone for hosting me and made my way outside with another close friend.

As we stood about to proceed to her apartment, a colleague drove past us with her husband. We waved to them. Then we saw them turn around and come back toward us. She ran out of the car to us as if on an errand. As we waited to hear her urgency, she expressed her admiration for our lives in ministry. As she made her way to leave, she looked at us convincingly and said: "Just follow the Lord." This time I felt sure the words were inspired. I finally made it home that night. Before I retired for the evening I called my dear friend Darlene to check in as customary. As we ended our conversation, she reminded me of Ruth's reward when she left everything she knew to go with her mother-in-law. She also encouraged me to "Follow the Lord." These reminders kept me encouraged that the Lord is with me.

My ministry vocations have allowed me to teach and preach to many people on the subject of faith. I have also not been shy in sharing my own personal experiences of how God has led me in my life. One thing became very clear to me in my journey of faith. It is in the valley which I have now found myself that my faith is truly going to be tested. It's easy to talk faith when the Lord is blessing and He is answering all my prayers. What happens when I cannot hear Him after calling on Him for months and the blessings seem withheld from me? This is exactly where I found myself. I knew that this situation was not one from which I could walk away.

As for a matter of fact, I literally felt stuck. I couldn't move forward and I couldn't go back. I had one choice and that was to call on

God and wait on Him. This was my plight in the spiritual warfare in which I providentially found myself. I believe that through this experience I discovered the depth of my faith, trust, and loyalty to God. Sometime in November I was brought back to a dream that I had just days before I left for my first interview. In the dream I was in Michigan. I headed home to my apartment. When I looked behind me, I saw two huge tornadoes coming from South Bend, Indiana heading in my direction with an excessive force. Though they were traveling at an excessively high speed mingled with an indescribable fury, they damaged nothing in their path. They traveled side by side. One tornado was extremely dark and fierce. The second one was a lighter shade and equally powerful as the first. They moved as if they had a destination in mind. As I saw the forces coming toward me, I panicked. I tried to remember how I should protect myself from a tornado, but before I could reach safety, both tornadoes struck just where I had been standing in my home. My home was the only one damaged of all the property in their paths. At their impact everything around me that I owned was damaged and destroyed.

As they vanished I had nothing left. I found myself curled in the middle of the slab left from where my home once stood, with both my hands still covering my head as if to shield myself. Debris lay all around, but I remained unharmed. As I stood up, I gazed in amazement at my life and it seemed destroyed. I remember waking up that morning and feeling disturbed and troubled in my spirit that God was showing me something. I pondered on the part of the dream where I lost everything. As I did this, a still small voice reminded me to focus on the fact that, though I had lost everything, I was unharmed. As I looked over the things I experienced in my journey to being hired, I saw evidences of this dream manifested in remarkable ways.

After graduation I returned to New York. Though I have a loving family and many friends here, I felt so unsettled, no longer having my own place. God blessed me tremendously financially while being home, however, by making it possible for me to preach, teach and evangelize. In spite of these blessings I found myself like a nomad from home to home trying to feel a sense of security. I looked at my life and saw that I truly had lost all for the sake of the gospel. My comfort, security, and possessions were now all scattered. I had nothing except my relationship with God and the many wonderful people He placed in my life. God reminded me that though I had nothing materially, in Him I had everything. In spite of my pain I felt peace. Although at times my peace was interrupted, one thing was certain. Regardless of how I felt, I never neglected an opportunity to share God with others or to tell them of His greatness and unfailing love. Each Sabbath that I entered a church to preach I met wonderful people of God. They showed me through their smiles, hugs, kisses and words of encouragement God's love for me. My trials continue to take me into painful places but I have the great assurance that God is always with me.

The Color of God's Love

In September of 2007 just a few weeks after my arrival at Andrews University, I had the privilege of going on the annual Battle Creek Tour. What a wonderful experience! I learned the history of our church and the brave pioneers who carved its movement. While I stood at the grave of Ellen White listening to our teacher, a gentle and pleasant voice greeted me. I smiled as I reintroduced myself to a lovely young pastor whom I had seen a few days before at chapel. I remembered my first few days of chapel services, curiously surveying the area to study the people with whom I would be associating for the next three years. It was then that I first caught a glimpse of the innocent look of this lovely individual. As we reacquainted ourselves that day, he reminded me of his name.

Remembering the prophetic words of my church elder in the weeks before my calling, "Maybe it is at Andrews that you may meet your husband," every son of God was a potential fulfillment to this promise. Since I have no dating preference as it relates to race I was open to whomever God placed in my path. I guess this would be true as long as God's will did not take me out of my comfort zone. As we talked briefly, he shared his challenges with his work load. Since I registered for a light schedule during my first semester, I offered my help with the writing and organization of his papers and classes. After we resumed classes I began working with him twice a week to assist him. We only met for three weeks before terminating our meetings but a beautiful Christian bond developed. Neither of us paid attention to the fact that we were of different races. It became a minute issue compared to the wonderful Christian interaction we were having.

Since we were getting along so well, we continued to stay in touch even after the sessions were over. The more time we spent together, the more we realized the similarities in our lives. I admired deeply the spiritual life of this individual and he expressed feeling the same way about mine. I never overwhelmed him with my burdens, but I knew I could have confided in him. He loved to pray and so did I. So we prayed many times together. I was having a spiritual experience that I had never shared with someone of the opposite sex. Throughout my male relationships, I had not had an opportunity to meet such a devoted Christian man. As my friendship with this person developed, I could not help but notice that he brought something into my life I greatly desired in a partner. He brought godliness and spirituality into our relationship. He lived a prayerful life immersed in the love of God.

As time passed, he shared with me beautiful cards which expressed how much he also admired my deep connection and relationship with God. He told me "he felt certain there were no such spiritual women left." I felt flattered and humbled by his words, because I know I am flawed and less than perfect. I enjoyed the beauty of a wholesome spiritual friendship. Whenever we were together, we laughed at the silliest things. We enjoyed some deep belly laughs together. I love to laugh. I never felt the need to impress him with the way I looked. Regardless of what I looked like on any given day, he barely seemed to notice. Whether I was nicely dressed or I looked like I could use a makeover, the focus was on the internal. That greatly impressed me. This was new and beautiful. Yet, a courtship with him was not something I desired unless I was completely sure God was drawing us together in that way. It was just comforting to have someone to talk to, go places with and even have a social life in the confines of the small town of Berrien Springs. For a couple of months we enjoyed this unplanned, yet developing Christian friendship-relationship.

A Colorful Awakening

Although I truly was not focused on having a romantic relationship with my new friend, I wasn't blind to the fact that he was interested in me in that way. Given his Christ-centered nature, this was flattering. I did not encourage a relationship, not because I didn't care about him, but because of my own reservations in dating someone younger than I am. I discovered early in our interactions that I was older. Since I always dated older men, I wrestled with this. I felt strongly at that time about dating someone even months younger than I am. I also felt this way because it seemed evident our maturity levels were a world apart in regards to dating. I did not have the energy or the desire to undertake this type of relationship at that time. My reservations made it difficult to open up fully to receive what I felt God was possibly offering, an opportunity for a wonderful Christ-centered relationship. I can at times be stubborn in my ways. The Lord is still helping me grow in this area.

I never openly discussed with him my concerns on the matter. I did not want to hurt him since he seemed so persistent in his pursuit. I also did not wish to interfere if God was working. I continued to pray intensely about his presence in my life. Since I was aware of my history with God in that He always seemed to challenge me in the areas in which I struggled most, I felt sure He was teaching me another object lesson. I believe that my heart needed to be open to all possibilities so that when God is ready to work on my behalf He is not hindered by my traditional, cultural, personal or even religious biases. If I was going to share in a sincere relationship with him, I had to learn that in Christ "there is no distinction" (Galatians 3:28) on the basis of race, color, creed, age or culture. I believe that my reservations in becoming involved were difficult for my new friend.

He never discussed his own challenges with me, but I discovered he also struggled with the fact that I was black. It is my understanding that he also had not explored dating a black girl at this point in his life. We were both experiencing something new. It seemed truly unusual that we would even be interested in each other. Still, our concerns or differences did not dissolve the wonderful spiritual bond we were developing. We continued to spend much time together visiting each other's churches, shopping, eating out, sitting together in our classes, attending different gatherings, praying and talking a lot on the phone. We were inseparable for a while. In spite of our differences, his heart was still set on exploring a relationship, and I was open to obeying God until the day he was reminded that I was black.

It happened one day while I sat waiting for him to leave a meeting with someone at school he saw as a trusted leader. I will never forget the

243

day he came out of this meeting looking as if he had been shot in the heart. I wish I could have recorded the expression on his face. Looking back, I could see that I became different to him at that moment. As we drove home he shared with me the details of the meeting. He told me that he was advised that sharing in a courtship with a black woman is like committing ministry suicide (this is my interpretation). In addition, he would not be accepted well in our denomination should he proceed in this direction. He was also cautioned that his chances of finding employment as a pastor would be jeopardized should he embark on this interracial relationship. He has never seen me or interacted with me the same since that meeting. Although we remained in each other's lives mainly due to his persistence, our friendship took a new direction.

Over time, it appeared the freedom he once felt in accompanying me publicly, became a major discomfort. His public distance was so blatant often it could not even be concealed. I cannot recall a time in my life that I was so openly and publicly rejected. It is my observation he did this to please his circle of influence and to avoid the possibilities of encouraging any further closeness with me.

I observed that my intensions were frequently questioned and my acts of kindness misinterpreted. This was difficult to cope with, since I was simply being my caring self. This was baffling to me, upsetting and frustrating. I also believe he truly didn't know how to handle the situation. I brought my observations about his behavior to his attention, but it always appeared that I was being too sensitive. Admittedly, I was at a very sensitive phase in my life. I tried to be patient in maintaining our friendship. Yet, I knew in my heart it was a matter of time before the relationship dissolved, should these discomforts continue. He did try hard to find understanding in the matter by searching scripture, and seeking further counsel. He is a spiritually guided individual. His efforts in pressing forward were fruitless and discouraging to him since his family, who are also devout Sabbath keeping Christians, failed to give their blessings. I learned that their position on interracial dating was very strong. I saw further evidence of their disapproval in the summer of 2009.

My friend called one Friday evening to ask me to join him in welcoming the Sabbath. He also informed me that his dad's parents were visiting from out of state with his aunt and her son. He picked me up at home as the family whom I never met drove behind us. We pulled up at a supermarket in a nearby town. We all met at the store entrance. Although I never met these individuals before, not one of them acknowledged my presence at any time and he seemed powerless to make an introduction. It was quite an unpleasant encounter. I said not a word and it was never discussed to this day. I don't think these things were comforting to my friend, since he is open to establishing friendships with all kinds of people.

This situation, along with the financial and other challenges I faced in my first few semesters at school, weighed heavily on me. I requested that we refrain from interacting with each other so we could pray and see where God was leading, or if we were simply following our own direction, particularly since we were experiencing such challenges. I also didn't feel peace about sharing in a courtship with him. The weeks we did not communicate were rough. I missed his friendship since we had been inseparable for a while. Yet, in some ways I felt relieved that I did not have the added pressure. I spent much time in prayer asking God what to do and how to interpret His leading in the matter. There was also much for which I needed to ask God's forgiveness regarding the situation. For example, when we first met and I struggled with the issue of age, I grew upset with God that when I finally encountered a devoted Christian man, as I had been praying for, He sent a situation with which I struggled. I remember one day in our first semester just before Thanksgiving, my friend asked me to go to a lake nearby to spend time with him. I found excuses each time he asked.

Josian Framton

One day in a frustrated prayer to God, I told Him I was going to ask my friend to accompany me to a lake about a half hour away to spend time together and there I would find out what his intentions were toward me. I felt the spirit of God pressing me to not run ahead of Him to know anything. He would reveal all in time. I did not listen. I called my friend anyway and asked him to come to the lake with me. I wanted to put an end to the uncertainties in our friendship and free myself of the added pressure to my studies. He was happy because he wanted to do this for some time. I never shared this with him till this day. As we drove, halfway to our destination, we had a flat tire.

We pulled onto a dirt road to put on the reserve tire. As he worked on repairing the flat, he recounted that he had lived in Michigan for many months before beginning his studies and never had a flat tire. We rolled the tire many times to see where it had popped or what had popped it, but it looked normal. We never found a damaged spot. Puzzled, he said, "I think it's a sign. Let's go back home." I felt sure this was a result of my disobedience to God, but I said nothing to him about it. Not too long after, when I had given up on interfering with God's business, we went for a drive. As we got close to a public park he pulled in and said he wanted us to talk. It was then he openly asked me what I thought of the time we had been spending together and my thoughts about our feelings for each other. I was caught completely off guard and almost didn't know what to say. I struggled to find words, but my response was unrehearsed because it came straight from the heart. God showed me that it is in His time, not mine, that He will bring things to pass.

It was about three weeks after our decision to pray about our friendship and where we felt God was leading us. Since I was the one who asked to take a break, it felt fair that I resume communication when I felt I heard from God. My confirmation came through three different

246

individuals who, not knowing anything about the situation we faced, within days without any initiation concerning my personal life, approached me to give me their endorsement of our relationship. I also remained in prayer and study of the word of God to guide me. Very early one morning, I called him to discuss my thoughts on the matter and how I felt God was leading. It was not the easiest thing to do at the time. I had concluded in my heart that I would never discuss such matters of love with anyone, unless I felt certain the person was sent by God.

Reluctantly, that morning I expressed to him how I felt about the situation based on my understanding of God's leading. I still had not felt any deep conviction that we should have a relationship beyond a regular friendship. He told me his feelings on the matter were not the same. I was only disappointed because I had moved in the direction I did, because I felt God's leading and not because I personally wanted to. We can at times misinterpret God. We agreed that we would continue to share in a regular friendship. This brought a challenging friendship over the course of our studies. I often felt frustrated. Realizing the sudden turn in our interactions, I asked many times over the course of our friendship for us to cut contact. Neither of us wanted to be out of each other's lives since we once shared in a wonderful friendship, but I did not care for the discomforts either.

He told me, "Our ability to laugh at anything and so freely interact with one another as well as our strong spiritual bond is rare." We both wanted to maintain that. I also felt a sense of responsibility in maintaining the friendship, since I had been somewhat cold that night in the spring of 2008 when we met to discuss the meeting with his confidant. The pressures of my early seminary journey had robbed me of my usual sensitivity as he brought all these things to my attention. After coldly dismissing him that night, I worked hard to redeem myself and show that I was sorry. I believe he interpreted my attempts to repair things as wanting to build a relationship, but I did not wish to take our friendship to that relational level. My initial thoughts on the matter had not changed. I simply valued his presence in my life, because he is a sincere human being and a genuine Christian. My reservations in having a courtship with him, however, still had not changed.

If it was God's will that we should have had the gift of a Christian courtship, I would have openly welcomed it. I try at best to be obedient to God. I would have obeyed God despite my own preferences. God knows what is best for us. "If we delight in Him, He will give our heart's desires" (Psalm 37:4). I prayed deeply about all these things. Sometime in 2009 my friend wrote me a letter of apology. In the letter he told me that he knew in his heart that I am a "godly woman" but that his behavior spoke very differently. He asked me if I could find it in my heart to forgive him for the way he treated me. I prayerfully accepted his apology and extended my forgiveness without any reservation. I valued his friendship; I did not wish to lose it. I also had lessons God intended to teach me in this situation. We continued to interact beautifully for a while, but in time I saw patterns manifesting themselves again. Maintaining the friendship under such circumstances became strenuous and further upsetting to my already challenging study life. I did all I could to not allow the friendship to die, but it seemed inevitable given the circumstances. Amidst the challenges I still saw God at work. It is clear that since our lives did not come together as a couple, this was not God's plan. There were other spiritual lessons God wanted each of us to learn by allowing our paths to cross. I am grateful for the lessons I have learned through this experience.

All Are Precious in His Sight

I learned a lot through this experience. God used this relationship to reveal my own immaturity in selecting a life partner and to expose the areas in my spirituality where I still needed to grow and mature. "God is no respecter of persons" and "in Him there is no distinction" (Acts 10:34; Galatians 3:28). There is no telling whom He may send into our lives; we must keep an open mind. If I profess to love God, which I do, then I must be like Him in all my conduct. In my ministry as a pastor I have been saddened that so many distinctions exist in the family of God on the basis of race, culture, ethnicity, gender and age, amongst many others. A close friend and prayer partner shared with me a few years ago that she traveled to a particular state in the South to conduct a prayer seminar. The church was a Caucasian congregation. While she sat at lunch after the service ended, the pastor asked her, "Do you really believe your kind are going to heaven?" She said, "I was shocked that in this day and age there are those who still believe the people going to heaven are the ones who think and look like them."

I was attending some revival meetings at a church one time when an African-American pastor share how he first woke to his own prejudices. He became ill, was unconscious and was taken to the hospital. When he awoke, he thought he had been in heaven until he heard the voices of white people around him. He said he realized then that he was not in heaven because he did not expect that white people would be in heaven. It may seem understandable that a black person would not expect to see the same white people in heaven who have contributed to their pain on this earth. Just like there are whites who are convinced that blacks are sub-human and could not possibly secure a place in heaven.

While I was preparing to begin pastoral work in the South, an African-American minister told me, "The people at the church where you are assigned will not love you because you are little, a foreigner and a woman." I immediately sensed that Satan sought to discourage me through this agent. While all he said could be true, I quickly dismissed his negative remark by reminding him, "I will still go to that location as long as God is leading me there." We expect that God should treat and regard others the same way that we do. We believe God shares our prejudices. But in Isaiah 55:9-11 we are reminded, "God's ways are not our ways and neither are His thoughts our thoughts."

God can use anyone, regardless of height, size, race, color, ethnicity, citizenship, country, nationality, etc. I pray the time will come when we will practice what we preach. Because of His love for His people, God will continue to find ways to show us how indifference to each other affects our ability to be true to our service for Him. In love He will design circumstances and bring experiences into our lives that will rid us of such prejudices. We are all precious to Him regardless of our background, culture, ethnicity, education, profession/vocation, religious affiliation, age or race. His love for us is not dependent on such human factors, since he loves us unconditionally. If He so loves us, we ought to love others in the same way. I thank God for teaching me this valuable life lesson through this process.

The Day the Bugs Came

No matter what was happening with me, I remained determined to enjoy my journey at Andrews University. I loved being at seminary. I enjoyed the beauty of the environment, the peace and calm it brought. I soaked in the love I felt from the many lovely, godly people who continually encouraged me and supported my work in ministry. I laughed more than I cried, and I cried a lot. Nothing, however, prepared me for the bug invasion I had in the summer of 2008. I had been out all Friday afternoon. and excitedly returned home to prepare for the Sabbath. Growing up as a Sabbath keeping Christian was often fun. I looked forward to Sabbaths mainly because I saw my friends after a long week.

As I grew older, I no longer found keeping the Sabbath fun. It became the day I could not do things. It seemed restricting and boring. Since the Sabbath begins on Friday evening at sunset and ends Saturday evening at the same time, I used to wish the sun would never set on a Friday evening and that it would rush down as quickly as possible on a Saturday evening. When my relationship with God transitioned from a religious experience to a deep, personal spiritual relationship with Him, I grew to love and appreciate the gift of the Sabbath rest. I now understand it as a wonderful day of rest from my secular life and labors, to commune with the God of heaven. The Sabbath has been given to humans at creation as a beautiful gift from God to rest from our laboring lives.

On Sabbaths, I enjoy the beauty of nature as I stroll through a park to see God's creative works. After laying aside anything that will disturb my time with God, I rest in quietness during those twenty-four hours. I read inspiring books on spiritual growth and other spiritual matters. I indulge in lovely gospel music centering my mind and focus on the promises of heaven. I meet often with friends for my best and largest meal of the week. I enjoy great conversation, laughter and fellowship. I mostly enjoy freedom from my secular labors such as house chores and handling tiring business affairs. I have become so grateful for the Sabbath rest, so it is not surprising that I loved Sabbaths at Andrews University. They were very special. There was something about knowing your entire community of faith is getting ready for the same occasion.

A friend shared with me how she lit candles as the sun went down each Friday. The brighter the candles became the closer the Sabbath drew. So each week I adopted this new art of welcoming the Sabbath. Then I took a special class with a wonderful teacher who spent a long time in Israel. She learned how they kept Sabbath there and shared some of their preparation secrets with us. How beautiful were the things I learned, how they blessed each one in the family and celebrated this beautiful gift of rest from God. What a wonderful feeling to rest from my labors of life and enter into the beautiful, peaceful rest God promised in the Bible. There was much I needed to rest from mentally and physically as I continued to settle in seminary life.

When I made it home in great anticipation this particular Friday evening, to prepare for my favorite day of the week, I never expected the scene from the horror movie I walked into in my apartment. An influx of ladybugs had mysteriously come through my mesh screen and sealed windows. I could not believe my eyes. Hundreds of these creatures covered my ceiling, windows, bedroom, and bathroom. Ladybugs were everywhere. Since the Housing Office was already closed, I had nowhere to turn. I could not call Campus Safety for a bug issue. I stood helpless in my living room with tear-filled eyes; quickly, I figured a course of action. I filled spray bottles with bleach and sprayed the bugs.

As the insects became irritated by the bleach, they began to fly on me and all over the apartment. I ran around like a crazy woman before collapsing in defeat on the floor, and just wept terribly in frustration and mental exhaustion from the chaos. Gradually, the bugs began to die from the bleach. I was able to brush some off my bed so I could sleep. It was a disgusting sight to behold as I looked up and saw hundreds of them trapped in the flat plate-like shade around the bulbs in my living room. I called my building manager to come look at my apartment. He seemed shocked. He said he did not know any other tenant who had this problem. I decided to ask some neighbors myself, to see if they had a ladybug problem of such magnitude, but no one reported having such a problem with the bugs.

Committed to Serve

My journey to becoming a pastor was unquestionably a most trying one. But one thing was clear from the day I began this journey. It was not about me. No matter the trial or test, as long as my body and brain functioned, I had to get up and do what I have been called to do. It has nothing to do with how I feel mentally or otherwise on any given day. It has everything to do with where God needs me to be on a particular day. This aspect of surrender and submission to the will of God has challenged every aspect of my own temperament, personality and comforts. So, when my journey of trials and testing began during my very first few days at school, I still had to proceed with a firm determination to serve no matter what came my way. Some of my religious experiences have left a negative impact on my ability to fully see and feel God's love. I purposed that I, with God's help, would not make other people feel the way that I have felt. I have not always been successful in accomplishing this. My ability to be truthful and honest with my thoughts and words has undoubtedly at times hurt others. It is never my intention to do so, but being human, I often fail in this area. For those reasons mentioned, I centered my attention on ministering to those who came to me seeking help. Seminary has many international students whose first language is not English. I spent many hours tutoring and mentoring such students. I assisted countless others with their term papers, even at times neglecting my own assignments to help them. I cooked and brought students home, male and female, for food whenever I had it. Although I lacked funds while studying, I never lacked food. It remains a mystery to me, but I was well cared for during my tough economic times.

One semester while in New York for the Christmas holidays, I learned that a box of food had been delivered to me by the University Church. I still do not know how they knew I needed this gift. I shared what I received with others. Whenever I was blessed, I always tried to remember to bless others. Sometimes I baked banana and other types of breads, which I cut into slices and took them to the classes to share with other students. I passed on many of my highly graded papers so that those struggling could get a sense of what was required to score high. Many students cautioned me that my work could be misused and that I was too trusting. I always reminded them that if I could not trust in that environment, then where could I be safe? I trusted them and they needed to trust themselves. I babysat free for students who could not afford babysitters, so they could study, all while having a full workload.

God blessed my service by allowing me to excel in my classes, although I struggled with the Greek and Hebrew languages. I was also helped by my fellow colleagues especially when it came to needing textbooks. I could not afford to purchase textbooks, and many students were so kind to loan me all the books I needed for certain semesters. When one student was returning to Australia after his program ended, he passed on all the books he felt I would need in my last year. I was so grateful. There was no condition to the commitment I made to service; I simply committed my life in service to God, and it is what I shall do until I breathe my last breath.

Glory Days

Despite Satan's attempts to make my ministry journey at seminary a most difficult and painful one, God worked doubly hard on my behalf to ensure that this became by far the most beautiful of all my life experiences. I can sincerely say I believe that it has been so. My determination to remain grounded in God helped this to be a possibility. Since "In the presence of God there is fullness of Joy" (Psalm 16:11), I stayed close to God to help me through the challenges I faced.

Thankfully, I did not lose my joy or my peace. I truly felt "the peace of God which surpasses all human understanding" (Philippians 4:7). I went about my daily life failing to succumb to murmuring or complaining. I remembered that "in all things I was to give thanks" (1 Thessalonians 5:18), and that I should rejoice in my circumstances. I felt strengthened in my faith in God. My trials paled in comparison to the beautiful encounters I had and the wonderful individuals I met along this journey at Andrews University and the Seminary.

For instance, while I served as President, my teachers, and the staff and students at the Seminary were so deeply caring and encouraging to my life and work in ministry. The camaraderie brought me sweet consolation. The level of respect extended by the overall community of faith kept me spiritually encouraged and energized. As the weight of my responsibilities increased, so did the support from students, teachers and staff. I felt the love of God shown toward me through these faithful followers of His. Whenever we had an event, countless numbers of our teachers and staff chipped in and participated in our endeavors to lighten the load of service. Many of them served, not seeking anything in return. They prayed with and encouraged me every step of the way as I sought to do the work before me. The frequent hugs from colleagues, staff and friends which often comforted my heart showed me the ever present love of God. Truly, "greater is He that is in me than he that is in the world" (1 John 4:4).

My circle of friends, associates and acquaintances increased, giving me a lovely social life. There is not a whole lot happening in Berrien Springs so it felt great having places to go and people with whom to spend time. I found ways to create fun experiences with the wonderful people with whom I was bonding. Potlucks (merging all kinds of dishes), were a signature activity at Andrews University. Never have I tried more exotic vegetarian meals. The Seminary is a diverse community enrolling students from almost every country around the world.

Our chapel services gave me something to look forward to each Tuesday morning as it became filled with students from all over the globe, literally. I caught a glimpse of what the kingdom of God finally will look like as every nation, kindred, tongue and people will gather before Him in the recreated earth. Friday evening worship to usher in the Sabbath brought a Sabbath appreciation to my life which I had not felt from the time I started keeping the Sabbath. Every event at Andrews University brought the most wonderful feeling of Christian fellowship. Foods of every kind accompanied each event. I just loved that. The spring weathers brought such excitement, as flowers encircled the University's grounds with beautiful colors overlooking the well-manicured green grass.

Oh, how I grew to love being in this atmosphere! Some of the most wonderful people I have met are at seminary. The study groups where we found humorous and creative ways to remember our Hebrew and Greek words brought sweet memories. The sweet sounds of the morning birds became my alarm clock as they sang a very distinct song each morning. My heart sank at the thought of not hearing them again. The echoes of large numbers of children from all racial backgrounds playing together created a beautiful picture of what heaven will be like. I learned to love life at Andrews University with its tranquil location in Berrien Springs. It shall forever be imprinted on my memory. This experience became so rich and beautiful that I wished it would never end. The positive encounters far outweighed the negatives. As I began packing for my final departure from Andrews after graduation, I wept each day thinking of being separated from such a beautiful environment, filled with wonderful godly people. I will never forget the beauty of this God led time in my life.

In 2007, I asked the Seminary if they made pastors.

A PASTOR IS MADE

Chapter 12

A Pastor is Made

In March 2007 when I called the Andrews University Theological Seminary, I asked them if they "made pastors." Almost three years later, as I prepared for graduation, it became clear to me that God had made me a pastor. It is indeed my greatest witness of a miracle. As I walked across the stage on May 2, 2010 to receive my diploma, I was overwhelmed with emotions. I looked back at all I had endured in order to make it to this point. The dedication service the day before had already brought me many tears. The weight of my journey rested heavily on me. The joys, pains, challenges and beauty all came into full view. My friends and I cried throughout the entire dedication service. My mother, Aunt Maria, Carmella, Mr. D (my former teacher), and spiritual parents Avis and Bruce, along with other friends and well-wishers were all present to help me celebrate. By graduation morning I was already emotionally spent.

The realization that with God's help I miraculously completed my studies without student loans or regular gainful employment, and also overcoming such trying and tempting times blew my mind. It also dawned on me that, despite the many hardships and circumstances threatening completion, I had miraculously overcome the odds against me. I stood amazed at the workings of God. I marveled at the reality that indeed my trust in Him had not been in vain. I tried to trace how all my semester tuitions had been paid over the course of my studies, but I could not figure it out. There was never one person who paid any semester's payment for me on any continuous or consistent basis. These things both baffled and intrigued me. My faith soared as I marveled at the many ways, and through the many people God had blessed me. It dawned on me that God had, in fact, led me on this journey of faith by using some amazing people to help me make it through this journey.

The Blessings of Christian Friendships

While at seminary God brought some wonderful people into my life. Darlene, who became my best friend during my studies and beyond, has unquestionably been led into my life by God. Though we still cannot fully trace how we became so close, one thing is clear; we were meant to be in each other's lives. We first met in our Spiritual Formation class our first semester. She sat very reserved and quiet in her place. She possessed a peace that I have not seen on a lot of faces. She had a calmness amidst the hassle and intensity of seminary life that which could only come from God. She never seemed ruffled, exhausted, frustrated or bothered. We had an opportunity to be in a few group sessions in class together, and every time she opened her mouth, I sensed a deep spirituality packed with words of wisdom. She also possessed a deep unshakable love, loyalty and commitment to God. I felt drawn to that. I saw her as someone who could be trusted. It is my belief that if someone is faithful to God, they will undeniably be faithful in their earthly relationships.

As time passed, a beautiful, unforced and natural bond was

developing between Darlene and me. We were able to confide in each other things we could not share with anyone else but God. She became a great source of support and strength for me throughout the many trials I experienced while studying. We comforted each other through hardships and we endeavored to stay close to God. She is a loving, caring person, so she ensured that my needs were also met and cared for whenever I approached her with a crisis. We were inseparable and still are. I never had to worry about anything I shared with her. She is one of the most trustworthy people I have ever met. I sometimes do not know how I would have survived my troubles if I did not have her as a sponge. She also tells me that she is unsure of how she would have survived without my presence in her life. I am often amazed at that since I felt that I needed her way more than she ever needed my support. Although graduation has taken us into our various ministry vocations in life, we continue to share in a most beautiful friendship. I have a love for Darlene imbedded deep in my heart. What a wonderful, incredible woman of God! As I continued in my studies, God continued to bless my life with wonderful godly and special people.

In my third year I met Everett. I call her by her last name, Samuels. Our friendship blossomed over Field School in New York in 2009. She is a sincere, trustworthy individual. A lovely friendship grew as we worked together. Though on the surface she appears to be a serious woman, she is a pleasant, funny person, easy to get along with. For a while our paths kept crossing but without developing a relationship. Part of it may have been my own reservations. Looking back, it is amazing how some things play themselves out. I received a call in my first year from a friend in New York. He needed my help in briefly housing a student, who would be beginning studies as a pastor. I gladly welcomed the idea, but the plans fell through and the student made other arrangements. That student is Samuels. Our friendship was slow in developing, but a beautiful bond has emerged. She always does something nice for me. Whenever she traveled even to New York, she would bring back something I loved. We realized that we shared much in common, particularly her very private nature. She has a strong, sincere spirit. She became a great support for me as I went through my difficulties after graduation. I have grown close to her and genuinely love her.

I am convinced that my connection with Eric has been providential. I see him as a true son of God. He is a deeply spiritual person, and his presence in my life has been used by God to enrich my own spiritual growth. I could always count on him to pray when I had a difficulty, whether he had knowledge of my concerns or not. He never intruded or tried to invade my privacy. He is a trustworthy person. He loves to pray, so he made himself available when I needed his prayers. He was the only one present to help me move my things out of my apartment back to New York after graduation. He took time from work with a friend to help me lift my heavy boxes without complaint. He assisted me a lot with packing. This made my moving a lot less stressful. He is a great example of a good Christian man and I appreciated these Christian attributes in him.

Simona, affectionately known as Mona, became my friend when she offered me a ride home one night. The rest is history. I never thought we could ever be good friends. Our personalities are a world apart. She is an extremely strong person who never backs down from a problem. Deep inside, however, she's a self-sacrificing and spiritually driven woman. My presence in her life may have brought her some frustrations, though she never mentioned it. I often left things behind when I visited her, or overlooked some important assignment. Since we took many classes together, she involuntarily became my memory box. I was a beneficiary of her study style, particularly as it related to effectively studying for several classes and exams. She was skilled at that. Sometimes I posed a challenge due to my pickiness and the perfectionist aspect of my personality.

One night she agreed to help me get my hair done. I had been braiding for a while and needed a break from the braids. She had almost involuntarily become my on campus hair dresser. She seemed impressed by my natural curls and wavy hair as well as its length. I gave her my history as to how I inherited my curls from my father. She tried encouraging me to wear my curls out, but I insisted on having extensions. She felt sure I did not need them. I guess just to please me she agreed to help. She had never put extensions in a person's hair before, so she had to follow my lead. Things got real complicated and we were up all night until day break and we had class early the next morning. Feeling terrible about it, I asked her to stop a few times and revisit it later in the day, but she persisted. She leaves nothing undone. I felt quite bad the next day. By morning we looked like zombies. It was not the last time we had one of these hair dressing moments. These experiences with her gave me insight into her resilience. Despite our personality differences we have been able to share in a lovely Christian friendship. We shared more than hair moments.

We often consoled ourselves about term papers, particularly "Exegesis papers." We tromped through snow up to our knees and reminisced on the homes and friends we left behind in New York. We shared joys and wallowed in self pity concerning the laid back life of Berrien Springs. We had a sleep over in which we watched movies, made smoothies and laughed crazily all night. Our times together have created bonds which I pray will last.

I met many other wonderful men and women who touched and inspired my life. I attended two colleges before becoming a student at Andrews University. In neither of them did I develop the rich bonds with students the way I did while at seminary. I am eternally grateful to have met such wonderful disciples and Christian friends.

Those Who Journeyed With Me

I would not have survived this ministry journey through seminary without the amazing support of the wonderful people God so strategically and deliberately placed in my path. I am so grateful for the influences of these people in my life. They have helped make my journey a bearable one. If it had not been for these earthly angels, my story would possibly be a different one. Although God has a million ways in which He can provide, he chose to use these human agents to bless me through this journey. My journey through seminary was truly a bitter-sweet experience. As a minister, finding people with whom you can be real and sincerely be yourself is an amazing challenge. Fake friends are not hard to come by and I have most certainly encountered a few. God in His wisdom knew I would need someone who would be for me what Darlene Thomas became, a most sincere, trustworthy, genuine, true woman of God.

She was there for me every step of the way. She understood who I was and never saw anything but good in my character. She had a deep sense of my heart and the things I am capable and incapable of. She has such a deep regard and respect for me. Her confidence in who I am as a person and pastor, helped me endure the many questions raised about my character by people who had only interacted with me from a distance. She believed in me and understood me in depth. She understood my connection with God. We prayed so many times together as she helped me though my struggles. She assisted me in many ways when I needed help on many levels. She has loved me in an unconditional way because even when she saw my flaws, she accepted me for the person that I am.

I could never have chosen her myself for a friend and made such a blessed choice. God would have had to choose her for me, for her to have been such a powerful blessing in my life. She's the only person I would let see me cry on so many occasions. I have had so many melt downs with her. When my journey after seminary began, she rallied behind me and became for me a tower of strength. God gave me Darlene as a gift, and what a beautiful gift she is. I thank her for seeing the very best in me. There is reserved in my heart a very special place for this woman of God.

While in school, I continued to travel around the country preaching, teaching and telling of God's awesomeness by sharing my experiences. Many people were inspired along the way. As a result, they donated in support of my ministry. My church family in New York supported me in ways which could only have been spiritual. Many remained consistent in their giving, pouring funds, cards, gifts, prayers and encouragement from the day I began until now. I do not want to fall into the temptation of singling anyone out and missing the opportunity of thanking all. Time would fail me to name them all, but I must thank the Best family, Sisters Hodge and Barrett whose financial and spiritual support remained consistent and ongoing throughout my studies. I am equally grateful to all who gave to me in various ways without seeking anything in return. Their giving was sacrificial given these tough economic times.

These saints occupy a very special place in my heart. I cannot forget my pastor at this church, Dr. Abraham Jules. He is someone I tremendously respect, love and appreciate. He has helped me to believe in my work as a woman in ministry. He has stood by me in tough situations and done all he could to provide the things I needed to succeed. I have never called on him for help and been turned away. He has always found a way to help me. Whenever I am home he uses me in our worship services and shows no reservation in having me preach. He encourages me to be my best. He believes in me and supports my dreams and ideas for ministry. I thank God for his being in my life. I have a sincere love for him because of the way he has helped my life and ministry. It is my heartfelt prayer that he and his family reap manifold blessings in this life and the one to come. I have a deep love for my church family and pastor at the Mount Vernon Seventh-day Adventist Church. I am eternally indebted to them.

God also blessed me with some wonderful church family members at the Philadelphia Seventh-day Adventist Church in The Bronx, New York. Like my pastor, Pastor Willkie and his family are very dear to me. He is a wonderful man of God. From the day we met, he has been a great supporter of my work as a woman in ministry. His humility is to be admired. He genuinely loves God and His people. He has helped me grow in my work as a pastor by allowing me to share his pulpit many times. It was his affirming words that helped seal my decision to accept Pastoral Ministry. I have a great respect and regard for this man of God. The members of his congregation have been so loving, supportive and caring towards me. Their care and love has truly helped confirm God's love for me and His endorsement for the work He has called me to do in pastoral ministry.

While in the Midwest, I had the opportunity to bond with a lovely group of people in Chicago, Illinois. The members of the Broadview Seventh-day Adventist Church and their pastor, Pastor Lowe, have inspired me to keep growing in ministry. He believes deeply in my calling as a pastor. His support of my work in ministry has been encouragement, consistent and empowering. This pastor always motivates me by reminding me of the power God has given me to do His work. He has allowed me to share his pulpit many times without any reservations. I looked forward to my Broadview visits. I love the people at this church and their pastor, my friend and brother, very much. Broadview is my Midwest home church away from New York.

God allowed me to meet a wonderful group of people at the All Nations Church in Berrien Springs, Michigan. I had the opportunity of serving there for two of my almost three years of study while in pastoral training. One family in particular, the Gashugis family, were especially kind to me. They befriended me from the time I began attending services there.

Brother Gashugis quickly involved me in teaching the adult lesson study on Sabbath mornings. He and his wife often invited me to join them for lunch on Sabbaths, and we became prayer partners. They opened their home and hearts to me and treated me as their own. I appreciate and love them and thank God for their Christian care for me. Countless other members in this church consistently gave their full support to my work as a pastor and respected me tremendously. Many often encouraged me and looked to me for spiritual support and guidance. I am blessed to have met such loving Christian people who through spiritual eyes acknowledged God's calling on my life and showed their support to me.

I found a brother in the pastor at the Maranatha Seventh-day Adventist Church in Brooklyn, New York, Pastor Vidal. We met while he served at the Mamaroneck Seventh-day Adventist Church in Mamaroneck, where I had my first Sabbath preaching assignment in 2007. He has supported my work in ministry by allowing me to share his pulpit many times. He pressed me to consider working as a pastor in a church when I expressed my resistance. He has been a great support for me during my many difficult moments. I truly see him as my brother. We share in a lovely respectable Christian bond. I continue to pray that the Lord will always bless him and his family, as I know he is a genuine man of God.

I am blessed to have met a wonderful group of Christians at the Sharon Seventh-day Adventist Church in The Bronx, New York. The

Pastor, Pastor Goulding (since moved on), and members have allowed me to minister to their congregation countless times without reservation. They have spoken powerful blessings into my life and have showed great support to my ministry. I see them as my family and I greatly enjoy my moments in their congregation. I thank God for this family in Jesus. There are many other pastors within our denomination, too numerous to mention, who have also been very supportive of my work and life in ministry. I am equally grateful for their support.

I thank God for the Stein-Fedele family in Pelham, New York. This family has shown their support to me in remarkable ways. They are always giving to me and showing their care in many beautiful ways. When I started school, I could not afford a cell phone. They gifted me with a cell for which they assumed all financial responsibilities throughout my entire three years of study. They made it possible for me to remain connected to my family and friends. Our friendship has deepened in beautiful ways with the progression of time. The list of their care and support toward me is quite long. I feel a deep connection with their entire family, including their two lovely children. I am truly indebted to them for such love and support. I pray for their family often and ask God to continue to bless and enrich their lives.

The encouragement and lovely friendship of the Lampson family in Pelham keeps me reminded that God shows us love through all his earthly children. Paula and Tim make sure I can grab some funds through babysitting whenever I am in town. They have been so kind to me during the twelve years we've known each other. Paula is always checking in to see how I am doing and how my life is advancing. She has been so loyal and supportive to me in beautiful ways. Her deep regard for me and her belief in my work as a pastor are wonderfully encouraging. Her girls show me such a respectful love; my heart feels so close to them. Our relationship has deepened since my pastoral journey began. She reminds me often of her prayers on my behalf. She has been delighted I decided to become a pastor. I continue to pray God's blessing over the whole Lampson family.

I am equally thankful for the Kuster family. We have also known each other for a few years now. Carol is such a gentle, loving person. We don't communicate often, but she always makes sure we have visits when I am in town. Their children have been very lovely and kind to me. They are always so happy when we see each other. We've had some fun times having supper and many road trips together. I am so thankful for the presence of these wonderful friends in my life. Our years of friendship have helped me in my understanding that they have been placed in my life by God.

I met a wonderful couple in the summer of 2009 when they were asked to host me while on a preaching assignment at their church in Chicago, Fred and Dora. Our connection was almost instant. They are a loving and caring couple who treated me kindly and made me feel most welcome whenever I was in their home. Since then, we have remained dear friends. I enjoyed my times with them. Whenever I wanted a feel of New York, their lovely home became my home away from home. I appreciate this couple a lot.

I am continually thankful to God for the unwavering support of my spiritual parents, Bruce and Avis Berry. From the day our paths crossed in 1997 they have remained a remarkable support in my life. God made them the parents I did not have in this country. They have made so many sacrifices on my behalf. Their love can only come from God. It is not surprising they journeyed with me throughout my seminary studies to ensure their successful completion. They helped me stay afloat when I often felt that I was definitely going to go under. They extended a self-sacrificing love to me which I cannot express in words. Their consistency in giving has encouraged me in my own care for others. There is never a time I have called on them and they turned me away. They did whatever was necessary to ensure that my request was met. I could never have chosen for myself such wonderful and godly Christian people to touch and enrich my life the way they have. They are indeed a great gift from God. I will forever be indebted to them for such unfailing and compassionate love. I am blessed to have been adopted into their family.

I became better acquainted with the Luke family while at Andrews. Since we are from the same country, we had a very good understanding of each other. He and his wife have been a great blessing to me. They ensured that I had fresh home grown produce in the fall each time I returned from New York after my summer breaks. This pastor prayed with and for me all along my journey. He visited me and helped me in my understanding of many scriptures. We had some humorous times as we indulged in certain deep Bible studies. He became a strong support for my ministry and assisted me in dealing with many personal concerns. He always provided godly counsel and wisdom. He has been such a powerful encouragement to my life in ministry. I always felt better after speaking with him. His family has been very kind to me. They opened their home as a place where I could retreat on many Sabbath afternoons. I literally felt I had in them a family in Berrien Springs. I truly appreciate this man of God.

I met Mr. Dwyer several years ago. He was my neighbor and a retiree. When I learned of his medical challenges and that he lived alone, I began caring for him. Since then, he remained a very kind and giving contributor to my life. He has been so supportive through my hardships and has been encouraging not just to me, but to the other members of my family that he met. I have a deep gratitude for him.

I met at seminary a wonderful group of Christian people. Although my overly private nature did not allow me to share with them the deep struggles, hardships and pains which accompanied my journey, they treated me as if they knew I needed care. One of the staff members expressed a love to me which often strengthened me. She is such a loving woman who had a deep yearning for the things of God. She was unquestionably one of my greatest seminary fans. She referred to me as "My Josie!" which warmed my heart. Countless other staff members, teachers and leaders showed me such love and encouragement which helped me to make it through seminary life as I served as President. Many others helped lighten my load by making themselves available whenever I needed their service. They never refused an opportunity to help in the kitchen when we had an event. I felt blessed to have met wonderful teachers with whom I could pray. I learned a lot through their teachings. I saw the Spirit of God in their work as teachers. Many sat with me, encouraged me and helped me to realize that God had a great plan for my life. They had no idea how their belief in me inspired and empowered me. The words of one particular teacher still ring in my ears. "You have come to the kingdom for such a time as this." Her words affirmed God's leading in my life and it strengthened my faith. Sometimes my struggles challenged my faith in remarkable ways, but God always sent someone to keep me reminded of His plans for my life. These individuals have all helped make my seminary life a beautiful experience.

The Director of Programs at the Seminary particularly brought a strong prayer support to my life. Throughout my entire time of study at seminary, Mr. Harris prayed with me and encouraged me along my journey. He believed strongly in my work as a pastor and felt convinced that God had called me to ministry. His belief in me inspired me in my studies and my preparation for pastoral work. I have great respect and regard for Him as a genuine man of God.

Whenever I think of my friendship with my former teacher in my undergraduate studies, I am more convinced that God brings people into our lives for specific reasons. I had the blessed privilege of taking a Database Management class with this teacher while at Monroe College. Our lives have been intertwined ever since. In spite of the great friendship we have shared for the past ten years, I have never stopped calling him "Mr. D." Although he did not have the slightest clue about the troubles I had in my life, he always inspired and encouraged me. He was the first person who birthed the idea in my head that I should be a motivational speaker. He even told me how I could go about starting off in this line of work. I did not see myself in public life, so I followed up only once on the idea simply to please him but not because I was interested. I never continued pursuing becoming a motivational speaker. I did not envision myself in this line of work. One time I asked him why he felt I would be good at this type of work and he said, "You have a voice of inspiration and a way of motivating and encouraging others." It is true that I did not wear my pain on my sleeves. I also didn't miss an opportunity to help someone feel better, though I myself did not always feel so good. I never fully understood it, but Mr. D always believed in me.

When my ministry journey began four years ago and I found myself touring the country teaching and preaching God's word, many concurred that I had a motivational approach to my teachings. It was because of his earlier influence that I had asked our youth leader about public speaking. My teacher saw the vision way before I ever did. Today motivational speaking is very much a part of my ministry. I thank God for the influence of Jeffery Donavan in my life. He has been a very powerful source of inspiration in my life and I appreciate him for it. It is my prayer that he and his wife find all the blessings that this life offers. There are also other wonderful teachers and friends at Monroe College who have encouraged me and believed in me as a person. I am also thankful for their support.

Last, but not least, I thank God for my biological family both here in the United States and in Dominica. God has unquestionably placed me in this family. My mother continues to commit herself to praying for the care and safety of her children. She has shown her love and support in the best ways she knows how and I am thankful to God for keeping her alive to see these changes in my life. To all my aunts and uncles, and extended family like Rohan, who were there from the beginning. I especially remember my uncle Gibbs, who was like a father to me as a young girl and through my teenage years. I have a love for my aunt Maria, who supported me greatly through her calls, cards and finances while at school. As I studied, my cousins Juliette, Carmella, Vanessa, Debbie B and Debbie J were undoubtedly helpful fans. They checked in consistently to see what I needed.

There are many other people whose names are not mentioned here who have undoubtedly cared for me and helped me in wonderful ways. My heart is equally grateful for their support. I will not forget their acts of kindness, love and generosity. As we move along the journey of life many people come along our path. We do not always know right away why these people are placed in our lives. One thing is certain. Regardless of whether these people are good, or bad, God will make their presence in our lives a blessing.

Amidst my turbulences I have learned to soar God's way.

SOARING WITH GOD

Soaring With God

My life in ministry has taken me on many trips around the country. Since it is necessary to fly to most of my destinations, I have become very familiar with the term "turbulence." On one of my flights I learned an interesting object lesson. The plane flew beautifully for a while. Everything went smooth as we glided through the air. Suddenly, out of nowhere a series of turbulences sent flight attendants on an aisle dance and passengers including me were staring at each other in anxiety. The pilot asked that the passengers remain securely fastened and not move until instructed. Regardless of how bad the turbulence was, no one asked to leave the airplane or made an attempt to abandon it. There was the understanding that no matter how terrible things became, we were going to follow the pilot's instructions and wait for the arrival of our intended destination.

My life as a Christian has been filled with many unexpected turbulences. They have raised my anxiety and caused me a lot of pain but I am going to wait on God. As my pilot, He steers my airplane of life and has instructed me to sit securely fastened because he has a sure destination in mind. He reminds me that "in this world I will have tribulations" (John

16:33); but victory is sure.

What a wonderful assurance to know that God has been the "Beginner and the Finisher of my faith" (Hebrews 12:2). He began this good work of ministry in me and He is faithfully carrying me through it (Philippians 1:6). This assurance has given me a confidence and freedom which can only be found in God through Jesus Christ. I am free from the guilt of past mistakes. I am free from life's judgments and condemnations. The attacks on my life and character have not hindered, but advanced me. I am also free from my lifelong fears. My emotional shackles have been broken. I am covered under the banner of Prince Emmanuel. This new life in God through Jesus Christ has shown me that there is no amount of teaching on God, no matter how scholarly or brilliant, which could have ever brought me into such a beautiful relationship with Him the way that He Himself has. I heard much concerning God; I read much about Him since my journey began with Him as a child. He revealed Himself to me in a way which will forever change my view of Him.

My whole life has been a search to fill an unexplainable void I possessed. This void has been filled by the beautiful presence of God. As a pastor I am at total peace with my calling. It is something I never feel the need to explain or defend. My searching has come to an end, since I have now found in God all I have been looking for in this life. I feel loved, cared for and appreciated by Him. He promises to "never leave nor forsake me" (Hebrews 13:5). I sense His protective care for me and I need not search any further. There are many things for which I am waiting on God as I grow in my relationship with Him. My desire to be joined in union with a faithful man of God has not diminished or changed. I would love to have an opportunity to model God's love here on earth through a loving Christian family of my own. I continue to pray and wait on God for this blessing. I look forward to enjoying financial security. I would love to be able to do more for the advancement of the work of His gospel. I wait on God for such things. As I wait, my patience is being tried in remarkable ways, but I must wait on God in order to reap my blessing.

The story is told of a man who discovered a great treasure. The treasure was buried very deep. It would take some long days and nights of digging before he got to this buried treasure. He set out with great enthusiasm to retrieve this fortune which could set him free from poverty. As he began his venture, he dug and dug and dug, day after day, after day. Days turned into long nights but no treasure. In frustration this adventurer gave up. Another man heard of this quitter and decided to continue with digging in hopes of finding this buried fortune.

This adventurer had barely dug for a few moments when there laid in full view a wealth of treasure. The man who gave up had done so just moments before earning a fortune which would have forever changed his life. He had centered his attention on the hardships, the frustrations and the pain which accompanied his journey. In time he gave up, failing to endure. Someone willing to pursue this treasure reaped its benefits, barely having worked a day. Through my difficulties I had to learn patience in waiting upon God. Sometimes we let go of the Lord's arm just moments before we reap our blessings.

What a blessed assurance to know that we do not serve God in vain. Through my trials I must understand, "The LORD is the everlasting God, the Creator of the ends of the earth. He will not grow tired or weary, and His understanding no one can fathom. He gives strength to the weary and increases the power of the weak. Even youths grow tired and weary, and young men stumble and fall; but those who hope in the LORD will renew their strength. They will soar on wings like eagles; they will run and not grow weary, they will walk and not be faint" (Isaiah 40:28-31). I have learned to soar above my struggles. A treasure awaits the people of God. It can only be obtained if we, despite hardships, choose to wait on Him.

Pleasures Evermore

One of my favorite passages of scripture is found in Psalms 16:11. "Thou will show me the path of life: In your presence is fullness of joy; in your right hand there are pleasures for evermore." How unfortunate that as children of God we scrape through the crumbs of life searching for residue when riches untold await us. God has been with me my entire life leading me on life's journey. He has led me through many hardships, struggles, trials, temptations, tribulations, dangers, toils, snares and even through the valley of the shadow of death. Spiritually blind, I could not trace His hands in my life affairs until He miraculously arrested my attention just a few short years ago.

The story is told of a young man who purchased a ticket for a ship to set sail on a long journey. While on board, he quietly ate the dry bread and other little stale foods his impoverished circumstances allowed him to afford. He sneaked up on the cold deck to catch some sleep at night. Each night, he painfully watched other passengers wined and dined on the large buffet prepared by the crew. Then they enjoyed the lovely cabins for a good night sleep. Oh, how he wished he was rich and could have partaken of this pleasure. On the last day of sailing, someone found him alone on deck and asked him why he had failed to join the luscious feast going on each night and why he would not join the other passengers in sharing in the lovely cabins prepared. He sadly responded, "I am too poor to afford such a luxurious life." The stranger replied, "These services came when you purchased your ticket for this ship. The beautiful cabin and the delicious buffets were all included in your ticket payment."

God in His love has paid a price a long time ago through His Son Jesus Christ. His ticket of love has awarded us wonderful privileges. Yet we have chosen to fall victim to our life's circumstances and live defeated lives. Upon recognizing God's plan for my life, I put my trust in Him, determined to live a life of purpose and meaning. As I serve as a pastor, I fail to allow the rejection, condemnation, criticism, accusations or judgments of others to rob me of the abundant life God has promised me. God has a plan for all His earthly beings and he is offering the privilege of the abundant life to all His children; they need only to reach out and embrace it.

This Will Not Be Taken From Me

I am of the firm conviction that when God gives something to His children, there is no one who can take it away. "For the LORD Almighty has purposed, and who can thwart (prevent or put a stop to) him? His hand is stretched out, and who can turn it back" (Isaiah 14:26-28). I have great confidence that "the things that are due me are in the hands of God and my reward is with God" (Isaiah 49:4). God is a real presence to me. He is not a myth or any figment of my imagination. The journey to becoming a pastor has undoubtedly been an amazing one. Yet God Himself has carried me through the many dangers, toils and snares which sought to ensnare and destroy me. Although Satan through some demonic human agents has worked relentlessly to destroy my character, integrity and reputation, God continues to elevate and prosper me.

Becoming a pastor is by far the greatest of all my life's accomplishments. It is also the greatest miracle I have witnessed God perform on my behalf. This new vocation in life has awarded me a peace which can only come from God. I have been so blessed by wonderful people. God's presence in my life through the kindness of His earthly ministering spirits has shown me first hand His love for me. As I travel around this country speaking to the hearts of God's people, they have spoken some powerful blessings into my life. Each time these words are spoken to me I feel deeply God's voice communicating His love and plans for me. Such encounters have given me even deeper insight into the work of the Holy Spirit. None of the attempts to destroy me have taken root. I am ever reminded, "No weapon formed against me will prosper and every tongue that is raised up against me in judgment will be condemned" (Isaiah 54:17).

God has continued to allow me to rise amidst the deliberate attempts of Satan to keep my head buried by his attempts to hurt my character. I can see in full view the promise of God found in Psalm 110:1, "Sit at my right hand until I make your enemies a footstool for your feet." Though my troubles are far from over, I handle them in new ways and with spiritual strength. All I have ever desired to do is tied into this one role. Where I felt rejected, embarrassed and pushed aside in times past, I see how God has lifted me above these difficulties by surrounding me with great and amazing relationships. The feelings of insignificance, low esteem, fears and defeat which had so long plagued my existence have vanished. God has given me "Beauty for my ashes" (Isaiah 61:1-3). It is only in the will of God that we are made free. Though I am not overly confident and still see areas in my life which can be improved, I do not feel the need to prove anything to anyone anymore. I am comfortable in my skin and "I am not ashamed of the Gospel of Jesus Christ" (Romans 1:16).

There is nowhere else I would rather be and there is nothing else I would rather be doing with my life. God has indeed blessed me by making me a pastor and a citizen of His eternal kingdom. I am "confident of this very thing, that God has begun this good work in me and He will perform it until the day of Jesus Christ" (Philippians 1:5-7).

APPENDIX

Scriptures Which Encouraged My Journey

Chapter 1

Jeremiah 1:5 "Before I formed you in the womb I knew you, before you were born I set you apart; I appointed you as a prophet to the nations."

Psalm 139:13 "For You created my inmost being; you knit me together in my mother's womb."

Psalm 139:13-16 "For You created my inmost being; you knit me together in my mother's womb. I praise you because I am fearfully and wonderfully made; your works are wonderful, I know that full well. My frame was not hidden from you . . . Your eyes saw my unformed body; all the days ordained for me were written in your book before one of them came to be."

Jeremiah 29:11 "'For I know the plans I have for you,'" declares the LORD, 'plans to prosper you and not to harm you, plans to give you hope and a future.'"

Matthew 10:30 "And even the very hairs of your head are all numbered."

2 Timothy 1:7 "For the spirit God gave us does not make us timid, but gives us power, love and self-discipline."

Lamentations 3:22 "Because of the LORD's great love we are not consumed, for his compassions never fail."

John 10:10 "The thief comes only to steal, kill and destroy; I have come that they may have life, and have it to the full."

Prayer

Lord, when we cannot trace your hand, we do not often trust your doings. Please teach us how, though we cannot trace your hand, we can always trust your heart. I thank You that You do not see things as we do, but that Your thoughts and Your ways are much higher than ours. When we fail to recognize Your presence, You do not go away from us, but in loving kindness You keep trying different ways to connect with us. I pray that You will remind us of the plans You have for our lives. They are good plans. It is never in Your will to cause us harm because Your thoughts for us are good. No matter how much pain we may experience in this life, remind us that You do not ever seek to cause us harm or pain. We thank you for coming divinely close to us and for answering our requests even when we do not know how to truly ask properly of You. We praise You in Your Son's name, Amen.

Chapter 2

Hebrew 13:5 "Keep your lives free from the love of money and be content with what you have, because God has said, 'never will I leave you; never will I forsake you.'"

Ezekiel 36:26 "I will give you a new heart and put a new spirit in you; I will remove from you your heart of stone and give you a heart of flesh."

Proverbs 23:7 "For as he thinks within himself, so he is."

1 Timothy 3:16 "Beyond all question, the mystery from which true godliness springs is great: He appeared in the flesh, was vindicated by the Spirit, was seen by angels, was preached among the nations, was believed on in the world, and was taken up in glory."

Romans 3:23 "For all have sinned and fall short of the glory of God."

Job 36:26 "How great is God—beyond our understanding! The number of His years is past finding out."

Prayer

Father, when the toils of life assail us, we look within and without instead of looking up to You; "From where our help comes." Our innocence and ignorance of Your providential workings cause us to suffer a lot longer than we are supposed to. Please teach us to be so in tune with You that we will recognize You in all of our life occurrences. Also, open the avenues by which we can recognize You in our experiences, and keep our hearts and our minds centered and focused on You. Forgive our unbelief and the times when we blame You for things You are not responsible for. Oh, Lord, please show us that it is never Your desire to inflict humanity with deliberate harm or pain. Let us see that you are allowing our trials to strengthen and grow us. Build our characters to bring us into a deeper relationship with You. We say thank you to You, in Your Son's name, Amen.

Chapter 3

Genesis 1:26 & Genesis 5:1 "Then God said, 'Let us make mankind in our image, in our likeness, so that they may rule over the fish in the sea and the birds in the sky, over the livestock and all the wild animals, and over all the creatures that move along the ground.'"

Psalm 139:14 "I praise you because I am fearfully and wonderfully made; your works are wonderful, I know that full well."

Romans 8:28 "And we know that in all things God works for the good of those who love him, who have been called according to his purpose."

Ephesians 6:12 "For our struggle is not against flesh and blood, but against the rulers, against the authorities, against the powers of this dark world and against the spiritual forces of evil in the heavenly realms."

John 5:2 "This is how we know that we love the children of God: by loving God and carrying out his commands."

Prayer

Father, how sad it is that we do not recognize Your image in us and Your providential workings in our lives. You have created us in Your likeness and Your image and I pray that You will continue to show us how we can receive and accept Your workings in and through us. We are sorry that we have failed You by our disobedience. May You give us a spirit that will serve You undividedly. Take away from us the effects of sin and the desires to continue. May we know that You have the ability to keep us from falling and to present us faultless before Your throne. We thank You and love You, in Jesus' name, Amen.

Chapter 4

2 Corinthians 6:14 "Do not be yoked together with unbelievers. For what do righteousness and wickedness have in common? Or what fellowship can light have with darkness?"

Proverbs 14:12 "There is a way that appears to be right, but in the end it leads to death."

Proverbs 12:15 "The way of fools seems right to them, but the wise listen to advice."

Job 36:11 "If they obey and serve him, they will spend the rest of their days in prosperity and their years in contentment."

John 13:17 "If ye know these things, happy are ye if you do them."

Prayer

Dear Lord, it is true that serving You and living a life of obedience can sometimes be a challenge when we do not fully know and understand Your will and plan. Often we also get confused about what You are asking us to do. This is because our desire to sin hinders our ability to be rational concerning spiritual matters. So, we stray quite often from You. I pray that You will help us to come into a genuine spiritual relationship with You so that we can fully accept Your will for our lives. Take away our desire for those things that cause us to falter, and teach us to want Your will and not ours, knowing that Your way always leads us to life and peace.

We ask these mercies in Your Son's name, Amen.

Chapter 5

Psalm 127:1 "Unless the LORD builds the house, the builders labor in vain. Unless the LORD watches over the city, the guards stand watch in vain."

2 Peter 2:9 "If this is so, then the Lord knows how to rescue the godly from trials and to hold the unrighteous for punishment on the Day of Judgment."

James 1:12 "Blessed is the one who perseveres under trial because, having stood the test, that person will receive the crown of life that the Lord has promised to those who love him."

2 Corinthians 10:4 "The weapons we fight with are not the weapons of the world. On the contrary, they have divine power to demolish strongholds."

Ecclesiastes 3:11 "He has made everything beautiful in its time. He has also set eternity in the human heart; yet no one can fathom what God has done from beginning to end."

Prayer

Dear Lord, I know often we follow our own passion and sinful desires. We act in our ignorance, but You have said You would not hold our times of ignorance against us. Please forgive our foolish ways. Yes, it is true we pursue what is right in our own eyes. I pray that You will not hold our sins against us and will continue to guide us in Your ways of righteousness so that we will not continue to make decisions that would hurt You. Convict us of wrong so that we never find comfort or pleasure in sinfulness. Above all, do not take Your Holy Spirit from us, and lead us in Your ways everlasting.

Chapter 6

Romans 12:2 "Do not conform to the pattern of this world, but be transformed by the renewing of your mind. Then you will be able to test and approve what God's will is—his good, pleasing and perfect will."

Luke 19:9-10 "Jesus said to him, 'Today salvation has come to this house, because this man, too, is a son of Abraham. For the Son of Man came to seek and to save the lost.'"

2 Corinthians 3:18 "And we all, who with unveiled faces contemplate the Lord's glory, are being transformed into his image with ever-increasing glory, which comes from the Lord, who is the Spirit."

1 Corinthians 2:14 "The person without the Spirit does not accept the things that come from the Spirit of God but considers them foolishness, and cannot understand them because they are discerned only through the Spirit."

John 8:36 "So if the Son sets you free, you will be free indeed."

Prayer

Dear Father, we thank You for your deliberate involvement in our lives. We also thank You for pursuing us with the intent of bringing us into a loving and spiritual relationship with You. Thank You that even when we do not understand all You are doing to save us, You do not hold our resistance and ignorance against us. Thank You for working through our temperamental weaknesses and personality flaws to bring us into a deep communion with You. Open our eyes to discern the spiritual. Continue to keep us in Your obedience I pray, in Your Son's Name and for His sake, Amen.

Chapter 7

Joshua 1:9 "Have I not commanded you? Be strong and courageous. Do not be terrified; do not be discouraged, for the LORD your God will be with you wherever you go."

2 Chronicles 15:2 "The LORD is with you when you are with him. If you seek him, he will be found by you, but if you forsake him, he will forsake you."

Acts 17:27 "God did this so that, they would seek him and perhaps reach out for him and find him, though he is not far from any one of us."

2 Corinthians 2:10-11 "Anyone you forgive, I also forgive. And what I have forgiven if there was anything to forgive I have forgiven in the sight of Christ for your sake, in order that Satan might not outwit us: for we are not unaware of his schemes."

Psalm 139:1-5 "You have searched me, LORD, and You know me. You know when I sit and when I rise; You perceive my thoughts from afar. You discern my going out and my lying down; You are familiar with all my ways. Before a word is on my tongue You, LORD, know it completely. You hem me in behind and before, and you lay your hand upon me."

Jeremiah 29: 13 "You will seek me and find me when you seek me with all your heart."

Prayer

Father in heaven, we falter in that we come to You with our sinful agendas. We do not know how to live in submission to You. So, we miss many of Your providential workings in our lives and in the world. Our finite minds cannot embrace the divine interventions and encounters of a mysterious and Holy God. Sadly, we allow culture, tradition and even our religious fanaticism and biases to determine our obedience. Please teach us, Lord, to listen and discern spiritual things. Put it in us to pursue Your purpose and to follow You first and always above any earthly voice. This we humbly ask in Your name, Amen.

Chapter 8

Deuteronomy 30:15-16 "See, I set before you today life and prosperity, death and destruction. For I command you today to love the LORD your God, to walk in obedience to him, and to keep his commands, decrees and laws; then you will live and increase, and the LORD your God will bless you in the land you are entering to possess."

Deuteronomy 6:18 "Do what is right and good in the LORD's sight, so that it may go well with you and you may go in and take over the good land the LORD promised on oath to your ancestors."

Philippians 4:19 "And my God will meet all your needs according to the riches of His glory in Christ Jesus."

Matthew 7:24-25 "Therefore everyone who hears these words of mine and puts them into practice is like a wise man who built his house on the rock. The rain came down, the streams rose, and the winds blew and beat against that house; yet it did not fall, because it had its foundation on the rock."

Romans 8:28 "And we know that in all things God works for the good of those who love him, who have been called according to His purpose."

Prayer

Our Father in heaven, Thank You for the unconditional love with which You have loved us. It seems so easy to disobey You when we do not fully know and understand what You are trying to do in our lives. We as Your earthly children can be very stubborn and stiff-necked at times. At times we cannot trace Your hands. When this happens, we mistrust You. Our feeble minds cannot understand Your ways. They are so high above ours. Please help our unbelief. We ask that You would come divinely close to us to make us aware of Your divine nature. It is not that we would know everything, but that we could cooperate with You to bring about the fulfillment of Your purposes in our sinful lives. We pray You forgive our spirits of disobedience, rebellion and mistrust. Give us a heart to follow after You. Amen.

Chapter 9

Jeremiah 31:15-16 "This is what the LORD says: 'A voice is heard in Ramah, mourning and great weeping, Rachel weeping for her children and refusing to be comforted, because they are no more. Restrain your voice from weeping and your eyes from tears, for your work will be rewarded,' declares the LORD. 'They will return from the land of the enemy."

Psalm 46:1-3 "God is our refuge and strength, an ever-present help in trouble. Therefore we will not fear, though the earth gives way and the mountains fall into the heart of the sea, though its waters roar and foam and the mountains quake with their surging."

Psalm 138:7 "Though I walk in the midst of trouble, you preserve my life. You stretch out your hand against the anger of my foes; with your right hand you save me."

Psalm 22:24 "For he has not despised or scorned the suffering of the afflicted one; he has not hidden his face from him but has listened to his cry for help."

Psalm 37:23-24 "The LORD makes firm the steps of the one who delights in him; though he may stumble, he will not fall, for the LORD upholds him with His hand."

Prayer

Dear God, Father, often when we are hurting we seem to be sure that we are forgotten by You. Yet, You never forget Your own. We wail as if we had no one for us. We become perplexed and nervous as if You had deserted us. Remind us, Lord, of your promises each time we become tempted to entertain such thoughts about You. Father, impress deep upon our hearts Your commitment to keeping the covenant that You have made with Your children. Remind us that You will not "withhold anything good from us." Teach each of us, Lord, to have faith in You, so secured, that we won't ever doubt You. Please keep us from the evil one and may we never waver in our belief in You, Amen.

Chapter 10

Philippians 4:19 "And my God shall supply all your need according to His riches in glory by Christ Jesus." KJV.

Isaiah 65:23-24 "They will not labor in vain, nor will they bear children doomed to misfortune; for they will be a people blessed by the LORD, they and their descendants with them. Before they call I will answer; while they are still speaking I will hear."

Jeremiah 33:3 "Call to me and I will answer you and tell you great and unsearchable things you do not know."

Proverbs 3:5-6 "Trust in the LORD with all your heart and lean not on your own understanding; in all your ways submit to him, and he will make your paths straight."

1 Peter 5:7 "Cast all your anxiety on him because he cares for you."

Matthew 6:31-32 "So, do not worry, saying, 'What shall we eat?' or 'What shall we drink?' or 'What shall we wear?' For the pagans run after all these things, and your heavenly Father knows that you need them."

Prayer

Dear Father, teach us to stay in prayer. Teach us not to come to You simply for what we can get from You, but show us how to come to develop a personal relationship with You. Please show us how to seek for You, not only when we are in hardships, crises and conflicts, but in our good times as well. Teach us to develop patience while we are waiting on You. Show us how to love all kinds of people in the same way You have loved us. Give us a healthy self-love so that we are able to love others the way we love ourselves. Above all, give us a spirit of peace at all cost. Help us to 'Keep our hearts and minds on You,' so that we shall be kept in Your perfect peace. We praise You for Your answer to our prayers, Amen.

Chapter 11

Lamentations 3:19-24 "I remember my affliction and my wandering, the bitterness and the gall. I well remember them, and my soul is downcast within me. Yet this I call to mind and therefore I have hope: Because of the LORD's great love we are not consumed, for his compassions never fail. They are new every morning; great is your faithfulness. I say to myself, 'The LORD is my portion; therefore I will wait for him.'"

Isaiah 49:4, 23 "But I said, 'I have labored in vain; I have spent my strength for nothing at all. Yet what is due me is in the LORD's hand, and my reward is with my God.' Kings will be your foster fathers, and their queens your nursing mothers. They will bow down before you with their faces to the ground; they will lick the dust at your feet. Then you will know that I am the LORD; those who hope in me will not be disappointed."

Psalm 121:1-2 "I lift up my eyes to the mountains - where does my help come from? My help comes from the LORD, the Maker of heaven and earth."

Psalm 103:13 "As a father has compassion on his children, so the LORD has compassion on those who fear him."

Isaiah 26:3 "You will keep in perfect peace those whose minds are steadfast, because they trust in you."

2 Timothy 3:12 "In fact, everyone who wants to live a godly life in Christ Jesus will be persecuted."

Isaiah 54:4-6 "Do not be afraid; you will not be put to shame. Do not fear disgrace; you will not be humiliated. You will forget the shame of your youth and remember no more the reproach of your widowhood. For your Maker is your husband—the LORD Almighty is his name - the Holy One of Israel is your Redeemer; he is called the God of all the earth. The LORD will call you back as if you were a wife deserted and distressed in spirit."

John 16:33 "I have told you these things, so that in me you may have peace. In this world you will have trouble. But take heart! I have overcome the world."

Prayer

Dear Father, living life as a Christian comes with many challenges. We have an enemy, Satan, who stops at nothing to make our walk with You an impossible one. His attacks on our lives often leave us confused and give us the feeling we are abandoned by You. Our perplexities cause us to misunderstand Your purpose in our sufferings. Father, help us to trust Your character when we are unable to trace Your hands in our troubles and trials. Keep our minds stayed on You. Keep our feet from evil and help them not to be ensnared. We know that Your thoughts toward us are good and not evil. Give us endurance and perseverance to stand like the brave with our faces to our foes. Teach us the insight to not respond to our circumstances but to look to You. You cannot ever fail, God, so we have victory in You. Like Paul, may we rejoice in our hardships knowing the trying of our faith brings patience. What a mighty and awesome God You are. We praise and adore You in Jesus' name, Amen.

Chapter 12

Hebrews 13:6-7 "So we say with confidence, 'The Lord is my helper; I will not be afraid. What can mere mortals do to me?' Remember your leaders, who spoke the word of God to you. Consider the outcome of their way of life and imitate their faith."

Job 21:22 "Can anyone teach knowledge to God, since he judges even the highest?"

Psalm 84:11 "For the LORD God is a sun and shield; the LORD bestows favor and honor; no good thing does he withhold from those whose walk is blameless."

Psalm 2: 8 "Ask Me, and I will make the nations your inheritance, the ends of the earth your possession."

Psalm 37:4-6 "Take delight in the LORD, and he will give you the desires of your heart. Commit your way to the LORD; trust in him and he will do this: He will make your righteous reward shine like the dawn, your vindication like the noonday sun."

Prayer

Father, please teach us not to be self-focused. Thank You for the beauty of Your promises. We know that there is power in Your word. May we take hold of them to bring Your power into our lives. Remove the spiritual blindness which has so long plagued us. Give us insight into how we could come up higher in our spiritual walk with You. Your purpose is to have relationships with Your earthly beings. Everything You do is unto salvation, keep us focused on You. Forgive us for the many times we have gone astray. We thank You for all the people You place along our paths in life; even those who have hurt us. They have each in some way contributed to the many life lessons that You want us to learn. What a wise God You are. We love and trust You, Amen.

Soaring With God

Isaiah 40:30-31 "Even youths grow tired and weary, and young men stumble and fall; but those who hope in the LORD will renew their strength. They will soar on wings like eagles; they will run and not grow weary, they will walk and not be faint."

Isaiah 30:21 "Whether you turn to the right or to the left, your ears will hear a voice behind you, saying, 'This is the way; walk in it.'"

Proverbs 16:9 "In their hearts humans plan their course, but the LORD establishes their steps."

Proverbs 1:23 "Repent at my rebuke! Then I will pour out my thoughts to you, I will make known to you my teachings."

John 14:16-17 "And I will ask the Father, and he will give you another advocate to help you and be with you forever, the Spirit of truth. The world cannot accept him, because it neither sees him nor knows him. But you know him, for he lives with you and will be in you."

Ezekiel 36:27 "I will put my Spirit in you and move you to follow my decrees and be careful to keep my laws."

Psalm 34:5 "Those who look to him are radiant; their faces are never covered with shame."

Prayer

Oh, God, our help in ages past and our future hope. I praise You for all that You do in and for Your children. I stand in awe at Your faithfulness. What a marvelous privilege it is to be called Your child. How humbling to be used by You. I am grateful for Your gifts, care and love for me and all Your people. Only You, God, know the end from the beginning, because You are the First and the Last. I am so blessed to have You on my side. Thank you for adopting me into Your family and for allowing me to participate with You in the work of salvation. I am amazed by Your power to make bleak situations bright and promising. Thank You for saving me. I will be eternally thankful and grateful to You. Keep me and all those You love on the straight and narrow way. Thank you for loving me and all Your children, Amen.

My seminary apartment the day I was moving out

Graduation from Undergrad 2002

My Grand Parents

Me and Aunt Maria (right), and Mother (left), at my Seminary Graduation

Me and best friend Darlene, at my Seminary Graduation in 2010

Me, before a
preaching
assignment after
graduation

My lifelong
friend, Bess

Me with best friend and cousin Juliette, when she visited me at Andrews University

Me and cousin, Debbie J,
With whom I stayed on my first visit to America

Me with Girls, Debbie B on (right), Carmella and Juliette on (left)

Me, at sixteen years old in Guadeloupe

My spiritual parents, Avis and Bruce Berry

Me with cousin Vanessa, with whom I shared an apartment before seminary

JOURNAL

Write Your Experiences with God

Journal Two

Journal Three

Journal Four

Journal Five

Journal Eight

Journal Nine

Journal Ten

Journal Eleven

Journal Twelve

29821728R00202

Made in the USA
Charleston, SC
25 May 2014